Study Guide

for

Siegel's

Criminology:
Theories, Patterns, and Typologies

Eighth Edition

David Mackey
Framingham State College

THOMSON

WADSWORTH

Australia • Canada • Mexico • Singapore • Spain • United Kingdom • United States

Printed in the United States of America
1 2 3 4 5 6 7 07 06 05 04 03

Printer: Victor Graphics

ISBN: 0-534-61579-1

For more information about our products, contact us at:
Thomson Learning Academic Resource Center
1-800-423-0563

For permission to use material from this text,
contact us by:
Phone: 1-800-730-2214
Fax: 1-800-731-2215
Web: http://www.thomsonrights.com

Asia
Thomson Learning
5 Shenton Way #01-01
UIC Building
Singapore 068808

Australia/New Zealand
Thomson Learning
102 Dodds Street
Southbank, Victoria 3006
Australia

Canada
Nelson
1120 Birchmount Road
Toronto, Ontario M1K 5G4
Canada

Europe/Middle East/South Africa
Thomson Learning
High Holborn House
50/51 Bedford Row
London WC1R 4LR
United Kingdom

Latin America
Thomson Learning
Seneca, 53
Colonia Polanco
11560 Mexico D.F.
Mexico

Spain/Portugal
Paraninfo
Calle/Magallanes, 25
28015 Madrid, Spain

TABLE OF CONTENTS

CHAPTER ONE
CRIME AND CRIMINOLOGY

LEARNING OBJECTIVES

1. Identify the study of criminology as an interdisciplinary field.
2. Identify the influences of the history of criminology on contemporary criminological theory.
3. Contrast criminology and criminal justice as academic fields.
4. Identify and describe the key principles associated with classical criminology.
5. Identify and appreciate the historical origins of criminology.
6. Identify and contrast the three perspectives on how crime is viewed.
7. Identify and understand the basic methodological approaches in criminological research.

CHAPTER SUMMARY

Criminology is the scientific study of criminal behavior and society's reaction to law violations and violators. It is essentially an interdisciplinary field; many of its practitioners were originally trained in other academic fields. Criminology has a rich history with roots in the utilitarian philosophy of Beccaria, the biological positivism of Lombroso, the social theory of Durkheim, and the political philosophy of Marx. Included among the various subareas that make up the criminological enterprise are criminal statistics, the sociology of law, theory construction, criminal behavior systems, penology, and victimology. In viewing crime, criminologists use one of three perspectives: the consensus view, the conflict view, or the interactionist view. The consensus view is that crime is illegal behavior defined by the existing criminal law, which reflects the values and morals of a majority of citizens. The conflict view is that crime is behavior created so that the economically powerful can retain their control over society. The interactionist view portrays criminal behavior as a relativistic, constantly changing concept that reflects society's current moral values. According to the interactionist view, criminal behaviors is behavior so labeled by those in power; criminals are people society chooses to label as outsiders or deviants. Criminologists use a variety of research methods. These methods include cross sectional surveys, longitudinal cohort research, experiments, and observational studies.

CHAPTER OUTLINE

I.   Introduction
      A.   The Carnegie Deli murders
            1.   the role of handguns in violent crime
            2.   the role of drugs and alcohol in the crime problem
            3.   the image of crime created and reinforced by the media
      B.   Criminology
            1.   the use of scientific methods to objectively study crime and criminals

II.   Criminology
      A.   Scientific approach to studying criminal behavior
      B.   Sutherland and Cressey definition
            1.   importance of criminal law in defining crime
            2.   the cause of law violation
            3.   the methods used to control law violations
            4.   use of verified principles and the scientific method stressed
      C.   Criminology is multi-disciplinary in nature

III.   Brief History of Criminology
    A.   Study of crime and criminality is relatively recent development
    B.   Middle Ages
        1.   superstition and demonic possession dominate philosophy
        2.   violators of social norms and practices were believed to be witches
        3.   witches were burned at the stake
        4.   100,000 people prosecuted for witchcraft in Europe
        5.   offspring also viewed as inferior due to inferior blood
        6.   torture to gain confessions and physical penalties common
    C.   Mid eighteenth century developments
        1.   emergence of utilitarianism
        2.   behavior seen as rational conduct
        3.   behavior was viewed as useful, rational, and reasonable
        4.   advent of deterrence
            a.   pain must counterbalance the pleasure obtained from crime
            b.   people have free will to choose crime
            c.   criminal solutions usually require less work than non-crime
            d.   penalties should be severe, certain, and swift
        5.   penalties became more proportionate to the severity of the offense
    D.   Nineteenth century positivism
        1.   observation and analyses used to understand behavior
        2.   human behavior is a function of internal and external forces
        3.   positivism relies on the scientific method to solve problems
        4.   positivists challenge concepts which cannot be objectively measured
        5.   Charles Darwin encouraged a cult of science
    E.   Positivist criminology
        1.   physiognomists and phrenologists were the first positivists in criminology
        2.   physiognomists and phrenologists' work largely discredited
        3.   Pinel coins the term psychopathic personality
    F.   Biological determinism
        1.   Lombroso is viewed as the father of criminology
        2.   serious offenders inherited criminal traits
        3.   criminals suffer from atavistic anomalies
        4.   believed direct heredity is the cause of criminality
        5.   biosocial theory links physical and mental traits, social environment to behavior
    G.   Social positivism
        1.   changes in society
        2.   population increases and trend toward urbanization
        3.   industrialization
    H.   Foundations of sociological criminology
        1.   Quetelet used data and statistics to conduct criminological research
        2.   he began the cartographic school
        3.   identified the association between age, sex, and crime
        4.   identified sociological variables linked to increased crime rates
        5.   Durkheim viewed crime as a normal and inevitable social event
        6.   crime is linked to differences within a society
        7.   crime allows for social change
        8.   increasing crime rates can call attention to social ills
        9.   two types of societies
            a.   mechanical- characterized by rural society
            b.   organic- characterized by urban society
        10.   anomie is produced during periods when values are unclear
    I.   Chicago school and beyond

<table>
<tr><td>1.</td><td>Park, Burgess, and Wirth pioneer work in social ecology</td></tr>
<tr><td>2.</td><td>social forces in urban areas create natural areas for crime</td></tr>
<tr><td>3.</td><td>disorganized neighborhoods associated with the breakdown of institutions</td></tr>
<tr><td></td><td>a.   social institutions not effective in controlling behavior of residents</td></tr>
<tr><td>4.</td><td>crime not linked to individual characteristics or traits</td></tr>
<tr><td>5.</td><td>education, family life, and peer relations prominent variables</td></tr>
<tr><td>6.</td><td>Sutherland believed that criminals learned from older more experienced criminals</td></tr>
<tr><td>7.</td><td>Reckless linked delinquency to an inadequate self-image</td></tr>
<tr><td>8.</td><td>most criminologists embraced either social ecology or socialization views</td></tr>
</table>

J. Conflict criminology
1. central figure is Karl Marx
2. character of every civilization is determined by its mode of production
3. most important relationship is between the bourgeoisie and proletariat
4. exploitation of working class leads to class conflict
5. economic systems produce conditions that support crime

IV. Contemporary Criminology
- A. Schools of thought developed over the last 200 years
  1. classical school evolved into rational choice and deterrence theory
  2. biological determinism has evolved into biosocial theory
  3. sociological theories include modeling, interaction, and bonds to society
- B. What criminologists do
  1. Wolfgang and Ferracutti definition of a criminologist
- C. Criminological enterprise
  1. criminal statistics measure reported and self reported involvement in crime
  2. sociology of law analyzes the relationship between social control and society
     - a. example of Dr. Kevorkian
  3. theory construction
     - a. there are diverse theories of crime causation
     - b. consider explaining criminal behavior as well as not engaging in crime
     - c. attempts to explain variations in the crime rate
  4. criminal behavior systems
     - a. research on specific crime types and patterns
     - b. Wolfgang and Sutherland's classic studies
     - c. research on the links between different types of crime and criminals
  5. penology
     - a. involves the correction and control of known criminal offenders
     - b. field of criminal justice overlaps with penology
  6. victimology
     - a. classic studies by Hans von Hentig and Stephen Schafer
     - b. victim behavior is often key determinant of criminal event
     - c. victim's action may often precipitate criminal event
     - d. use of victim surveys to measure criminal behavior
     - e. create probabilities of victimization risk
     - f. study victim culpability
     - g. assist in creating victim services

V. How Criminologists View Crime
- A. Consensus view of crime
  1. crimes are behaviors which are repugnant to all members of society
  2. substantive criminal law reflects the values of society
  3. Sutherland and Cressey's view of criminal law and crime
  4. consensus view links criminal law to social harm
  5. social harm helps distinguish deviant behavior from criminal behavior

<ol start="6">
<li>illegal behavior may often begin as deviant behavior before criminalized</li>
<li>many contend that victimless crimes undermine the social fabric of society</li>
</ol>

B.   Conflict view of crime

1.   criminal law reflects and protects power and privilege
2.   society viewed as collection of diverse groups in constant conflict
3.   criminal law is designed to protect the haves from the have nots
4.   poor go to prison for minor offenses while the wealthy receive lenient treatment
5.   criminal law is shaped by those with political power
6.   identifies a list of real crimes

C.   Interactionist view of crime

1.   people act according to their own interpretation of reality
2.   they observe how others react to it
3.   reinterpret their behavior according to the meaning learned from others
4.   there would be no objective reality
5.   crimes are outlawed behavior because society has defined them that way
6.   moral crusaders use their influence to shape criminal law
7.   crime has no meaning unless people react to it negatively

VI.   How Criminologists Study Crime

A.   Survey research

1.   involves self report surveys and interviews
2.   sampling of populations is a critical concept
3.   cross sectional research gathers data from diverse sample at one time
4.   self report surveys ask people to report their involvement in criminal activity

B.   Cohort research

1.   gathers information from a group of people over a period of time
2.   can gather data about events which preceded the onset of offending
3.   retrospective cohort study asks participants to report about events in the past
4.   official data and self report data can be used in cohort research

C.   Aggregate data research

1.   large social science databases can provide information about trends in crime
2.   Uniform Crime Report is annual report of crimes reported to the police
3.   UCR is published by the Federal Bureau of Investigation

D.   Experimental research

1.   uses random selection to a treatment condition to control for threats to validity
2.   changes in state law may create natural experimental conditions
3.   time series design examines data before and after an event
4.   experimental designs in criminal justice are considered rare

E.   Observational and interview research

1.   observing criminals to gain insight into their motivations and activities
2.   participants can be brought into a lab setting and observed

VII.   Ethical Issues in Criminology

A.   Political and social consequences of research

1.   who, what, and how questions are important
2.   funding research efforts assists research but can also limit what is studied
3.   ethical concerns with the participants in studies
4.   experimental conditions may differentially impact the participants

KEY TERMS

atavistic anomalies: According to Lombroso, the physical characteristics that distinguish born criminals from the general population and are throwbacks to animals or primitive people.

bourgeoisie: The owners of the means of production.

cartographic school: This approach made use of social statistics that were being developed in Europe in the early nineteenth century that provided important demographic information on the population, including density, gender, religious affiliations, and wealth. Many of the relationships between crime and social phenomena identified then still serve as a basis of criminology today.

Chicago school: A group of urban sociologists who studied the relationship between environmental conditions and crime.

classical criminology: The theoretical perspective suggesting that people have free will to choose criminal or conventional behaviors; people choose to commit crime for reasons of greed or personal need; and crime can be controlled only by the fear of criminal sanctions.

cohort: A sample of subjects whose behavior is followed over a period of time.

conflict view: The view that human behavior is shaped by interpersonal conflict and that those who maintain social power will use it to further their own needs.

consensus view: The belief that the majority of citizens in a society share common ideals and work toward a common good and that crimes are acts that are outlawed because they conflict with the rules of the majority and are harmful to society.

crime typology: The study of criminal behavior involving research on the links between different types of crime and criminals. Some typologies focus on the criminals, suggesting the existence of offender groups, such as professional criminals, psychotic criminals, occasional criminals, and so on. Others focus on the crimes, clustering them into categories such as property crimes, sex crimes, and so on.

criminal anthropology: Early efforts to discover a biological basis of crime through measurement of physical and mental processes.

criminal justice: The decision making points from the initial investigation or arrest by police to the eventual release of the offender and his or her reentry into society; the various sequential criminal justice stages through which the offender passes.

criminologists: Use scientific methods to study the nature, extent, causes, and control of criminal behavior.

criminology: The scientific study of the nature, extent, cause, and control of criminal behavior.

cross sectional research: Survey data that derive from all age, race, gender, and income segments of the population being measured simultaneously. Since people from every age group are represented, age-specific crime rates can be determined. Proponents believe that this is a sufficient substitute for the more expensive longitudinal approach that follows a group of subjects over time in order to measure crime rate changes.

deviant behavior: Behavior that departs from the social norm.

interactionist view: The perspective that one's perception of reality is significantly influenced by one's interpretations of the reactions of others to similar events and stimuli.

interdisciplinary: Involving two or more academic fields.

longitudinal research: Research that tracks the development of a group of subjects over time.

lumpen proletariat: The fringe members at the bottom of society who produce nothing and live, parasitically, off the work of others.

mandatory sentences: A statutory requirement that a certain penalty shall be set and carried out in all cases on cases for conviction for a specific offense or series of offenses.

moral crusades: Efforts by interest group members to stamp out behavior they find objectionable. Typically, moral crusades are directed at public order crimes, such as drug abuse or pornography.

phrenologists: Scientists who studied the shape of the skulls and bumps on the head to determine whether these physical attributes were linked to criminal behavior.

physiognomists: Scientists who studied the facial features of criminals to determine whether the shape of ears, nose, and eyes and the distance between them were associated with antisocial behavior.

positivism: The branch of social science that uses the scientific method of the natural sciences and suggests that human behavior is a product of social, biological, psychological, or economic forces.

psychopathic personality: A personality characterized by a lack of warmth and feeling, inappropriate behavior responses, and an inability to learn from experience. While some psychologists view psychopathy as a result of childhood trauma, others see it as a result of biological abnormality.

Self report survey: A research approach that requires subjects to reveal their own participation in delinquent or criminal acts.

social ecology: Environmental forces that have a direct influence on human behavior.

substantive criminal law: A body of specific rules that declare what conduct is criminal and prescribe the punishment to be imposed for such conduct.

time series design: Choosing an event in time (such as passage of a DWI law) and examining specific data prior to and subsequent to this event to determine whether the law can be linked to a change in behavior.

Uniform Crime Report: Large data based, compiled by the Federal Bureau of Investigation, of crimes reported and arrests made each year throughout the United States.

utilitarianism: The view that people's behavior is motivated by the pursuit of pleasure and the avoidance of pain.

white collar crime: Illegal acts that capitalize on a person's status in the marketplace. White collar crimes can involve theft, embezzlement, fraud, market manipulation, restraint of trade, and false advertising.

MULTIPLE CHOICE

1. According to Lombroso, the physical characteristics, called _____ anomalies, that distinguish born criminals from the general population; criminals are throwbacks to animals or primitive people.
    A. atavistic   C. biosocial
    B. moralistic   D. fiduciary

2. According to the _____ view, the law defines crime, agreement exists on outlawed behavior, and laws apply equally to all citizens.
    A. interactionist   C. conflict
    B. consensus   D. pragmatic

3. According to the _____ view, the law is a tool of the ruling class, crime is a politically defined concept, 'real crimes' are not outlawed, and the law is used to control the underclass.
    A. interactionist   C. conflict
    B. consensus   D. pragmatic

4. According to the _____ view, moral entrepreneurs define crime, crimes are illegal because society defines them that way, and criminal labels are life transforming events.
    A. interactionist   C. conflict
    B. consensus   D. pragmatic

5. _____ refers to the study of agencies of social control that handle criminal offenders.
    A. criminology   C. criminological enterprise
    B. criminal justice   D. crime typologies

6. During the Middle Ages, what was the prescribed method noted in the text for dealing with witches or the possessed?
    A. prison   C. burning at the stake
    B. electronic monitoring   D. dropping a house on them

7. Which of the following is not identified as an element of Sutherland and Cressey's definition of criminology?
    A. the development of criminal law   C. methods used to control criminal behavior
    B. the cause of law violation   D. the creation of social deviance

8. _____ explains the origin, extent, and nature of crime in society.
    A. criminology   C. sociology of law
    B. criminal justice   D. penology

9. _____ believed that people seek pleasure and avoid pain; to deter crime, one must administer pain in an appropriate amount to counterbalance the pleasure gained from crime.
    A. Durkheim   C. Beccaria
    B. Sutherland   D. Siegel

10. What does the philosophy of utilitarianism emphasize?
    A. a fair, rational, and balanced approach to punishment
    B. the use of cruel and excessive punishments
    C. reliance on capital punishment to deter crimes
    D. identifying physical and mental traits associated with criminality

11. Which of the following takes the position that criminal solutions are frequently more attractive than conventional (pro-social) ones because they usually require less work for greater reward?

  A. positive criminology   C. criminal anthropology

  B. classical criminology   D. criminological enterprise

12. According to classical criminologists, what are the three qualities of formal punishments needed to deter people from committing crime?

  A. calm, cool, and collected   C. brutal, unjust, and physical

  B. swift, certain, and severe   D. weak, coddling, and minimal

13. _____ is noted as the father of criminology.

  A. Marx   C. Durkheim

  B. Beccaria   D. Lombroso

14. Who was identified as the first social scientist to use objective mathematical techniques to investigate the influence of social factors on the propensity to commit crimes?

  A. Beccaria   C. Sutherland

  B. Bentham   D. Quetelet

15. Which of the following subareas of criminology concerns itself with measuring the forces which can change law and society?

  A. penology   C. victimology

  B. sociology of law   D. theory construction

16. Several subareas of criminology exist within the broader arena of criminology; taken together these subareas make up the _____.

  A. criminological enterprise   C. criminal justice system

  B. criminology family tree   D. academic diversity index

17. Which research design makes extensive use of random selection of participants, a control or comparison group, and an experimental condition?

  A. experimental design   C. cohort study

  B. observational studies   D. self report survey

18. A criminologist is most likely to use a _____ design to find out if the drunk driving rate was affected by the passage of a law increasing the penalties for driving drunk.

  A. observational   C. time series

  B. self administered survey   D. cohort

19. Which of the following terms best describes a group of people who share a similar or like characteristic, such as being born in Boston in 1964?

  A. sample   C. research participants

  B. cohort   D. gaggle

20. Which of the following best describes a crime typology?

  A. research on the links between different types of crimes and criminals

  B. the measure of crime as it relates to geographic distribution

  C. the scientific study of agencies of social control

  D. measuring the forces which can change criminal law and society

21. Which of the following best describes deviant behavior?
   A. results in social harm
   B. behavior that departs from social norms
   C. behaviors that are banned by those with political power
   D. behavior that violates the laws of society power

22. Siegel notes that the world population was 600 million in 1700 and had risen to _____ in 1800.
   A. 650 million
   B. 750 million
   C. 900 million
   D. 2.3 billion

23. Who stated that crime is a necessary and normal social event for a society?
   A. Beccaria
   B. Durkheim
   C. Lombroso
   D. Quetelet

24. The criminologists at the University of Chicago used the _____ approach to studying patterns of crime.
   A. conflict
   B. functionalism
   C. social ecology
   D. rational choice

25. What is the Marxist term for the owners of the means of production?
   A. the proletariat
   B. the bourgeoisie
   C. criminaloids
   D. the chosen ones

TRUE/FALSE

1. Both suspects in the Carnegie Deli murders were first time offenders.
   A. True   B. False

2. Both suspects in the Carnegie Deli murders had extensive criminal records.
   A. True   B. False

3. The author notes that criminology and criminal justice refers to the same area of study and concern.
   A. True   B. False

4. Beccaria believed that people seek pleasure and avoid pain; to deter crime, one must administer pain in an appropriate amount to counterbalance the pleasure gained from crime.
   A. True   B. False

5. The goal of criminology is to study criminal behavior and criminals from a subjective viewpoint.
   A. True   B. False

6. Utilitarian philosophers seek to identify the physical and mental traits associated with criminality.
   A. True   B. False

7. Siegel notes that the world population was 600 million in 1700 and had risen to 900 million in 1800.
   A. True   B. False

8. Several subareas of criminology exist within the broader arena of criminology; taken together these subareas make up the criminological enterprise.
   A. True   B. False

9. Retrospective cohort designs make extensive use of random selection of participants, a control or comparison group, and an experimental condition to gather data.
     A. True   B. False

10. A criminologist is most likely to use an observational design to find out if the drunk driving rate was affected by the passage of a law increasing the penalties for driving drunk.
     A. True   B. False

11. Physiognomists are scientists who studied the shape of the skulls and bumps on the head to determine whether these physical attributes were linked to criminal behavior.
     A. True   B. False

12. Phrenologists are scientists who studied the facial features of criminals to determine whether the shape of ears, nose, and eyes and the distance between them were associated with antisocial behavior.
     A. True   B. False

13. According to Marx, the bourgeoisie are the fringe members at the bottom of society who produce nothing and live, parasitically, off the work of others.
     A. True   B. False

14. The perspective that one's perception of reality is significantly influenced by one's interpretations of the reactions of others to similar events and stimuli is called the interactionist view.
     A. True   B. False

15. Several subareas of criminology exist within the broader arena of criminology; taken together these subareas make up the criminal justice system.
     A. True   B. False

16. Experiments in criminology are the most common research design because they are relatively easy and cost-effective to conduct.
     A. True   B. False

17. The author notes that there are no ethical issues in criminology.
     A. True   B. False

18. The primary purpose of interviews and observational studies in criminology is to get incriminating evidence and confessions from research participants.
     A. True   B. False

19. The Uniform Crime Report is published annually by the Central Intelligence Agency.
     A. True   B. False

20. The consensus view contends that crime is a tool of the ruling class.
     A. True   B. False

FILL IN

1. _____ is a large data based, compiled by the Federal Bureau of Investigation, of crimes reported and arrests made each year throughout the United States.

2. _____ is the view that people's behavior is motivated by the pursuit of pleasure and the avoidance of pain.

3. Choosing an event in time (such as passage of a DWI law) and examining specific data prior to and subsequent to this event to determine whether the law can be linked to a change in behavior best describes a _____ design.

4. _____ are scientists who studied the shape of the skulls and bumps on the head to determine whether these physical attributes were linked to criminal behavior.

5. _____ are scientists who studied the facial features of criminals to determine whether the shape of ears, nose, and eyes and the distance between them were associated with antisocial behavior.

6. _____criminal law refers to a body of specific rules that declare what conduct is criminal and prescribe the punishment to be imposed for such conduct.

7. _____ research refers to survey data that derive from all age, race, gender, and income segments of the population being measured simultaneously.

8. According to Lombroso, the physical characteristics that distinguish born criminals from the general population and are throwbacks to animals or primitive people; these were called _____ anomalies.

9. A _____ cohort study starts with an intact group of known offenders and examines their early life experiences using educational, family, police, and hospital records.

10. According to the _____ view, the law defines crime, agreement exists on outlawed behavior, and laws apply equally to all citizens.

11. According to the _____ view, the law is a tool of the ruling class, crime is a politically defined concept, 'real crimes' are not outlawed, and the law is used to control the underclass.

12. According to the _____ view, moral entrepreneurs define crime, crimes are illegal because society defines them that way, and criminal labels are life transforming events.

13. _____ is the scientific approach to studying criminal behavior.

14. _____ refers to the study of agencies of social control that handle criminal offenders.

15. The criminologists at the University of _____ used the social ecology approach to studying patterns of crime.

ESSAY

1. If a criminologist learns of a serious crime during the course of an interview with a research participant, should he or she be obligated to report that information to the police?

2. According to classical criminologists, formal penalties must be swift, certain, and severe to deter people from crime. Do most people refrain from crime due to the fear of formal sanctions? Explain.

3. Durkheim contends that crime is functional for society. What functions does crime provide for society?

4. Identify and discuss some of the ethical considerations confronted by criminologists during the course of their research.

5. How would the consensus view, conflict view, and interactionist view interpret contemporary drug laws in the United States?

CHAPTER ONE
CRIME AND CRIMINOLOGY
ANSWER KEY

MULTIPLE CHOICE ITEMS

1. A	6. C	11. B	16. A	21. B
2. B	7. D	12. B	17. A	22. C
3. C	8. A	13. D	18. C	23. B
4. A	9. C	14. D	19. B	24. C
5. B	10. A	15. B	20. A	25. B

TRUE FALSE ITEMS

1. B	6. B	11. B	16. B
2. A	7. A	12. B	17. B
3. B	8. A	13. B	18. B
4. A	9. B	14. A	19. B
5. B	10. B	15. B	20. B

FILL IN ITEMS

1. Uniform Crime Report	6. substantive	11. conflict
2. utilitarianism	7. cross sectional	12. interactionist
3. time series	8. atavistic	13. criminology
4. phrenologists	9. retrospective	14. criminal justice
5. physiognomists	10. consensus	15. Chicago

CHAPTER TWO
THE CRIMINAL LAW AND ITS PROCESSES

LEARNING OBJECTIVES

1. Identify and understand the legal system in England prior to and after the Norman Conquest in 1066.
2. Identify and appreciate the origins and development of the common law system.
3. Identify and understand the different functions of criminal law.
4. Contrast excuses and justifications for defenses in criminal law.
5. Differentiate between the different legal tests of insanity.

CHAPTER SUMMARY

The substantive criminal law is a set of rules that specifies the behavior society has outlawed. The criminal law can be distinguished from the civil law on the basis that the former involves powers given to the state to enforce social rules, while the latter controls interactions between private citizens. The criminal law serves several important purposes: It represents public opinion and moral values, it enforces social controls, it deters criminal behavior and wrongdoing, it punishes transgressors, and it banishes private retribution. The criminal law used in US jurisdictions traces its origin to the English common law. Common law was formulated during the Middle Ages when King Henry II's judges began to use precedents set in one case to guide actions in another; this system is called stare decisis.

In the US legal system, common-law crimes have been codified by lawmakers into state and federal penal codes. Today, most crimes fall into the category of felony or misdemeanor. Felonies are serious crimes usually punished by a prison term, whereas misdemeanors are minor crimes that carry a fine or a light jail sentence. Common felonies include murder, rape, assault with a deadly weapons, and robbery; misdemeanors include larceny, simple assault, and possession of small amounts of drugs.

Every crime has specific elements. In most instances, these elements include the actus reus (guilty act), which is the actual physical part of the crime (for example, taking money or burning a building) and the mens rea (guilty mind), which refers to the state of mind of the individual who commits a crime- more specifically , the person's intent to do the act.

At trial, accused individuals can defend themselves by claiming to have lacked mens rea and, therefore, were not responsible for the criminal actions. One type of defense is excuse for mental reasons, such as insanity, intoxication, necessity, or duress. Another defense is justification by reason of self-defense or entrapment. For all defenses, insanity is perhaps the most controversial. In most states, persons using an insanity defense claim that they did not know what they were doing when they committed a crime or that their mental sate did not allow them to tell the difference between right and wrong (the M'Naghten Rule). Insanity defenses can also include the claims that the offender was motivated by an irresistible impulse or lacked the substantial capacity to conform his or her conduct to the criminal law. Regardless of the insanity defense used, critics charge that mental illness is separate from legal responsibility and that the two should not be equated. Supporters counter that the insanity defense allows mentally ill people to avoid penal sanctions.

The criminal law is undergoing constant reform. Some acts are being decriminalized-their penalties are being reduced- while laws are being reviewed to make penalties for some acts more severe. The law must confront social and technological change.

CHAPTER OUTLINE

I.   Introduction
    A.   Trial of Garcia and question of degree of criminal responsibility
          1.   shot his former girlfriend on the day of her wedding to another guy
          2.   highlights the importance of the criminal intent and mental state
          3.   social relations must conform to the legal code

II.   The Origin of Law
    A.   Preliterate societies
          1.   mores and folkways were the equivalent of law
          2.   customs followed long after their original meaning is lost
    B.   Code of Hammurabi
          1.   punishment based on lex talionis
          2.   officials were made responsible for apprehending and punishing the transgressors
          3.   officials would be required to make amends if guilty not punished
    C.   Mosaic Code
          1.   Covenant between God and the Israelites
          2.   10 commandments
          3.   serves as a basis of contemporary criminal law in the United States
    D.   Twelve tables
          1.   commission of ten noble Roman men
          2.   formed by pressures from the plebeians' accusation of unfair treatment
          3.   patricians were the wealthy who served as magistrates
    E.   Early crime, punishment, and law
          1.   most formal legal codes lost during the Dark Ages
          2.   wergild developed as measure of compensation for crime
          3.   guilt determined by two methods
               a.   compurgation
              b.   ordeal
              c.   trial by combat
          4.   physical punishments common
          5.   peasants faced harsh penalties for crimes against their masters
          6.   vagabonds faced harsh penalties
    F.   Origins of common law
          1.   English law decentralized during the Dark Ages
          2.   English system of law enforcement based on tithings, hundred, and shire
          3.   early English system of courts
               a.   hundred-gemot
               b.   shire-gemot
              c.   hali-gemot
               d.   holymotes or ecclesiastics
          4.   early system of compensation similar to contemporary civil law
               a.   depends on the type of crime and the nature of harm
          5.   wergild divided into two parts
               a.   bot is the amount paid to compensate for loss or injury
               b.   part (were) went to the king
               c.   part (wite) went to the victim
               d.   became a precursor to the contemporary fine system
          6.   important persons received more as victims and also paid more as defendants
    G.   Norman Conquest
          1.   William, Duke of Normandy invades England in 1066
          2.   royal courts created to handle more serious criminal matters
          3.   royal courts used local customs and traditions to guide decisions

             4.   concept of stare decisis- to stand by decided cases

III.   Common Law
- A.   During the reign of King Henry II
  1. established body of law to gain control from local land owners
  2. established circuit courts for traveling judges
  3. three central royal courts
     a. Exchequer, King's Bench and Common Pleas
  4. juries investigated crimes, accused suspects, gave testimony, and decided cases
  5. royal prosecutors were introduced into the process
     a. could intimidate witnesses and juries
- B.   Common law
  1. merged local customs with Norman laws
  2. judicial decisions began to be written and published
  3. judge made law using precedents would eventually become case law
- C.   Common law and statutory law
  1. common law is still the law of the land in England
  2. common law was seen as constantly evolving
     a. Rex v. Scofield 1784 attempt to burn down a house
     b. question was whether attempted crimes were still crimes
     c. created the category of inchoate offenses
  3. statutory laws were enacted by Parliament
     a. Waltham Black Act- harsh penalties against the peasant class
- D.   Common law and statutory law in America
  1. American colonies were ruled under British common law
  2. common law was converted to statutory law to allow modernization and modification
     a. an example with the Harrison Act in 1914
     b. an example with the Marijuana Tax Act in 1937

IV.   Classification of Law
- A.   Crimes and torts
  1. two large categories of laws: civil and criminal
  2. civil law includes all other types of law except criminal
     a. property law and contract law
  3. of all civil law types, tort law is closest to criminal law
  4. tort is civil action in which person asks to be compensated for a harm or injury
     a. libel- false and injurious writing
     b. slander- false and injurious statements
  5. a person can be sued for damages even if not found guilty of a criminal act
  6. a person can be held criminally and civilly liable for one action
- B.   Similarities
  1. both attempt to control people's behaviors
- C.   Differences
  1. criminal law gives the power to the state whereas a tort is a private matter
  2. the state brings action in a criminal matter whereas the victim initiates action in a tort
  3. burden of proof is different
     a. preponderance of the evidence
     b. beyond a reasonable doubt
- D.   Felonies and misdemeanors
  1. the distinction is based on seriousness
  2. felonies punished by more than 1 year in state prison
  3. misdemeanors punished by less than 1 year in county jail
- E.   Mala in se and mala prohibitum
  1. mala in se crimes referred to as natural law

2. mala prohibitum crimes refers to statutory crimes
3. easier to link mala in se crimes to issues of morality

V. Functions of Criminal Law
    A. Enforcing social control
        1. primary purpose of substantive criminal law is to control behavior
        2. written statement of rules to which people must conform
        3. prohibits behaviors believed to threaten the social well-being
    B. Discouraging revenge
        1. the law shifts the burden of revenge from the individual to the state
    C. Expressing public opinion and morality
        1. criminal law is used to codify changes in public morality and values
        2. difficult in terms of protecting the rights of the minority
        3. the development of vagrancy laws reflect the debate
    D. Deterring criminal conduct
        1. law has a social control function
        2. law can punish and correct law violators
    E. Punishing wrongdoing
        1. law gives the state the authority to punish violations
        2. it need not fulfill a utilitarian purpose to justify its existence
    F. Maintaining the social order
        1. ownership and transfer of property
        2. capitalist system supported by criminal law by protecting private capital
            a. Carrier's case 1473

VI. Legal Definition of a Crime
    A. Elements of a crime
        1. to fulfill legal requirements of guilt, all elements of a crime must be proven
    B. Actus reus
        1. failure to perform a legally required duty, which is based on relationship or status
        2. imposition by statute
        3. a contractual relationship
    C. Mens rea
        1. act must be done with criminal intent
        2. includes situations in which recklessness or negligence establishes required intent
    D. Strict liability
        1. several crimes do not require mens rea
        2. person is guilty by simply doing what is prohibited
        3. purpose is to protect the public from harm

VII. Criminal Defenses
    A. Basics
        1. refute one or more elements of the crime
        2. defendants may deny the actus reus
        3. person may have lacked the criminal intent (mens rea)
        4. may contend the act was justified and therefore without criminal liability
    B. Self defense
        1. a person defending himself has limits on use of force in self defense
            a. only such force as is reasonably necessary to prevent personal harm
        2. danger must be immediate
        3. escape
    C. Ignorance or mistake
        1. general rule ignorance is no excuse
        2. failure to publicize new law possible exception

    3. new arrivals to the US are expected to know the laws
  D. Insanity plea
    1. the defendant's state of mind negates his criminal responsibility
    2. insanity is a legal category
    3. person can have a diagnosed mental illness but still be legal sane
    4. specific insanity rules
      a. M'Naghten Rule
      b. Irresistible Impulse Test
      c. Substantial Capacity Test

VIII. Changing the Criminal Law
  A. Decriminalized
    1. some crimes have decreased penalties for offenses
    2. some offenses have been legalized altogether
  B. New areas
    1. obitiatry
    2. stalking
    3. community notification laws
    4. sexual predator laws
    5. technological changes can produce new areas for crime
  C. New defenses
    1. Battered women's syndrome and adopted child syndrome
    2. premenstrual syndrome defense

KEY TERMS

actus reus: An illegal act. The actus reus can be an affirmative act, such as taking money, or the failure to act, such as failing to take proper precautions while driving a car.

appellate court: Courts that reconsider a case that has already been tried to determine whether the measures used complied with accepted rules of criminal procedure and were in line with constitutional doctrines.

arson: The intentional or negligent burning of a home, structure, or vehicle for criminal purposes such as profit, revenge, fraud, or criminal concealment.

assault: An attack that may not involve physical contact; includes attempted battery or intentionally frightening the victim with word or deed.

battery: A physical attack that includes hitting, punching, or slapping, or other offensive touching of the victim.

beyond a reasonable doubt: Degree of proof required for conviction of a defendant in criminal and juvenile delinquency proceedings. It is less than absolute certainty but more than high probability. If there is doubt based on reason, the accused is entitled to the benefit of that doubt by acquittal.

bot: Under Anglo-Saxon law, the restitution paid for killing someone in an open fight.

case law: When judicial decisions began to be written and published, judicial precedents were established, and more concrete examples of common law decisions began to emerge. Together these cases and decisions filtered through the national court system and produced a fixed body of legal rule and principles, or case law.

circuit: A specific route traveled by King Henry's circuit judges who heard cases which had previously been under the jurisdiction of local courts.

circuit judges: Traveling judges appointed by King Henry of England.

civil law: All law that is not criminal; including torts (personal wrongs), contract, property, maritime, and commercial law.

Code of Hammurabi: The first written criminal code developed in Babylonia about 2000 B.C.

commercial theft: Business theft that is part of the criminal law; without such laws the free enterprise system could not exist.

common law: Early English law, developed by judges, that incorporated Anglo-Saxon tribal custom, feudal rules and practices, and the everyday rules of behavior of local villages. Common law became the standardized law of the land in England and eventually formed the basis of the criminal law in the United States.

community notification laws: Recent legislative efforts that require convicted sex offenders to register with local police when they move into an area or neighborhood.

compurgation: In early English law, a process whereby an accused person swore an oath of innocence while being backed up by a group of 12 to 25 oath-helpers who would attest to his character and claims of innocence.

contract law: The law of personal agreements.

criminal attempt law: The intent may make an act, innocent in itself, criminal; also called inchoate crimes.

decriminalization: Reducing the penalty for an act but not actually legalizing it.

embezzlement: A type of larceny that involves taking the possessions of another (fraudulent conversation) that have been placed in the thief's lawful possession for safekeeping.

felony: A serious offense that carries a penalty of incarceration in a state prison, usually for one year or more. Persons convicted of felony offenses lose such rights as the rights to vote, hold elective office, or maintain certain licenses.

fraud: Taking the possessions of another through deception or cheating, such as selling a person a desk that is represented as an antique but is known to be a copy.

folkways: Generally followed customs that do not have moral attachments to them, such as not interrupting people when they are speaking.

hali-gemot: The manorial court of the local noblemen in England in the eleventh century.

holy-motes: Acts of a spiritual nature were judged by clergymen and church officials in these courts in England in the eleventh century; they were also called ecclesiastics.

house of correction: A county correctional institution generally used for the incarceration of more serious misdemeanants, whose sentences are usually less than one year.

hundred-gemot: Literally, the hundred group whose courts tried petty cases of the criminal court.

hundred: In Medieval England, a group of 100 families who were responsible for maintaining the order and trying minor offenses.

inchoate crimes: Incomplete or contemplated crimes such as criminal solicitation or criminal attempts.

juries: In England, groups of local landowners whom the circuit judges called not only to decide the facts of cases but also to investigate the crimes, accuse suspected offenders, and even give testimony at trials.

justification: A defense to a criminal charge in which the accused maintains that his or her actions were justified by the circumstances and therefore he or she should not be held criminally liable.

larceny: Taking for one's own use the property of another by means other than force or threat of force on the victim or forcibly breaking into a person's home or workplace; theft.

legal code: The specific laws that fall within the scope of criminal law.

lex talionis: Physical retaliation; an eye for an eye.

libel: False or injurious writing.

mala in se: Acts that are outlawed because they violate basic moral values, such as rape, murder, assault, and robbery.

mala prohibitum: Acts that are outlawed because they clash with current norms and public opinion, such as tax, traffic, and drug laws.

manorial courts: The local hundred who dealt with most secular violations in eleventh century England.

mens rea: Guilty mind. The mental element of a crime or the intent to commit a criminal act.

morals: Generally followed behavior based on societal codes of conduct; societal norms.

mores: In preliterate societies, common custom and traditions that were equivalents of law.

Mosaic Code: The laws of the ancient Israelites, found in the old testament of the Judeo-Christian bible.

natural law: Laws rooted in the core values inherent in Western civilization; actions contrary to natural law are viewed as mala in se crimes.

norms: Unwritten rules of conduct and universally followed behavior.

obitiatry: According to Jack Kevorkian, the practice of helping people take their own lives.

ordeal: Based on the principle of divine intervention and the then prevalent belief that divine forces would not allow an innocent person to be harmed, this was a way of determining guilt.

patricians: In ancient Rome, the wealthy classes who served as magistrates.

pedophiles: Sexual offenders who target children.

plebeians: In ancient Rome, the name for the lower classes.

preponderance of the evidence: The level of proof in civil cases; more than half the evidence supports the allegations of one side.

prison: A state or federal correctional institution for incarceration of felony offenders for terms of one year or more.

probation: A sentence entailing the conditional release of a convicted offender into the community under the supervision of the court (in the form of a probation officer), subject to certain conditions for a specified time. The conditions are usually similar to those of parole. Violations of the conditions of probation may result in revocation of probation.

property law: The law governing transfer and ownership of property.

reeve: In early England, the senior law enforcement figure in a county, the forerunner of today's sheriff.

royal prosecutors: Representatives of the crown who submitted evidence and brought witnesses to testify before the jury during the reign of King Henry II.

sexual predator law: Law that allows authorities to keep some criminals convicted of sexually violent crimes in custody even after their sentences are served.

shire: Counties in England and much of Europe in the eleventh century.

shire-gemot: During the Middle Ages, an assemblage of local landholders who heard more serious and important criminal cases.

slander: False and injurious statements.

social control function: The view that people commit crime when the forces that bind them to society are weakened or broken.

stalking: A pattern of behavior directed at a specific person that includes repeated physical or visual proximity, unwanted communications, and/or threats sufficient to cause fear in a reasonable person.

stare decisis: To stand by decided cases; the legal principle by which the decision or holding in an earlier case becomes the standard by which subsequent similar cases are judged.

state prison: A facility where felony offenders are held.

statute of limitations: Specifies the amount of time by which action must be taken by the state in a criminal matter.

statutory crimes: Laws created by legislative bodies to meet changing social conditions, public opinion, and custom.

strict liability crimes: Illegal acts whose elements do not contain the need for intent, or mens rea; they are usually acts that endanger the public welfare, such as illegal dumping of toxic wastes.

substantive criminal law: A body of specific rules that declare what conduct is criminal and prescribe the punishment to be imposed for such conduct.

tithings: During the Middle Ages, groups of about ten families who were responsible for maintaining order among themselves and dealing with disturbances, fires, wild animals, and so on.

tort: The law of personal wrongs and damage. Tort actions include negligence, libel, slander, assault, and trespass.

tort law: The law of personal wrongs and damage; most similar in intent and form to criminal law.

Twelve Tables: A special commission of 10 noble Roman men formulated the Twelve Tables in 451 B.C. in response from pressure from the lower classes, who believed an unwritten code gave arbitrary and unlimited power to the wealthy classes.

treasonous acts: Siding with an enemy in a dispute over territory or succession.

vagrancy: The crime of being a vagrant or homeless person. The first vagrancy laws were aimed at workers from leaving their estates to secure higher wages elsewhere. They punished migration and permissionless travel.

wergild: Under Medieval law, the money paid by the offender to the victim and the state for the criminal offense.

wite: The portion of the wergild that went to the victim's family.

TEST BANK

MULTIPLE CHOICE

1. The portion of the wergild that went to the victim's family is called _____.
    A. wite
    B. wergild
    C. bot
    D. tithings

2. Under Medieval law, the money paid by the offender to the victim and the state for the criminal offense is called the _____.
    A. wite
    B. wergild
    C. bot
    D. tithings

3. A special commission of 10 noble Roman men formulated the Twelve Tables in 451 B.C. in response from pressure from the lower classes, who believed an unwritten code gave arbitrary and unlimited power to the wealthy classes led to the development of the _____.
    A. Patricians aplenty
    B. Ten Commandments
    C. Twelve Tables
    D. Ecclesiastic Court

4. During the Middle Ages, groups of about ten families who were responsible for maintaining order among themselves and dealing with disturbances, fires, wild animals, and so on were called _____.
    A. wite
    B. wergild
    C. bot
    D. tithings

5. _____ is the body of specific rules that declare what conduct is criminal and prescribe the punishment to be imposed for such conduct.
    A. procedural criminal law
    B. substantive criminal law
    C. substantive civil law
    D. procedural natural law

6. _____ are illegal acts whose elements do not contain the need for intent, or mens rea; they are usually acts that endanger the public welfare, such as illegal dumping of toxic wastes.
    A. substantive criminal law
    B. natural law
    C. stare decisis
    D. strict liability crimes

7. _____ are laws created by legislative bodies to meet changing social conditions, public opinion, and custom.
    A. statutory crimes
    B. common law
    C. case law
    D. natural law

8. To stand by decided cases; the legal principle by which the decision or holding in an earlier case becomes the standard by which subsequent similar cases are judged is called _____.
    A. stare decisis
    B. mens rea
    C. actus reus
    D. lex talionis

9. A facility where felony offenders are held is called _____.
    A. state prison
    B. county jail
    C. purgatory
    D. reformatory

10. The _____ specifies the amount of time by which action must be taken by the state in a criminal matter.
    A. statute of limitations
    B. substantive criminal law
    C. lex talionis
    D. stare decisis

11. _____ is false and injurious statements.
    A. slander
    B. libel
    C. stalking
    D. inchoate offenses

12. During the Middle Ages, an assemblage of local landholders who heard more serious and important criminal cases were called _____.
    A. hali-gemot   C. holy-motes
    B. hundred-gemot   D. shire-gemot

13. The level of proof in civil cases is called _____; it occurs when more than half the evidence supports the allegations of one side.
    A. beyond a reasonable doubt   C. probable cause
    B. preponderance of the evidence   D. lex talionis

14. In ancient Rome, the name for the lower classes was the _____.
    A. obitiatry   C. plebeians
    B. juries   D. patricians

15. In ancient Rome, the wealthy classes who served as magistrates.
    A. obitiatry   C. plebeians
    B. juries   D. patricians

16. Based on the principle of divine intervention and the then prevalent belief that divine forces would not allow an innocent person to be harmed, this was a way of determining guilt is called _____.
    A. ordeal   C. obitiatry
    B. justification   D. holy-motes

17. According to Jack Kevorkian, the practice of helping people take their own lives is called _____.
    A. obitiatry   C. plebeians
    B. pseudo-suicide   D. patricians

18. In England, groups of local landowners whom the circuit judges called not only to decide the facts of cases but also to investigate the crimes, accuse suspected offenders, and even give testimony at trials; they were called _____.
    A. knights   C. plebeians
    B. juries   D. patricians

19. Incomplete or contemplated crimes are called _____; they include criminal solicitation or criminal attempts.
    A. justifications   C. inchoate crimes
    B. excuses   D. mulligans

20. A defense to a criminal charge in which the accused maintains that his or her actions were justified by the circumstances and therefore he or she should not be held criminally liable are called _____.
    A. justifications   C. inchoate crimes
    B. excuses   D. mulligans

21. In Medieval England, a group of 100 families, called a _____, were responsible for maintaining the order and trying minor offenses.
    A. hundred   C. gaggle
    B. tithing   D. shire

22. A county correctional institution, called a _____, is generally used for the incarceration of more serious misdemeanants, whose sentences are usually less than one year.
    A. prison   C. work camp
    B. reformatory   D. house of correction

23. Acts of a spiritual nature were judged by clergymen and church officials in these courts in England in the eleventh century called _____; they were also called ecclesiastics.

    A. hali-gemot   C. holy-motes

    B. hundred-gemot   D. shire-gemot

24. _____ was literally, the hundred group whose courts tried petty cases of the criminal court.

    A. hali-gemot   C. holy-motes

    B. hundred-gemot   D. shire-gemot

25. The manorial court of the local noblemen in England in the eleventh century was called _____.

    A. hali-gemot   C. holy-motes

    B. hundred-gemot   D. shire-gemot

TRUE/FALSE

1. The portion of the wergild that went to the victim's family is called the tithings.

    A. True   B. False

2. Under Medieval law, the money paid by the offender to the victim and the state for the criminal offense is called the wergild.

    A. True   B. False

3. A special commission of 10 noble Roman men formulated the Twelve Tables in 451 B.C. in response from pressure from the lower classes, who believed an unwritten code gave arbitrary and unlimited power to the wealthy classes led to the development of the Twelve Tables.

    A. True   B. False

4. During the Middle Ages, groups of about ten families who were responsible for maintaining order among themselves and dealing with disturbances, fires, wild animals, and so on were called the wite.

    A. True   B. False

5. Procedural criminal law is the body of specific rules that declare what conduct is criminal and prescribe the punishment to be imposed for such conduct.

    A. True   B. False

6. Stare decisis are illegal acts whose elements do not contain the need for intent, or mens rea; they are usually acts that endanger the public welfare, such as illegal dumping of toxic wastes.

    A. True   B. False

7. Strict liability crimes are illegal acts whose elements do not contain the need for intent, or mens rea; they are usually acts that endanger the public welfare, such as illegal dumping of toxic wastes.

    A. True   B. False

8. Statutory crimes are laws created by legislative bodies to meet changing social conditions, public opinion, and custom.

    A. True   B. False

9. Common law was law created by legislative bodies to meet changing social conditions, public opinion, and custom.

    A. True   B. False

10. To stand by decided cases; the legal principle by which the decision or holding in an earlier case becomes the standard by which subsequent similar cases are judged is called lex talionis.
     A. True   B. False

11. The statute of limitations specifies the amount of time by which action must be taken by the state in a criminal matter.
     A. True   B. False

12. A facility where felony offenders are held is called county jail.
     A. True   B. False

13. To stand by decided cases; the legal principle by which the decision or holding in an earlier case becomes the standard by which subsequent similar cases are judged is called stare decisis.
     A. True   B. False

14. Slander is false and injurious statements.
     A. True   B. False

15. The manorial court of the local noblemen in England in the eleventh century was called a hali-gemot.
     A. True   B. False

16. Holy-motes were literally, the hundred group whose courts tried petty cases of the criminal court.
     A. True   B. False

17. In Medieval England, a group of 100 families, called a hundred, were responsible for maintaining the order and trying minor offenses.
     A. True   B. False

18. Guilty mind is the mens rea; the mental element of a crime or the intent to commit a criminal act.
     A. True   B. False

19. Mala in se are acts that are outlawed because they violate basic moral values, such as rape, murder, assault, and robbery.
     A. True   B. False

20. Lex talionis is physical retaliation, such as an eye for an eye.
     A. True   B. False

FILL IN

1. _____ is an illegal act such as taking money, or the failure to act, such as failing to take proper precautions while driving a car.

2. _____ courts reconsider a case that has already been tried to determine whether the measures used complied with accepted rules of criminal procedure and were in line with constitutional doctrines.

3. _____ is a type of larceny that involves taking the possessions of another (fraudulent conversation) that have been placed in the thief's lawful possession for safekeeping.

4. _____ involves reducing the penalty for an act but not actually legalizing it.

5. _____ is the law of personal agreements.

6. In early English law, a process whereby an accused person swore an oath of innocence while being backed up by a group of 12 to 25 oath-helpers who would attest to his character and claims of innocence is called _____.

7. _____ laws are recent legislative efforts that require convicted sex offenders to register with local police when they move into an area or neighborhood.

8. Early English law developed by judges, called _____, incorporated Anglo-Saxon tribal custom, feudal rules and practices, and the everyday rules of behavior of local villages; it became the standardized law of the land in England and eventually formed the basis of the criminal law in the United States.

9. _____ was the first written criminal code developed in Babylonia about 2000 B.C.

10. All law that is not criminal law is called _____ law; it includes torts (personal wrongs), contract, property, maritime, and commercial law.

11. _____ is the intentional or negligent burning of a home, structure, or vehicle for criminal purposes such as profit, revenge, fraud, or criminal concealment.

12. An attack that may not involve physical contact; includes attempted battery or intentionally frightening the victim with word or deed is called an _____.

13. A physical attack that includes hitting, punching, or slapping, or other offensive touching of the victim is called _____.

14. The degree of proof required for conviction of a defendant in criminal and juvenile delinquency proceedings is called _____.

15. Under Anglo-Saxon law, the restitution paid for killing someone in an open fight is called _____.

ESSAY

1. Describe the legal system in England prior to the Norman Conquest in 1066.

2. Discuss the early development of common law in England.

3. Discuss the similarities and differences between criminal law and torts.

4. Identify and discuss the functions of criminal law.

5. Identify and discuss some of the controversy associated with the insanity defense.

CHAPTER TWO
THE CRIMINAL LAW AND ITS PROCESSES
ANSWER KEY

MULTIPLE CHOICE ITEMS

1. A	6. D	11. A	16. A	21. A
2. B	7. A	12. D	17. A	22. D
3. C	8. A	13. B	18. B	23. C
4. D	9. A	14. C	19. C	24. B
5. B	10. A	15. D	20. A	25. A

TRUE FALSE ITEMS

1. B	6. B	11. A	16. B
2. A	7. A	12. B	17. A
3. A	8. A	13. A	18. A
4. B	9. B	14. A	19. A
5. B	10. B	15. A	20. A

FILL IN ITEMS

1. actus reus	6. compurgation	11. arson
2. appellate	7. community notification	12. assault
3. embezzlement	8. common law	13. battery
4. decriminalization	9. Code of Hammurabi	14. beyond a reasonable doubt
5. contract law	10. civil	15. bot

CHAPTER THREE
THE NATURE AND EXTENT OF CRIME

LEARNING OBJECTIVES

1. Identify the three sources of crime data.
2. Understand the nature, purpose, trends, and problems associated with the three sources of crime data.
3. Understand the relationship between firearms and interpersonal violence.
4. Identify and appreciate the controversy associated with crime and social class.
5. Identify and appreciate the controversy associated with crime and age.
6. Identify and understand gender differences in criminality.

CHAPTER SUMMARY

There are three primary sources of crime statistics: the Uniform Crime Report based on police data accumulated by the FBI, self-reports from criminal behavior surveys, and victim surveys. They tell us that there is quite a bit of crime in the United States, although the amount of violent crime decreased until 2001. Each data source has its strengths and weaknesses, and although quite different from one another, they actually agree on the nature of criminal behavior.

The data sources show stable patterns in the crime rate. Ecological patterns show that some areas of the country are more crime prone than others, that there are seasons and times for crime, and that these patterns are quite stable. There is also evidence of gender and age gaps in the crime rate: men commit more crime than women, and young people commit more crime than the elderly. Crime data show that people commit less crime as they age, but the significance and cause of this pattern is still not completely understood.

Similarly, racial and class patterns appear in the crime rate. However, it is still unclear whether these are true differences or a function of discriminatory law enforcement. One of the most important findings in the crime statistics is the existence of the chronic offender, a repeat criminal responsible for a significant amount of all law violations. Chronic offenders begin their careers early in life and, rather than aging out of crime, persist into adulthood. The discovery of the chronic offender has led to the study of developmental criminology—why people persist, desist, terminate, or escalate their deviant behavior.

CHAPTER OUTLINE

I.   Introduction
    A.   Farrington and Welsh study the effects of street lighting on crime
        1.   systematic review and a meta analysis
        2.   studies indicate neighborhoods which improve their street lighting show less crime
        3.   Improving lighting caused the crime rate to go down during the day as much as night
        4.   illustrates the need for comprehensive and accurate crime data

II. Measuring Crime
    A.   Official data: Uniform Crime Report
        1.   Federal Bureau of Investigation's Uniform Crime Report (UCR)
            a.   best known and most widely cited source of official criminal statistics
        2.   Part I crimes and index offenses
            a.   murder and non-negligent manslaughter, rape, robbery, and aggravated assault
            b.   burglary, larceny, arson, and motor vehicle theft
    B.   Collecting data for the Uniform Crime Report
        1.   each month law enforcement agencies report data

          a.   based on the number of index crimes known to the police
- 2. police report how many crimes were cleared
- 3. crimes are cleared in two ways
  - a. when person is arrested, charged, and turned over to the court or
  - b. by exceptional means
- 4. just over 20 % of all reported index crimes are cleared by arrest each year
  - a. violent crimes are more likely to be solved than property crimes
- 5. UCR uses three methods to express crime data
  - a. expressed as raw figures
  - b. crime rates per 100,000 people are computed
  - c. changes in the number and rate of crime over time

C. How accurate are the Uniform Crime Reports?
1. reporting practices
2. many victims do not report these incidents to police
3. others do not have property insurance and don't see a point in reporting
4. some victims fear reprisals
5. less than 40% of all criminal incidents are reported to police
6. some contend it is a private matter

D. Law enforcement practices
1. from 1948 and 1952 dramatic crime increase in NYC
2. burglaries increased from 2,726 to 42,491
3. larcenies increased from 7,713 to 70,949
4. some departments define crimes loosely
5. arson may be seriously underreported
6. many fire departments do not report to the FBI
7. police officials may deliberately alter reported crimes
8. efforts to improve their department's public image
9. boosting police efficiency and professionalism may increase crime rates
10. increased confidence in police may increase reporting
11. a rising crime rate may be simply an artifact
12. improved police record-keeping

E. Methodological issues
1. no federal crimes are reported
2. reports are voluntary and vary in accuracy
3. not all police departments submit reports
4. FBI uses estimates in its total crime projections
5. for multiple crimes only the most serious is recorded
6. each act is listed as single offense for some crimes but not others
7. incomplete acts are lumped together with completed ones
8. differences exist between FBI's and states' definition of certain crimes

F. Future of the Uniform Crime Report
1. National Incident-Based Reporting System (NIBRS)
2. 22 crime patterns
3. hate or bias crimes

III. Victim Surveys: The National Crime Victimization Survey
A. Utility
1. victim surveys get at the unknown figures of crime
2. sponsored by the Bureau of Justice Statistics
3. large sample size
4. in 2001, 43,680 households and 79,950 people
5. age 12 or older were interviewed
6. households remain in the sample for about three years
7. new homes rotate into the sample continually
B. Issues

1.   NCVS finds that many crimes go unreported to police
2.   less than half of all violent crimes are reported to police
3.   one-third of personal theft crimes are reported to police
4.   half of household thefts are reported to police
5.   over-reporting due to victims' misinterpretation of events
6.   under-reporting due to the embarrassment

IV.   Self-Report Survey
      A.   Techniques
           1.   mass distribution of questionnaires
           2.   most are given anonymously
           3.   self-report instruments contain items measuring key variables
           4.   includes: subjects' attitudes, personal characteristics, and behaviors
      B.   Key uses
           1.   testing theories
           2.   measuring attitudes toward crime
           3.   computing the association between crime and important social variables
           4.   evaluate the distribution of criminal behavior
                a.   across racial, class, and gender lines
      C.   Are self-reports accurate
           1.   critics suggest it is unreasonable to expect people to admit illegal acts
           2.   some people may exaggerate their criminal acts
           3.   forget some of criminal acts
           4.   can be confused about what is being asked
           5.   overabundance of trivial offenses
      D.   Various techniques have been used to verify self-report data
           1.   known group method
           2.   use peer informants who can verify the subject's answers
           3.   test-retest method
           4.   questions designed to reveal respondents who are lying
           5.   polygraphs
           6.   compare the answers youths give with their official police records
      E.   Issues
           1.   significant portion of the school's population of persistent high-rate offenders
                a.   more likely to refuse to participate
                b.   absent the day of survey administration
           2.   offenders with the most extensive prior criminality
                a.   are likely to be "poor historians" of their own crime commission rates
           3.   institutionalized youths not generally represented in the self-report surveys
           4.   substance abusers tend to under-report the frequency of their drug use

V.   Compatibility of Crime Statistics Sources
      A.   Differences
           1.   UCR collects information on individuals arrested for offenses
           2.   UCR misses crimes that go unreported to the police
           3.   NCVS provides information on unreported crimes
           4.   NCVS results based on a sample of individuals rather than actual counts
           5.   NCVS does not collect information on murder and drug offenses
           6.   self-report data provides information on offenders' personal characteristics
      B.   Similarities
           1.   self-reports provide information on the personal characteristics
           2.   data sources measure different concepts associated with crime
VI.   Trends
      A.   Trends in crime
           1.   studies have indicated a gradual increase in the crime rate

        2.   crime rate increased significantly for about 15 years following the Civil War

        3.   another crime wave was recorded around the Depression (about 1930)

        4.   homicide rate increased in the 1960s through the 1970s

        5.   1991 police recorded about 14.6 million crimes

        6.   overall crime rate is about 25 percent less than a decade ago

B.   Criminological enterprise: Crime trends

        1.   teenagers have extremely high crime rates

        2.   crime rate follow the proportion of young males in the population

        3.   a poor economy may actually help lower crime rates

        4.   definitive relationship between unemployment and crime

            a.   most research finds a weak association between the two variables

        5.   crime linked to social problems

            a.   single-parent families, dropout rates, racial conflict, and teen pregnancies

        6.   research by Donohue and Levitt on recent drop in crime rates

            a.   attributed to the availability of legalized abortion

        7.   there are more than 850,000 gang members in the United States

        8.   increases in violent crime between 1980 and 1990 attributed to crack

        9.   availability of violent media can influence the direction of crime rates

        10.   research indicates the more TV watch kids the more they get into fights

        11.   quality of health care can have a significant impact on murder rates

        12.   reduction in crime rates attributed to aggressive police practices

C.   Trends in violent crime

        1.   from 2000 to 2001 the volume of violent crime remained unchanged

        2.   murder rate increased between 2000-2001

        3.   homicides peaked in 1991 with over 24,000 murders

D.   Trends in property crime

        1.   property crime rates have declined in recent years

        2.   motor vehicle theft increased 5.7 percent

E.   Trends in victimization data

        1.   NCVS reports 24.2 million violent and property victimizations in 2001

        2.   lowest number of criminal victimization recorded since the 1973

F.   Self report findings

        1.   offenders seem to engage in a "mixed bag" of crime and deviance

        2.   self-report study Monitoring the Future youths report

            a.   about 30 percent report stealing in the last 12 months

            b.   about 20 percent said they were involved in a gang fight

            c.   about 10 percent injured someone badly

            d.   almost 25 percent engaged in breaking and entering

        3.   Fox predicts a significant increase in teen violence based on current trends

        4.   Levitt disputes the contribution of the population's age makeup to crime rates

        5.   materialism is being replaced by "kinder and gentler" cultural values

VII.   Ecology of Crime

    A.   Day, season and climate

        1.   most reported crimes occur during the warm summer months

        2.   people spend more time outdoors during warm weather

        3.   crime rates also may be higher on the first day of the month

    B.   Temperature

        1.   association resembles an inverted U-shaped curve

        2.   long stretch of highly uncomfortable weather is related to homicide rates

    C.   Population density

        1.   large urban areas have the highest violence rates

        2.   exceptions are low population areas with large transient populations

    D.   Region

        1.   southern crime rates once again lead the nation

VIII.   Use of Firearms
    A.   Dominant role
        1.   about two thirds of all murders involved firearms
        2.   Kleck and Gertz, maintain that handguns are an effective deterrent to crime
        3.   400,000 people per year use guns where saved lives
    B.   Policy and practice: Should guns be controlled
        1.   more than 200 million guns are in private hands
        2.   cheap mass-produced handguns known as Saturday night specials
        3.   Federal Gun Control Act of 1968
        4.   minors, ex-felons, and drug users prohibited from owning guns
        5.   Brady Handgun Violence Prevention Act enacted in 1993
        6.   instant check to determine whether prohibited purchaser
        7.   Massachusetts Bartley-Fox Law
            a.   mandatory one-year prison term
        8.   California's "10-20-life" law
        9.   U.S. v. Rodriguez-Moreno (1998)
        10.   Kleck argues that guns actually inhibit violence
        11.   research on jurisdictions that allow citizens to carry concealed weapons
            a.   have lower violent crime rates
        12.   guns in violent situation more likely to produce a negative outcome
            a.   compared to any other kind of weapon

IX.   Social Class and Crime
    A.   Lower-class phenomenon
        1.   lowest SES has the greatest incentive to commit crimes
        2.   linked to instrumental crimes add expressive crimes
    B.   Class and self reports
        1.   Short and Nye did not find a direct relationship between social class and crime
        2.   socioeconomic class related to official processing
        3.   studies concluded that a class-crime relationship did not exist
        4.   self-report instruments include trivial offenses
    C.   Class-crime controversy
        1.   methods employed to measure social class vary widely
        2.   association between class and crime more complex than a simple linear relationship
    D.   Does class matter
        1.   lower class are more likely to suffer psychological abnormality
        2.   lower class turn to criminal behavior to relieve their frustration

X.   Age and Crime
    A.   Age is inversely related to criminality
        1.   younger people commit crime more often than their older peers
        2.   elderly crime rate has remained stable for the past 20 years
        3.   relationship is constant: regardless of their demographic characteristics
            a.   commit less crime as they age
            b.   aging out is a function of the natural history
        4.   people who maintain successful marriages are more likely to desist from crime
    B.   Early onset
        1.   people who commit crimes at a very early age at risk to become chronic offenders

XI.   Gender and Crime
    A.   Gender and crime
        1.   male crime rates are much higher than those of females
        2.   male-female arrest ratio is about 3.5 male offenders to 1 female offender
        3.   serious violent crimes, the ratio is closer to 5 males to 1 female

                4.   murder arrests are 8:1 male
        B.   Explaining gender differences
                1.   early criminologists identified emotional, physical, and psychological differences
                2.   masculinity hypothesis
                3.   female criminals were viewed as either sexually controlling or sexually naive
                4.   chivalry hypothesis
                5.   link antisocial behavior to hormonal influences
        C.   Socialization
                1.   young girls are socialized to avoid being violent and aggression
                2.   girls supervised more closely by parents
        D.   Cognitive differences
                1.   girls higher in verbal ability
                2.   boys test higher in visual-spatial performance
                3.   girls acquire language faster
                4.   girls less likely to have reading problems
                5.   females display more self-control than males
        E.   Socialization differences
                1.   girls respond to provocation by feeling anxious and depressed
                2.   females more likely targets of sexual and physical abuse
                3.   society polarizes males and females
                        a.   provides them with mutually exclusive gender roles or scripts
                4.   boys are expected to be "masculine"
        F.   Feminist views
                1.   lower crime rate for women explained by their "second-class" position
                2.   as women's social roles changed, crime rates would converge
                3.   pattern of female criminality is similar to males
                4.   between 1991 and 2000 the male arrest rate declined by 3.8 percent
                        a.   female rate increased by 17.6 percent
                        b.   male arrests for violent crimes actually dropped by 17.1 percent
                        c.   while the female rate rose 32.7 percent

XII.   Race and Crime
        A.   Minorities and crime
                1.   minority group members involved in a disproportionate share of crime
                2.   research found no relationship between race and self-reported delinquency
                3.   arrest statistics may indicate a differential selection policy by police
                4.   police use "racial profiling" to stop African Americans
        B.   Racism and discrimination
                1.   some view black crime as a function of socialization in society
                2.   Bosket committed more than 200 armed robberies and 25 stabbings in his teens
                3.   young African American males are treated more harshly by the system
                4.   13 percent of all African American males have lost the right to vote
        C.   Economic disparity
                1.   lower-class African Americans are left out of the economic mainstream
        D.   Family dissolution
                1.   low employment rates places a strain on marriages

XIII.   Criminal Careers
        A.   Career criminals or chronic offenders
                1.   Delinquency in a Birth Cohort
                2.   cohort of 9,945 boys born in Philadelphia in 1945
                3.   54 percent (1,862) of the sample's delinquent youths were repeat offenders
                4.   627 boys arrested five times or more
                5.   chronic 6% responsible for 5,305 offenses, or 51.9 percent of all the offenses
        B.   Who are the career criminals

        1.   kids exposed to a variety of personal and social problems at an early age
- C.   Continuity of crime
  - 1.   persistent juvenile offenders most likely to continue crime into adulthood
  - 2.   youthful offenders who persist are more likely to:
    - a.   abuse alcohol, get into trouble while in military service;
    - b.   become economically dependent, have lower aspirations;
    - c.   get divorced or separated and have a weak employment record
  - 3.   best predictor of future behavior is past behavior
- D.   Implications of chronic offender concept
  - 1.   central focus of crime control policy
  - 2.   three strikes and you're out

KEY TERMS

aging out: The process by which individuals reduce the frequency of their offending behavior as they age. It is also known as spontaneous remission, because people are believed to spontaneously reduce the rate of their criminal behavior as they mature. Aging out is thought to occur among all groups of offenders.

career criminal: A person who repeatedly violates the law and organizes his or her lifestyle around criminality.

chivalry hypothesis: The idea that low female crime and delinquency rates are a reflection of the leniency with which police treat female offenders.

chronic offender: According to Wolfgang, a delinquent offender who is arrested five or more times before he or she is 18 and who stands a good chance of becoming an adult criminal; such offenders are responsible for more than half of all serious crimes.

cleared crimes: Crimes are cleared in two ways: 1) when at least one person is arrested, charged, and turned over to the court for prosecution; 2) by exceptional means, when some element beyond police control precludes the arrest of the offender (for example, the offender leaves the country).

continuity of crime: The view that crime begins early in life and continues throughout the life course. Thus, the best predictor of future criminality is past criminality.

early onset: the term that refers to the assumption that a criminal career begins early in life and that people who are deviant at a very young age are the ones most likely to persist in crime.

expressive crimes: A crime that has no purpose except to accomplish the behavior at hand.

index crimes: The eight crimes that, because of their seriousness and frequency, the FBI reports the incidence of in the annual Uniform Crime Reports. Index crimes include murder, rape, assault, robbery, burglary, arson, larceny, and motor vehicle theft.

instrumental crimes: Offenses designed to improve the financial or social position of the offender.

liberal feminist theory: This theory suggested that the traditionally lower crime rate for women could be explained by their second class economic and social position. As women's social roles changed and their lifestyle became more like those of males, it was believed that their crime rates would converge.

masculinity hypothesis: The view that women who commit crimes have biological and psychological traits similar to those of men.

National Crime Victimization Survey (NCVS): The ongoing victimization study conducted jointly by the Justice Department and the U.S. Census Bureau that surveys victims about their experiences with law violation.

National Incident-Based Reporting System (NIBRS): A new program that will require local police agencies to provide a brief account of each incident and arrest within 22 crime patterns, including incident, victim, and offender information.

Part I crimes: Another term for index crimes.

Part II crimes: All crimes other than ndex and minor traffic offenses. The FBI records annual arrest informtion for part II offenses.

persistence: The idea that those who started their delinquent careers early and who committed serious violent crimes throughout adolescence were the most likely to persist as adults.

self-report survey: A research approach that requires subjects to reveal their own participation in delinquent or criminal acts.

three strikes and you're out: Policy whereby people convicted of three felony offenses receive a mandatory life sentence.

Uniform Crime Report (UCR): Large database, compiled by the Federal Bureau of Investigation, of crimes reported and arrests made each year in the United States.

TEST BANK

MULTIPLE CHOICE

1. What is the best known and most widely cited source of crime statistics?
   A. the UCR
   B. the NCVS
   C. the ICR
   D. the BJS

2. Which of the following is not reported in the Uniform Crime Reports?
   A. arrestee's age
   B. arrestee's race
   C. arrestee's gender
   D. arrestee's class

3. Murder, forcible rape, and aggravated assault are examples of which category of crime classification according to the Uniform Crime Reports?
   A. misdemeanors
   B. Type II crimes
   C. violent crimes
   D. index crimes

4. When a person is arrested, charged, and turned over to the court for prosecution, the FBI considers the case
_____.
   A. cleared
   B. solved
   C. resolved
   D. settled

5. Which one of the following types of crimes is most likely to be cleared by arrest?
   A. property crimes
   B. violent crimes
   C. Type II crimes
   D. traffic crimes

6. What does a hypothetical murder rate of 7 in the Uniform Crime Report mean?
   A. about 7,000 people were murdered in that given year
   B. about 7% of all murders were cleared that year
   C. about 7 in 100,000 citizens were murdered that year
   D. about 7 in 1,000 citizens were murdered that year

7. Which of the following is a legitimate concern identified by the author regarding the validity of the Uniform Crime Report?
   A. victims die and are no longer available for incident based information
   B. offenders are not interviewed
   C. witnesses are not interviewed
   D. definitions of index crimes vary across jurisdictions

8. What is the National Incident Based Reporting System?
   A. a victim survey designed to measure the dark figure of crime
   B. a victim hotline which anonymously chronicles criminal incidents
   C. an offender database which lists information on offenders and their habits
   D. an improved UCR with expanded crime categories and more information on each offense

9. Which of the following databases collects information about drug offenses and hate/bias crimes?
   A. NIBRS
   B. UCR
   C. ICPEWC
   D. NCVS

10. A criminologist is most likely to use what measurement method to chart the extent of substance abuse in the US population.
    A. UCR data
    B. self report studies
    C. victim surveys
    D. participant observation studies

11. Self reports are viewed as a mechanism to get at what type of data?
    A. victimization rates
    B. participants' behaviors, attitudes, and characteristics
    C. incarceration rates
    D. police effectiveness

12. Who is considered the most readily available participants of self report studies?
    A. active residential burglars
    B. people who have just been arrested
    C. people who have been the victim of crime
    D. students

13. In general, how do self report findings compare to the official crime statistics?
    A. self report surveys find greater amounts of crime
    B. self report surveys generally find less crime
    C. the findings between the two are almost identical
    D. official statistics generally report more crime than self reports

14. Which method tests the validity of self report responses by comparing incarcerated youths' answers with a normal sample to see if there are differences between their responses?
    A. test retest method   C. missing case test
    B. static group comparison   D. known group method

15. Which method tests the validity of self report responses by comparing a youth's response to a survey question to his previous response for a similar survey item?
    A. test retest method   C. missing case test
    B. static group comparison   D. known group method

16. The missing case issue concerns the failure of self reports to measure what type of offender?
    A. female offenders   C. serious chronic offenders
    B. under 21 offenders   D. student who are occasional offenders

17. What victim survey is conducted jointly by the US Census Bureau and the Bureau of Justice Statistics?
    A. Uniform Crime Reports
    B. National Crime Report on Victims of Crime
    C. National Crime Victimization Survey
    D. President's Crime Survey

18. Which of the following was not identified by the author as a criticism of the National Crime Victimization Survey?
    A. a sample doesn't allow criminologists to identify accurate trends
    B. over-reporting offenses due to victims' misinterpretation of events
    C. under-reporting offenses due to victims' embarrassment
    D. sampling errors

19. Which of the following was identified by the author as the best source of data on murder in the US?
    A. Uniform Crime Reports
    B. National Crime Victimization Survey
    C. Self Report surveys
    D. victimization surveys

20. What year did the murder rate peak in the United States?
    A. 1930   C. 1985
    B. 1968   D. 1991

21. What single factor is usually considered to have the greatest impact on the general crime rate?
   A. age distribution of the population
   B. drug abuse rate
   C. unemployment rate
   D. amount of elderly residents

22. Based on our current crime trends, what does James Fox predict will happen?
   A. as our population continues to get older, crime will decrease
   B. crime rates will decrease as the economy slows down
   C. crime rates will increase with the increase in the youthful population
   D. it is impossible to predict

23. When are crime rates the highest?
   A. winter   C. summer
   B. spring   D. fall

24. Resort areas with large transient populations are exceptions to what factor linked to high crime rates?
   A. high temperatures   C. high population density
   B. increased gang activity   D. increased personal gun ownership

25. Selling drugs so that the dealer could buy expensive jewelry, a car, and a stereo is an example of what type of crime?
   A. expressive   C. conventional
   B. instrumental   D. capitalistic

TRUE/FALSE

1. Property crimes are more likely to be solved than violent crime.
   A. True   B. False

2. Police efficiency and professionalism may actually increase crime rates as measured by the Uniform Crime Reports.
   A. True   B. False

3. No federal crimes are reported in the Uniform Crime Reports.
   A. True   B. False

4. Age is inversely related to criminality.
   A. True   B. False

5. The three major sources of crime data agree that male crime rates are higher than female crime rates.
   A. True   B. False

6. Willie Bosket committed more than 200 armed robberies and 25 stabbings in his teens.
   A. True   B. False

7. The author notes that just over 20 % of all reported index crimes are cleared by arrest each year.
   A. True   B. False

8. The author notes that about 75 % of all reported index crimes are cleared by arrest each year
   A. True   B. False

9. An expressive crime is an offense designed to improve the financial or social position of the offender.
   A. True   B. False

10. An instrumental crime is a crime that has no purpose except to accomplish the behavior at hand.
   A. True   B. False

11. The masculinity hypothesis is the view that women who commit crimes have biological and psychological traits similar to those of men.
   A. True   B. False

12. The chivalry hypothesis is the idea that low female crime and delinquency rates are a reflection of the leniency with which police treat female offenders.
   A. True   B. False

13. Liberal feminist theory suggests that the traditionally lower crime rate for women could be explained by their 'second-class' economic and social position relative to men.
   A. True   B. False

14. According to liberal feminism, as women's social roles changed and their lifestyle became more like those of males, it was believed that their crime rates would converge.
   A. True   B. False

15. According to the findings of the study Delinquency in a Birth Cohort, the chronic 6% were responsible for 5,305 offenses, or 51.9 percent of all the offenses for the cohort.
   A. True   B. False

16. According to the author, the male-female arrest ratio is about 3.5 male offenders to 1 female offender, and for serious violent crimes, the ratio is closer to 5 males to 1 female.
   A. True   B. False

17. The author notes that less than 40% of all criminal incidents are reported to police.
   A. True   B. False

18. The author notes that 13 percent of all African American males have lost the right to vote.
   A. True   B. False

19. The author notes that the overall crime rate is about 25 percent less than a decade ago.
   A. True   B. False

20. There are about 150,000 gang members in the United States.
   A. True   B. False

FILL IN

1. The _____ is a large database, compiled by the Federal Bureau of Investigation, of crimes reported and arrests made each year in the United States.

2. When at least one person is arrested, charged, and turned over to the court for prosecution, the crime is considered _____.

3. _____ is a new program that will require local police agencies to provide a brief account of each incident and arrest within 22 crime patterns, including incident, victim, and offender information.

4. A _____ survey is a research approach that requires subjects to reveal their own participation in delinquent or criminal acts.

5. The eight crimes that, because of their seriousness and frequency, the FBI reports their incidence in the annual Uniform Crime Reports; they are known collectively as _____ crimes.

6. _____ crimes are offenses designed to improve the financial or social position of the offender.

7. _____ is the process by which individuals reduce the frequency of their offending behavior as they age.

8. _____ crime is a crime that has no purpose except to accomplish the behavior at hand.

9. The term, _____, refers to the assumption that a criminal career begins early in life and that people who are deviant at a very young age are the ones most likely to persist in crime.

10. According to the _____ hypothesis, women who commit crimes have biological and psychological traits similar to those of men.

11. According to the _____ hypothesis, low female crime and delinquency rates are a reflection of the leniency with which police treat female offenders.

12. According to liberal feminist theory, as women's social roles changed and their lifestyle became more like those of males, it was believed that their crime rates would _____.

13. According to _____ feminist theory the traditionally lower crime rate for women could be explained by their second class economic and social position.

14. A _____ criminal is a person who repeatedly violates the law and organizes his or her lifestyle around criminality.

15. According to Wolfgang, a _____ offender is a delinquent offender who is arrested five or more times before he or she is 18 and who stands a good chance of becoming an adult criminal.

ESSAY

1. Identify and define the two methods when a crime is cleared by the police.

2. Discuss the three ways used to express crime data in the Uniform Crime Reports.

3. Discuss how law enforcement practices and methodological problems may adversely impact the validity of the Uniform Crime Reports.

4. Describe the recent changes to the Uniform Crime Reports.

5. Describe the findings of the research Delinquency in a Birth Cohort.

CHAPTER THREE
THE NATURE AND EXTENT OF CRIME
ANSWER KEY

MULTIPLE CHOICE ITEMS

1. A	6. C	11. B	16. C	21. A
2. D	7. D	12. D	17. C	22. C
3. D	8. D	13. A	18. A	23. C
4. A	9. A	14. D	19. A	24. C
5. B	10. B	15. A	20. D	25. B

TRUE FALSE ITEMS

1. B	6. A	11. A	16. A
2. A	7. A	12. A	17. A
3. A	8. B	13. A	18. A
4. A	9. B	14. A	19. A
5. A	10. B	15. A	20. B

FILL IN ITEMS

1. Uniform Crime Report	6. instrumental	11. chivalry
2. cleared	7. aging out	12. converge
3. NIBRS	8. expressive crimes	13. liberal
4. self-report	9. early onset	14. career
5. index	10. masculinity	15. chronic

CHAPTER FOUR
VICTIMS AND VICTIMIZATION

LEARNING OBJECTIVES

1. Identify and appreciate the financial, psychological, and social costs of victimization.
2. Identify and understand the various theories to explain violent victimization.
3. Identify and appreciate the role of victim life-style in explaining victimization.
4. Identify various programs and services available to crime victims.

CHAPTER SUMMARY

Criminologists now consider victims and victimizations a major focus of study. More than 25 million US citizens suffer from crime each year, and the social and economic costs of crime are in the billions of dollars. Like crime, victimization has stable patterns and trends. Violent crime victims tend to be young, poor, single males living in large cities. Crime takes place more often at night in open public places. Many victimizations occur in the home, and many victims are the target of relatives and loved ones.

There are a number of theories of victimization. One view, called victim precipitation, is that victims provoke criminals. Lifestyle theories suggest that victims put themselves in danger by engaging in high-risk activities, such as going out late at night, living in a high-crime area, and associating with high-risk peers. The routine activity theory maintains that a pool of motivated offenders exits and that they will take advantage of unguarded, suitable targets. The major theories of victimization are summarized in Table 4.4.

Numerous programs help victims by providing court services, economic compensation, public education, and crisis intervention. Some advocates have gone so far as to suggest that the US Constitution be amended to include protection of victims' rights. Rather than depend on the justice system, some victims have attempted to help themselves. In some instances, this self-help means community organization for self-protection. In other instances, victims have armed themselves and fought back against their attackers. There is evidence that fighting back reduced the number of completed crimes but is also related to victim injury.

CHAPTER OUTLINE

I.   Introduction
    A.   Giordano case
        1.   325,000 youths sexually exploited in the US each year
        2.   key to understand the victim's role in the criminal event
    B.   Victimology
        1.   focus is on victims and their relationship to the justice system
        2.   victimization data provides insight into nature and extent of problem
        3.   discussion of the relationship between victims and offenders
        4.   theories explain the role of victims in crime problem

II. Problems of Crime Victims
    A.   Loss
        1.   residents 12 years and older experienced 25.9 million crimes in 2000
        2.   75% were property crimes and 24% were violent crimes
        3.   FBI estimates that victims lost about 12 billion in property
        4.   4 billion of losses eventually recovered
        5.   lost wages due to victimization brings the total to 100 billion
        6.   long term suffering and death brings total losses to about 450 billion yearly
        7.   averages to $1,800 per US citizen

8.   each heroin addict costs society about 135,000 per year
9.   costs are based on tangible direct costs and indirect costs
10.   victimization during adolescence can impact later adult earnings
   a.   affects achievement and success
B.   Suffering
   1.   10 million violent crime victims in the US each year
   2.   2.6 million receive some type of injury
   3.   nearly 1 in 5 violent crime injuries received medical treatment
   4.   victimization at te hands of the justice system
   5.   some rape victims report feeling re-raped after their treatment by system
   6.   victim may suffer from stress and anxiety after event
   7.   long term emotional trauma and sexual and physical assault
   8.   post crime stress disorder suffered by both men and women
   9.   anxiety disorders and obsessive compulsive disorders reported by victims
   10.   physical injuries and disabilities
C.   Fear
   1.   Canadian study of sexual harassment reported 80% victimization rate
   2.   heightened fear after experience
   3.   spillover effect- develop fear of criminal victimization for other crimes
   4.   victims can also develop altruistic fear of crime
D.   Antisocial behavior
   1.   victims are more likely to become criminals themselves
   2.   young males sexually and physically abused more likely to engage in:
      a.   smoke, drink, and take drugs
   3.   childhood cycle of violence

III.   Nature of Victimization
A.   National Crime Victimization Survey
   1.   violent crime rates fell 15% from 1999 to 2000
   2.   victimization rates for 2000 are lowest rates recorded since 1973
B.   Social ecology of victimization
   1.   where, when, and how it occurs
   2.   serious violent crime occurs after 6pm
   3.   slightly more likely site for all crime was an open, public area
   4.   urban residents significantly higher rates of theft and violence
      a.   drugs and gangs more common in cities
   5.   murder victimization higher in disorganized inner city areas
C.   Victim's household
   1.   most vulnerable to crime
      a.   larger, higher income, African-American, western, and urban areas
   2.   least vulnerable to crime
      a.   poor, rural, white, northeast areas
      b.   home owners at lower risk than renters for victimization
   3.   population movements and changes possible explanation for patterns
      a.   move to less urban areas
      b.   25% of all households are single persons
   4.   US society has become more mobile with smaller families
D.   Victim characteristics
   1.   gender
      a.   men were twice as likely to be victims of robbery and assault
      b.   men were most likely to be attacked by a stranger
      c.   women were most likely to be attacked by a relative
      d.   women were 6 times more likely to experience rape or sexual assault
   2.   age
      a.   victimization risk diminishes rapidly after age 25

        b.   people over 65 make up 15% of population

        c.   people over 65 experience 1 % of violent victimization

3.   social status

        a.   least affluent are most likely to be victims of violent crimes

        b.   wealthy are more likely to be targets of personal theft crimes

4.   marital status

        a.   married people and widows are less likely to be victimized

        b.   married women are at greater risk of domestic violence

        c.   young at high risk but often too young for marriage

        d.   single young people go out more in public in high risk places

5.   race and ethnicity

        a.   African-Americans are more likely to be victims of violent crime

        b.   Hispanics are twice as likely to be robbed than non-Hispanics

        c.   differences may be due to urban residence

        d.   African-American males 5-8 times higher homicide risk than white males

6.   repeat victimization

        a.   maintaining certain patterns create chronic victims

        b.   past victimization is a strong predictor of future victimization

        c.   vulnerability, gratifiability, and antagonism risk factors

E.   Victims and their criminal

1.   victims report crimes were committed by single offender over age 20

2.   crimes tend to be intra-racial

3.   substance abuse was high among criminals

4.   60% of violent crimes were committed by strangers

5.   40% were committed by someone well known to the victim

IV.   Theories of Victimization

A.   Victim precipitation theory

1.   some people may initiate confrontation

2.   active precipitation occurs when victims act provocatively

        a.   uses threats, fighting words, or attacks first

3.   Active precipitation and rape

4.   Amir suggested that female victims often contributed to their attack

B.   Passive precipitation

1.   victim unknowingly threatens the attacker

2.   mere presence threatens attacker's status

3.   link to hate or bias crime

C.   Lifestyle theories

1.   people's lifestyle increases their exposure to criminal offenders

2.   crime is a function of behavior and target action

D.   High risk lifestyles

1.   adolescents hang out at high risk locations

2.   drinking, drug use and criminality can increase person's risk for victimization

3.   engaging in high risk behaviors increases victimization chances

E.   Deviant place hypothesis

1.   neighborhood risk factors for criminal victimization

2.   poor, densely populated, transient population, and mixed use

3.   home for demoralized groups of people who are easy targets of crime

4.   more affluent people avoid living in areas marked by high crime rates

V.   Routine Activity Theory

A.   Cohen and Felson

1.   three key variables increase likelihood of victimization

        a.   suitable targets

        b.   absence of capable guardians

     c. presence of motivated offenders
   2. routine activities and lifestyle choices (bars, late nights)
   3. change in lifestyle may change their exposure to crime
   4. hotspots are areas where motivated offenders hang out
     a. people who live in high crime areas
     b. go out late at night
     c. carry valuables
     d. engage in risky behavior
     e. without friends and family to watch them
   5. moral guardianship may deter crime
     a. help people refrain from opportunities
     b. socialized to hold conventional values
     c. peer disapproval linked to date rape on college campuses

 B. Lifestyle, opportunity and routine activities
   1. person's living arrangements can affect victimization risk
   2. proximity to potential offenders
   3. time at risk
   4. attractiveness as a target
   5. ability to be protected

 C. Empirical support
   1. crime rates increased from 1960 to 1980
   2. increases associated with female participation in the workforce
   3. suburbanization leads to less community supervision
   4. easily transportable goods

VI. Caring for the Victim
 A. NCVS
   1. notes almost every American will be victim at some point
   2. 75% have been victimized by crime at least once
   3. 25% of victims developed post traumatic stress
     a. psychological symptoms lasted for more than a decade

 B. Government's response
   1. 1982 Task Force on Victims of Crime
   2. Omnibus Victim and Witness Protection Act
   3. Comprehensive Crime Control Act and Victims of Crime Act

 C. Victim service programs
   1. 2,000 victim-witness assistance programs developed

 D. Victim compensation
   1. compensation includes medical, wages, future earnings, and counseling
   2. programs exist in 45 states

 E. Court services
   1. work to familiarize the victim with the justice system
   2. escorts

 F. Public education
   1. familiarize the general public with their services

 G. Crisis intervention
   1. provide immediate service to the victim
   2. phone hotlines
   3. service 24 / 7

 H. Victim-Offender-Reconciliation Programs
   1. use mediators for face to face contact
   2. encourages restitution and reconciliation

 I. Victim's rights
   1. ensuring basic rights for law abiding citizens
   2. victim involvement in the justice system

3.   victim advocacy

4.   creating a Victim's Bill of Rights

VII.   Self Protection

    A.   Active Role

        1.   citizen crime control groups

        2.   making one's home and business crime-proof

        3.   target hardening

    B.   Fighting back

        1.   contrasting effects of fighting back

        2.   those who escaped crime used reason or guns not fists

        3.   Kleck's research indicates using guns victims kill more suspects than police

    C.   Community organization

        1.   neighborhood patrols and block watch programs

        2.   little effect on crime rates

        3.   more successful when integrated into larger effort

KEY TERMS

active precipitation: The view that the source of many criminal incidents is the aggressive or provocative behavior of victims.

altruistic fear: Fear for others.

capable guardians: Effective deterrents to crime, such as police or watchful neighbors.

chronic victimization: Those who have been crime victims maintain a significantly higher chance of future victimization than people who have remained nonvictims.

crisis intervention: Emergency counseling for crime victims.

cycle of violence: The idea that victims of crime, especially childhood abuse, are more likely to commit crimes themselves.

date rape: Forcible sex during a courting relationship.

elder abuse: A disturbing form of domestic violence by children and other relatives with whom elderly people live.

motivated offenders: The potential offenders in a population.

obsessive compulsive disorder: An extreme preoccupation with certain thoughts and compulsive performance of certain behaviors.

passive precipitation: The view that certain people become victims because of personal and social characteristics that make them attractive targets for predatory criminals.

posttraumatic stress disorder: Psychological reaction to a highly stressful event; symptoms may include depression, anxiety, flashbacks, and reoccurring nightmares.

restitution agreements: A condition of probation in which the offender repays society or the victim of crime for the trouble the offender caused. Monetary restitution involves a direct payment to the victim as a form of compensation. Community service restitution may be used in victimless crimes and involves work in the community in lieu of more severe criminal sanctions.

siblicide: Sibling homicide.

suitable targets: According to routine activity theory, a target for crime that is relatively valuable, easily transportable, and not capably guarded.

target hardening: Making one's home or business crime proof through the use of locks, bars, alarms, and other devices.

victim compensation: The victim ordinarily receives compensation from the state to pay for damages associated with the crime. Rarely are two compensation schemes alike, however, and many state programs suffer from both lack of adequate funding and proper organization with the criminal justice system.

victimization (by the justice system): While the crime is still fresh in their minds, victims may find that the police interrogation following the crime is handled callously, with innuendos and insinuations that they were somehow at fault. Victims have difficulty knowing what is going on in a case; property is often kept for a long period of time as evidence and may never be returned. Some rape victims report that the treatment they receive from the legal, medical, and mental health services is so destructive that they can't help but feel re-raped.

victimologist: A person who studies the victim's role in criminal transactions.

victim precipitation view: The idea that the victim's behavior was the spark that ignited the subsequent offense, as when the victim abused the offender verbally or physically.

victim-witness assistance program: Government programs that help crime victims and witnesses; may include compensation, court services, and/or crisis intervention.

TEST BANK

MULTIPLE CHOICE

1. The author notes that about _____ youths sexually exploited in the US each year.
    - A. 125,000
    - B. 325,000
    - C. 35,000
    - D. 1.2 million

2. According to the NCVS, US residents 12 years and older experienced _____ crimes in 2000.
    - A. 2.3 million
    - B. 1.5 million
    - C. 25.9 million
    - D. 38.9 million

3. Psychological reaction to a highly stressful event; symptoms may include depression, anxiety, flashbacks, and reoccurring nightmares is called _____.
    - A. posttraumatic stress disorder
    - B. cognitive disorder
    - C. affective disorder
    - D. borderline personality

4. The view that the source of many criminal incidents is the aggressive or provocative behavior of victims is called
_____.
    - A. passive participation
    - B. victim tautology
    - C. victimology
    - D. active precipitation

5. _____ is the view that certain people become victims because of personal and social characteristics that make them attractive targets for predatory criminals.
    - A. passive participation
    - B. victim tautology
    - C. victimology
    - D. active precipitation

6. According to _____, a target for crime that is relatively valuable, easily transportable, and not capably guarded is most likely to be stolen.
    - A. routine activity theory
    - B. subcultural theory
    - C. victimology
    - D. active precipitation

7. The FBI estimates that victims lost about _____ in property in 2000.
    - A. 2 billion
    - B. 12 billion
    - C. 36 trillion
    - D. 890 billion

8. The FBI estimates of the total loss experienced by US citizens about _____ of losses were eventually recovered.
    - A. 800,000
    - B. 1 billion
    - C. 126 billion
    - D. 4 billion

9. The cost of crime to US citizens if long term suffering and death is included brings total losses to about _____ yearly.
    - A. 1.2 billion
    - B. 450 billion
    - C. 890 billion
    - D. 3.4 trillion

10. The average cost of crime in the United States is equal to _____ per citizen.
    - A. $1,800
    - B. $800
    - C. $4,800
    - D. $12,500

11. It was noted that there were _____ violent crime victims in the US each year.
    - A. 10 million
    - B. 15 million
    - C. 30 million
    - D. 65 million

12. According to the National Crime Victimization Survey, what was the pattern of <u>violent</u> crime trends from 1999 to 2000?
        A. rates fell 15%   C. rates increased 15%
        B. rates fell 30%   D. rates decreased 30%

13. People over 65 make up 15% of population, and they experience _____ % of violent victimizations.
        A. 1   C. 20
        B. 15   D. 35

14. Which of the following is an example of an indirect cost of criminal victimization?
        A. property loss   C. productivity loss
        B. medical bills   D. long term psychological pain

15. Target _____ refers to the victims' physical weakness or psychological distress renders them incapable of resisting or deterring crime and makes them easy targets.
        A. vulnerability   C. antagonism
        B. gratifiability   D. acquisition

16. Target _____ refers to the condition when some victims have characteristics that increase their risk because they have some quality, possession, skill, or attribute that an offender wants to obtain, use, have access to, or manipulate.
        A. vulnerability   C. antagonism
        B. gratifiability   D. acquisition

17. Target _____ refers to the condition when some characteristics increase risk because they arouse anger, jealousy, or destructive impulses in the offender.
        A. vulnerability   C. antagonism
        B. gratifiability   D. acquisition

18. Although 82 percent of the US population has siblings, murder among siblings constitute about _____ percent of all homicides annually.
        A. 2   C. 32
        B. 12   D. 54

19. An extreme preoccupation with certain thoughts and compulsive performance of certain behaviors is called _____.
        A. post traumatic stress disorder   C. obsessive compulsive disorder
        B. anxiety disorder   D. borderline personality

20. Making one's home or business crime proof through the use of locks, bars, alarms, and other devices is called _____.
        A. target hardening   C. victim precipitated prevention
        B. bunker mentality   D. tertiary prevention

21. Which of the following areas has the highest rate of criminal victimization?
        A. central city   C. suburban
        B. rural   D. small town

22. What is the most likely site for criminal victimization?
        A. an open, public area   C. the workplace
        B. a school   D. your home

23. Widom refers to the phenomenon in which child victims later become adult criminals as the _____.
        A. masculinity hypothesis   C. cycle of violence
        B. chivalry hypothesis   D. copy cat syndrome

24. Spousal abuse victims may suffer an emotional disturbance following exposure to stresses outside the normal human experience. What is this condition called?
    A. obsessive compulsive disorder
    B. hyper-arousal syndrome
    C. post traumatic stress syndrome
    D. anxiety disorder

25. Which of the following is an example of an indirect cost of criminal victimization?
    A. the loss of a $65 VCR stolen from your apartment
    B. missing three days of work due to a broken arm suffered during a mugging
    C. a hospital bill for fixing your broken arm after being mugged
    D. increased fear of strangers after being assaulted in a parking lot

TRUE/FALSE

1. The author notes that about 325,000 youths sexually exploited in the US each year.
    A. True   B. False

2. Passive precipitation is the view that the source of many criminal incidents is the aggressive or provocative behavior of victims.
    A. True   B. False

3. Active precipitation is the view that certain people become victims because of personal and social characteristics that make them attractive targets for predatory criminals.
    A. True   B. False

4. According to routine activity theory, a target for crime that is relatively valuable, easily transportable, and not capably guarded is most likely to be stolen.
    A. True   B. False

5. According to the National Crime Victimization Survey, victimization rates for 2000 are lowest rates recorded since 1973.
    A. True   B. False

6. The FBI estimates of the total loss experienced by US citizens about $450,000 of losses were eventually recovered.
    A. True   B. False

7. The cost of crime to US citizens if long term suffering and death is included brings total losses to about 1.2 billion yearly.
    A. True   B. False

8. According to the NCVS, US residents 12 years and older experienced 25.9 million crimes in 2000.
    A. True   B. False

9. The average cost of crime in the United States is equal to $1,800 per citizen.
    A. True   B. False

10. It was noted that there were 30 million violent crime victims in the US each year.
    A. True   B. False

11. According to the National Crime Victimization Survey, the rates of <u>violent</u> crime fell 15% from 1999 to 2000.
    A. True   B. False

12. The author notes that a Canadian study of sexual harassment reported 15% victimization rate among its participants.
        A. True   B. False

13. People over 65 make up 15% of population, and they experience 18 % of violent victimizations.
        A. True   B. False

14. The NCVS notes that almost every American will be victim at some point and 75% have been victimized by crime at least once.
        A. True   B. False

15. It was noted that 60% of violent crimes were committed by strangers.
        A. True   B. False

16. Long term psychological pain and suffering is an example of an indirect cost of criminal victimization.
        A. True   B. False

17. Spousal abuse victims may suffer an emotional disturbance following exposure to stresses outside the normal human experience, called post traumatic stress syndrome.
        A. True   B. False

18. Widom refers to the phenomenon in which child victims later become adult criminals as the masculinity hypothesis.
        A. True   B. False

19. The workplace is the most likely site for criminal victimization.
        A. True   B. False

20. The central city has the highest rate of criminal victimization.
        A. True   B. False

FILL IN

1. _____ may be used in victimless crimes and involves work in the community in lieu of more severe criminal sanctions.

2. _____ involves a direct payment to the victim as a form of compensation.

3. _____ are a condition of probation in which the offender repays society or the victim of crime for the trouble the offender caused.

4. Psychological reaction to a highly stressful event; symptoms may include depression, anxiety, flashbacks, and reoccurring nightmares is known as _____.

5. _____ is the view that certain people become victims because of personal and social characteristics that make them attractive targets for predatory criminals.

6. _____ disorder is an extreme preoccupation with certain thoughts and compulsive performance of certain behaviors.

7. _____ percent of all households are single persons.

8. A disturbing form of domestic violence by children and other relatives with whom elderly people live is called _____.

9. Forcible sex during a courting relationship is called _____.

10. The _____ of violence is the idea that victims of crime, especially childhood abuse, are more likely to commit crimes themselves.

11. Emergency counseling for crime victims is called _____.

12. Those who have been crime victims maintain a significantly higher chance of future victimization than people who have remained non-victims; they suffer from _____.

13. According to routine activity theory, effective deterrents to crime, such as police or watchful neighbors are called _____.

14. _____ fear is fear for others.

15. The view that the source of many criminal incidents is the aggressive or provocative behavior of victims is called _____.

ESSAY

1. Discuss the recent trends in criminal victimization in the United States.

2. Discuss the role of the criminal justice system in caring for the victims of crime.

3. Identify and define victim precipitated crime. Provide an example to demonstrate familiarity with the concept.

4. What does it mean when someone is victimized by the system?

5. What can people do to decrease their risk of becoming a victim of crime?

CHAPTER FOUR
VICTIMS AND VICTIMIZATION
ANSWER KEY

MULTIPLE CHOICE ITEMS

1. B	6. A	11. A	16. B	21. A
2. C	7. B	12. A	17. C	22. A
3. A	8. D	13. A	18. A	23. C
4. D	9. B	14. D	19. C	24. C
5. A	10. A	15. A	20. A	25. D

TRUE FALSE ITEMS

1. A	6. B	11. A	16. A
2. B	7. B	12. B	17. A
3. B	8. A	13. B	18. B
4. A	9. A	14. A	19. B
5. A	10. B	15. A	20. A

FILL IN ITEMS

1. Community service restitution	6. obsessive compulsive	11. crisis intervention
2. Monetary restitution	7. Twenty five	12. chronic victimization
3. restitution agreements	8. elder abuse	13. capable guardians
4. posttraumatic stress disorder	9. date rape	14. altruistic
5. passive precipitation	10. cycle	15. active precipitation

CHAPTER FIVE
CHOICE THEORY

LEARNING OBJECTIVES

1. Identify and understand the principles associated with classical criminology.
2. Identify and understand the principles associated with situational crime prevention.
3. Identify and understand the types of designs and findings of research testing deterrence concepts associated with capital punishment.
4. Identify and appreciate the concept of selective incapacitation.

CHAPTER SUMMARY

Choice theory assumes that criminals carefully choose whether to commit criminal acts. However, people are influenced by their fear of the criminal penalties associated with being caught and convicted for violating the law. The more severe, certain, and swift the punishment, the more likely it is to control crime. Crime can be prevented or displaced by convincing potential criminals that the risks of violating the law exceed the benefits. The choice approach is rooted in the classical criminology of 18th Century social philosophers Beccaria and Bentham.

Deterrence theory holds that if criminals are indeed rational, an inverse relationship should exist between punishment and crime. However, a number of factors confound the relationship. For example, if people do not believe they will be caught, even harsh punishment may not deter crime. Deterrence theory has been criticized on the groups that it wrongfully assumes that criminals make a rational choice before committing crimes, it ignores the intricacies of the criminal justice system, and it does not take into account the social and psychological factors that may influence criminality. Research designed to test the validity of the deterrence concept has not indicated that deterrent measures actually reduce the crime rate.

Specific deterrence theory holds that the crime rate can be reduced if known offenders are punished so severely that they never commit crimes again. There is little evidence that harsh punishments actually reduce the crime rate. Incapacitation theory maintains that if deterrence does not work, the best course of action is to incarcerate known offenders for long periods of time so that they lack criminal opportunity. Choice theory has been influential in shaping public policy. The criminal law is designed to deter potential criminals and fairly punish those who have been caught engaging in illegal acts.

CHAPTER OUTLINE

I.   Introduction
        A.   Drug war
                1.   1 billion dollars of aid to Colombia to aid in fighting drugs
                2.   price per kilo of cocaine held stable since aid began
        B.   Crime as rational choice
                1.   cool, calculated actions designed to maximize profits and minimize losses
                2.   decision to engage in crime based on a number of reasons
                3.   crime results when profit exceeds the potential costs
                4.   crime can be fun, rewarding, and satisfying

II.   Development of Rational Choice
        A.   Classical theory of crime
                1.   crime is a result of rational choice
                2.   classical school theory developed by Beccaria
                3.   theory based on choice

　　　　4.　　fair and certain punishment to control crime
　　　　5.　　crime and punishment must be proportionate
　　B.　　Bentham
　　　　1.　　concept of utilitarianism explains human conduct
　　　　2.　　punishment has four objectives
　　　　　　a.　　to prevent all criminal offenses
　　　　　　b.　　to convince an offender to commit a less serious offense
　　　　　　c.　　to convince an offender to use no more force than is necessary
　　　　　　d.　　to prevent crime as cheaply as possible
　　　　3.　　brought about reforms in several justice systems
　　　　4.　　lost popularity to positivism as leading explanation of crime
　　C.　　Choice theory emerges
　　　　1.　　mid 1970s brings the return of choice theory
　　　　2.　　questions arise about the effectiveness of rehabilitation
　　　　3.　　rise in crime and fear of crime
　　D.　　Thinking About Crime
　　　　1.　　James Q. Wilson debunks positivist thinking
　　　　2.　　emphasis on formal sanctions to deter illegal conduct
　　　　3.　　famous observation 'wicked people exist'
　　E.　　Impact on crime control
　　　　1.　　conservative shift in nation with the election of Reagan
　　　　2.　　tough laws were passed and nation's prison population booms
　　F.　　Concepts of rational choice
　　　　1.　　potential offenders consider personal and situational factors before crime
　　　　2.　　reasoning criminal weighs the potential costs and benefits of their action
　　　　3.　　offense specific means that offenders react selectively to offense characteristics
　　　　4.　　offender specific criminals decide whether they have the necessary prerequisites
　　　　5.　　distinction made between crime and criminality

III.　　Structuring Criminality
　　A.　　Economic opportunity
　　　　1.　　motivation by economic gains
　　　　2.　　perceptions of the lack of legitimate alternatives
　　B.　　Learning and experience
　　　　1.　　criminals learn the limits of their powers
　　　　2.　　Morgan and Joe's study of female drug dealers
　　　　　　a.　　control over their lives, economic independence, and professional pride
　　C.　　Knowledge of criminal techniques
　　　　1.　　criminals learn techniques to avoid detection
　　　　2.　　drug dealers learn techniques to avoid detection and losses
　　　　3.　　female crack dealers' arrest avoidance techniques
　　　　　　a.　　projected self image
　　　　　　b.　　stashing
　　　　　　c.　　selling hours
　　　　　　d.　　routine activities/ staged behaviors
　　　　4.　　dealing drugs in porno movie theaters
　　　　5.　　playing the peep game to identify potential threats
　　　　6.　　benefits of drug dealing alone or in a group
　　　　7.　　some burglars like thefts in permeable neighborhoods
　　　　　　a.　　offer potential to escape without detection

IV.　　Structuring Crime
　　A.　　Choosing the type of crime
　　　　1.　　some criminals are specialists
　　　　2.　　some criminals are generalists

3.   crime may be structured by the immediacy of the need for cash
B.   Choosing the time and place of crime
      1.   burglars prefer working between 9am and 11am and in early afternoon
      2.   Saturdays are not a good day since people are likely to be home
      3.   burglars may choose to break in when events are planned
      4.   rational choice evident in burglary target selection
          a.   secluded houses
          b.   free standing buildings
          c.   near stop signs
      5.   burglars are unlikely to travel long distances for crime
          a.   they don't have familiarity with the area
          b.   criminals have familiarity with police capabilities

C.   Choosing the target of crime
      1.   criminals aware of target vulnerability
      2.   people engaging in antisocial activity are at increased risk for victimization
          a.   offenders are unlikely to call the police
      3.   avoid people who are potentially armed to defend themselves

V.   Is Crime Rational?
A.   Are street crimes rational
      1.   some crimes display calculated planning
      2.   random acts of opportunity versus well thought out conspiracies
      3.   even unplanned acts can be the product of careful risk assessment
      4.   robbers more likely to choose targets who are vulnerable
          a.   avoid those who may be armed
      5.   robbers aware of awareness space
B.   Is drug use rational
      1.   onset of drug use controlled by rational choice
      2.   benefits include fun, excitement, and thrills
      3.   in the drug business
          a.   mutual societies
          b.   periodic markets
          c.   fixed site neighborhoods
          d.   drug marts
C.   Can violence be rational
      1.   case of Brandon Wilson who killed 9 year old boy
      2.   weapons possession for protection- rational choice
      3.   anger, aggression, and rational planning
      4.   serial killers select their targets emphasizing the powerless
D.   Rational rapists
      1.   travel an average of 3 miles to their target
      2.   crime has an allure that some cannot resist
      3.   edgework seen as a benefit and motivator of crime
E.   Benefits of crime
      1.   criminal way of life beneficial to some people
      2.   crime provides mastery over their environment
      3.   crime may boost their self esteem
      4.   people may engage in antisocial acts as problem solving mechanism
      5.   crime becomes a less attractive problem solving device as people get older
      6.   Katz identifies the immediate benefits of crime
          a.   labeled the seductions of crime
          b.   crime can provide sneaky thrills of crime
          c.   situational inducements important for explaining juvenile behavior

VI.   Eliminating Crime
    A.   Situational crime prevention
        1.   attempts to convince offenders to avoid specific targets
        2.   offenders are denied access to suitable targets
        3.   potential offenders are carefully monitored
        4.   Newman coins the term defensible space
            a.   architectural can reduce criminal opportunities
        5.   1992 book by Clarke, Situational Crime Prevention
        6.   A total community situational crime prevention model
        7.   16 techniques of situational crime prevention
    B.   Targeting specific crimes
        1.   four categories of crime prevention
            a.   increase the effort to commit crimes
            b.   increase the risk of committing crime
            c.   reduce the rewards of committing crimes
            d.   induce guilt or shame for committing crimes
    C.   Crime discouragers
        1.   directly influence crime prevention
        2.   guardians, handlers, and managers
        3.   with aids and assistance can impact crime rates
    D.   Diffusion and discouragement
        1.   diffusion- efforts to reduce one crime impact another
        2.   discouragement- criminals forego criminal activity
            a.   impression crime does not pay
            b.   example with SMART program and LOJACK
    E.   Displacement, extinction, and fear
        1.   people may choose alternative targets for crime
        2.   extinction provides a short term positive impact
        3.   fear of crime or retaliation can negatively impact program implementation

V.   General Deterrence
    A.   General deterrence
        1.   people will violate the law if left free and unrestricted
        2.   people will fear formal sanctions to crime
        3.   severity, certainty, and speed of legal sanctions impact crime rates
    B.   Certainty of punishment
        1.   likelihood of punishment outweighs possible benefits
        2.   criminals realize there is only a small chance they will be caught
        3.   police may not make an arrest if they are aware of the offense
        4.   good chance of receiving a lenient sentence if caught
        5.   tipping point is when the certainty of apprehension reaches critical percent
    C.   Does police activity deter crime
        1.   question whether the amount of police has impact on crime rates
        2.   high crime places may add additional officers confounding issue
        3.   increased police presence can lower crime rates long term
        4.   Kansas City Police Study
            a.   variations in level of patrol had no effect on outcome measures
        5.   crackdowns- increased police presence to increase potential for apprehension
    D.   Severity of punishment and deterrence
        1.   severity of punishment should lower crime rates
        2.   inverse relationship between crime rates and probability to go to prison
        3.   others question the effect of deterrence
            a.   relatively low odds of getting caught
    E.   Capital punishment
        1.   capital punishment viewed as the ultimate deterrent

2. immediate impact
   a. capital punishment may increase homicides immediately following execution
3. comparative research
   a. little difference in murder rates across jurisdictions
   b. murder rates decline in nations following abolition of capital punishment
4. time series studies
   a. failed to show a significant difference over time

F. Rethinking the deterrent effect
   1. murder is seen as an expressive crime of passion
   2. some contend the deterrent effect has been hidden in comparisons

G. Informal sanctions
   1. informal sanctions may have greater impact than formal sanctions
   2. offenders face embarrassment, guilt and shame
   3. legal mechanisms can reinforce informal mechanisms

H. Shame and humiliation
   1. shame and embarrassment can be powerful deterrents
   2. personal shame and public humiliation
   3. spousal abusers fear social costs of crime
   4. women feel shame and guilt more than males
   5. shame can influence instrumental crimes

I. Critique of general deterrence
   1. purpose of the system is to create threat system
   2. rationality
      a. personality disorders may minimize rational choice
      b. highly emotional state
   3. need
      a. offenders may lack education and skills
      b. lack of options may limit the impact of formal penalties
      c. formal sanctions become irrelevant
   4. greed
      a. some may feel benefits are worth the risks
   5. severity and speed
      a. system is not very effective in apprehending offenders
      b. juvenile system is more lenient

VI. Concept of Specific Deterrence
   A. Specific deterrence
      1. criminal sanctions deter future acts by criminals
      2. questions arise over the failure to deter offenders who have been punished
      3. incarceration may slow or delay recidivism
      4. overall probability of recidivism remains unchanged
      5. punishment may increase re-offending for some offenders
   B. Incapacitation
      1. theory that more prisoners should reduce crime rates
      2. incapacitation effect
      3. more than 2 million people behind bars
      4. crime may be influenced by other factors rather than imprisonment rates
   C. Can incapacitation reduce crime
      1. benefits of incapacitation remains inconclusive
      2. if prison population cut in half, crime rates projected to increase 4 %
      3. other studies report different conclusions with regard to prison populations
   D. Logic behind incarceration
      1. criminals unable to commit crimes while in prison
      2. offenders may be more likely to commit crimes when released
      3. expose younger inmates to more experienced offenders

4.   someone ready to take the place of offenders who are imprisoned
5.   most crime committed by offenders with less chance of getting a prison sentence
6.   huge financial costs associated with incapacitation
E.   Selective incapacitation
1.   selective incapacitation removes high rate offenders
2.   three strikes

VII.   Policy Implications of Choice Theory
A.   Just desert
1.   Von Hirsch book Doing Justice
2.   those who violate the rights of others deserve to be punished
3.   we should not add to human suffering
4.   punishment adds to suffering
5.   punishment may prevent more suffering
6.   just desert does not involve offenders' future actions only their past

KEY TERMS

crack downs: The concentration of police resources on a particular problem area, such as street level drug dealing, to eradicate or displace criminal activity.

crime: A violation of societal rules of behavior as interpreted and expressed by a criminal legal code created by people holding social and political power.

crime discouragers: Discouragers can be grouped into three categories: guardians who monitor targets, handlers who monitor potential offenders, and managers who monitor places.

crime displacement: An effect of crime prevention efforts in which efforts to control crime in one area shift illegal activities to another area.

criminality: A personality trait of the individual as distinct from a crime which is considered an event.

defensible space: The principle that crime prevention can be achieved through modifying the physical environment to reduce the opportunity individuals have to commit crimes.

deterrence theory: The view that the probability of arrest, conviction, and sanctioning increases, crime rates should decline.

diffusion of benefits: An effect that occurs when an effort to control one type of crime has the unexpected benefit of reducing the incidence of another crime.

discouragement: An effect which occurs when an effort made to eliminate one type of crime also controls others, because it reduces the value of criminal activity by limiting the access to desirable targets.

edge work: The excitement or exhilaration of successfully executing illegal activities in dangerous situations.

extinction: The phenomenon in which a crime prevention effort has an immediate impact which then dissipates as criminals adjust to new conditions.

general deterrence: A crime control policy that depends on the fear of criminal penalties.

incapacitation effect: The idea that keeping offenders in confinement will eliminate the risk of their committing further offenses.

informal sanctions: Disapproval, stigma, or anger directed toward an offender by significant others, resulting in shame, embarrassment, and loss of self respect.

just desert: The philosophy of justice that asserts that those who violate the rights of others deserve to be punished. The severity of punishment should be commensurate with the seriousness of the crime.

offender specific: The idea that offenders evaluate their skills, motives, needs, and fears before deciding to commit a crime.

offense specific: The idea that offenders react selectively to the characteristics of particular crimes.

permeable neighborhood: Areas with a greater than usual number of access streets from traffic arteries into the neighborhood.

rational choice: The view that crime is a function of a decision making process in which the potential offender weighs the potential costs and benefits of an illegal act.

reasoning criminal: According to the rational choice approach, law violating behavior occurs when an offender decides to risk breaking the law after considering both personal factors and situational factors.

selective incapacitation: The policy of creating enhanced prison sentences for the relatively small group of dangerous chronic offenders.

situational crime prevention: A method of crime prevention that stresses tactics and strategies to eliminate or reduce particular crimes in narrow settings.

specific deterrence: A crime control policy suggesting that punishment be severe enough to convince convicted offenders never to repeat their criminal activity.

suitable targets: According to routine activity theory, a target for crime that is relatively valuable, easily transportable, and not capably guarded.

three strikes and you're out: Policy whereby people convicted of three felony offenses receive a mandatory life sentence.

utilitarianism: The view that people's behavior is motivated by the pursuit of pleasure and the avoidance of pain.

TEST BANK

MULTIPLE CHOICE

1. Which of the following is not considered one of the four main objectives of criminal punishment according to Bentham?
   - A. to brutally punish an offender for his transgression
   - B. to convince an offender to commit a less serious offense
   - C. to convince an offender to use no more force than is necessary
   - D. to prevent crime as cheaply as possible

2. Coinciding with the publication of James Q. Wilson's book, Thinking About Crime, was a conservative shift in national politics which resulted in the election of _____ to the presidency.
   - A. Jimmy Carter
   - B. Gerald Ford
   - C. Howard Taft
   - D. Ronald Reagan

3. Martinson's report What Works? was critical of which school of though?
   - A. general deterrence
   - B. specific deterrence
   - C. positivism
   - D. just deserts

4. Disapproval, stigma, or anger directed toward an offender by significant others, resulting in shame, embarrassment, and loss of self respect best characterizes _____.
   - A. informal sanctions
   - B. general deterrence
   - C. just deserts
   - D. positivism

5. _____ is the view that people's behavior is motivated by the pursuit of pleasure and the avoidance of pain.
   - A. specific deterrence
   - B. positivism
   - C. utilitarianism
   - D. just deserts

6. The phenomenon in which a crime prevention effort has an immediate impact which then dissipates as criminals adjust to new conditions best describes which concept?
   - A. displacement
   - B. extinction
   - C. discouragement
   - D. displacement

7. Areas with a greater than usual number of access streets from traffic arteries into the neighborhood are called _____.
   - A. a permeable neighborhood
   - B. a transitory area
   - C. projects or ghettos
   - D. crime generators

8. The philosophy of justice that asserts that those who violate the rights of others deserve to be punished, and the severity of punishment should be commensurate with the seriousness of the crime is called _____.
   - A. just desert
   - B. general deterrence
   - C. positivism
   - D. specific deterrence

9. The origins of choice theory can be traced to the writings of which utilitarian philosophers?
   - A. Beccaria and Bentham
   - B. Marx and Engels
   - C. Courtright and Mackey
   - D. Lombroso and Quetlet

10. Beccaria was convinced that fair and certain punishment would _____.
   - A. prevent the onset of criminality
   - B. deter criminals
   - C. achieve social justice
   - D. control recidivism

61

11. Theories that have at their core the rational decision making of motivated criminals can trace their origin to what school of criminology?
- A. positivist school
- B. classical school
- C. determinism school
- D. conflict school

12. What British philosopher helped to popularize Beccaria's utilitarian views?
- A. Wilson
- B. Van den Haag
- C. Lombroso
- D. Bentham

13. Since punishment is harmful to a society, Bentham suggests that it is justified only when it satisfies what condition?
- A. if it is administered arbitrarily to keep criminals on their toes
- B. when it promises to prevent a greater evil than it creates
- C. when it utilizes a capricious scale of severity
- D. when it induces harm that is much greater than the harm caused by the criminal act

14. A review of rehabilitation programs which concluded that they failed to prevent future criminal activity was called _____.
- A. Rehab programs: The untold story
- B. Treatment programs, electric socks, and other wastes
- C. What Works
- D. The truth about rehabilitation programs

15. _____ are aimed at making potential criminals fear the consequences of crime; the threat of punishment is aimed at convincing potential criminals that crime does not pay.
- A. situational crime prevention
- B. general deterrence
- C. specific deterrence
- D. selective incapacitation

16. _____ refers to punishing known criminals so severely that they will never be tempted to repeat their offenses.
- A. situational crime prevention
- B. general deterrence
- C. specific deterrence
- D. selective incapacitation

17. New credit cards often have the cardholders picture on it; this crime prevention strategy would fall under what category of crime prevention?
- A. target hardening
- B. target reduction
- C. inducing guilt
- D. selective incapacitation

18. According to situational crime prevention concepts, a _____ monitors targets.
- A. guardian
- B. handler
- C. custodian
- D. manager

19. According to situational crime prevention concepts, a _____ monitor potential offenders.
- A. guardian
- B. handler
- C. custodian
- D. manager

20. According to situational crime prevention concepts, a _____ monitor particular places.
- A. guardian
- B. handler
- C. custodian
- D. manager

21. Which of the following best describes selective incapacitation?
    A. idea that keeping offenders in confinement will eliminate the risk of their committing further offenses
    B. disapproval, stigma, or anger directed toward an offender by significant others, resulting in shame, embarrassment, and loss of self respect
    C. policy of creating enhanced prison sentences for the relatively small group of dangerous chronic offenders
    D. crime control policy suggesting that punishment be severe enough to convince convicted offenders never to repeat their criminal activity

22. Which of the following best describes a crackdown?
    A. crime control policy that depends on the fear of criminal penalties
    B. view that the probability of arrest, conviction, and sanctioning increases, crime rates should decline
    C. concentration of police resources on a particular problem area, such as street level drug dealing, to eradicate or displace criminal activity.
    D. philosophy of justice that asserts that those who violate the rights of others deserve to be punished

23. Which of the following best describes specific deterrence?
    A. idea that keeping offenders in confinement will eliminate the risk of their committing further offenses
    B. disapproval, stigma, or anger directed toward an offender by significant others, resulting in shame, embarrassment, and loss of self respect
    C. policy of creating enhanced prison sentences for the relatively small group of dangerous chronic offenders
    D. crime control policy suggesting that punishment be severe enough to convince convicted offenders never to repeat their criminal activity

24. Which of the following best describes incapacitation effect?
    A. idea that keeping offenders in confinement will eliminate the risk of their committing further offenses
    B. disapproval, stigma, or anger directed toward an offender by significant others, resulting in shame, embarrassment, and loss of self respect
    C. policy of creating enhanced prison sentences for the relatively small group of dangerous chronic offenders
    D. crime control policy suggesting that punishment be severe enough to convince convicted offenders never to repeat their criminal activity

25. Which of the following best describes just deserts?
    A. crime control policy that depends on the fear of criminal penalties
    B. view that the probability of arrest, conviction, and sanctioning increases, crime rates should decline
    C. concentration of police resources on a particular problem area, such as street level drug dealing, to eradicate or displace criminal activity.
    D. philosophy of justice that asserts that those who violate the rights of others deserve to be punished

TRUE/FALSE

1. Beccaria believed crime and punishment must be proportional; if not, people would be encouraged to commit more serious offenses.
    A. True   B. False

2. Coinciding with the publication of James Q. Wilson's book, Thinking About Crime, was a conservative shift in national politics which resulted in the election of Jimmy Carter to the presidency.
    A. True   B. False

3. Younger rapists who have less experience committing crimes travel less distances to their victims and are therefore more at risk for detection.
    A. True   B. False

63

4. Bentham believed that people choose actions on the basis of whether they produce pleasure and happiness and help them avoid pain and unhappiness.

      A. True   B. False

5. According to Bentham, formal punishment has the objective to prevent all criminal offenses.

      A. True   B. False

6. Disapproval, stigma, or anger directed toward an offender by significant others, resulting in shame, embarrassment, and loss of self-respect best characterizes just deserts.

      A. True   B. False

7. Beccaria coined the term defensible space.

      A. True   B. False

8. Research in several nations around the world found little evidence that countries with a death penalty have lower violence rates than those without it; homicide rates actually decline after capital punishment is abolished.

      A. True   B. False

9. The philosophy of just deserts contends that people who commit crimes, even relatively minor offenses, should be severely punished in order to teach other people that crime does not pay.

      A. True   B. False

10. Research indicates that choice theory applies to property crime but does not apply to property crimes or drug offenses.

      A. True   B. False

11. Research indicates that corner homes, usually near traffic lights or stop signs, are the ones most likely to be burglarized.

      A. True   B. False

12. The Kansas City patrol study revealed that adding police presence resulted in more arrests, lower fear of crime, and lower crime rates.

      A. True   B. False

13. Crime is a personality trait of the individual as distinct from a crime which is considered an event.

      A. True   B. False

14. A permeable neighborhood is an area with a greater than usual number of access streets from traffic arteries into the neighborhood.

      A. True   B. False

15. Defensible space is an area with a greater than usual number of access streets from traffic arteries into the neighborhood.

      A. True   B. False

16. Criminality is a violation of societal rules of behavior as interpreted and expressed by a criminal legal code created by people holding social and political power.

      A. True   B. False

17. Edge work is the excitement or exhilaration of successfully executing illegal activities in dangerous situations.

      A. True   B. False

18. Edge work is a method of crime prevention that stresses tactics and strategies to eliminate or reduce particular crimes in narrow settings.

    A. True   B. False

19. The principle that crime prevention can be achieved through modifying the physical environment to reduce the opportunity individuals have to commit crimes is called defensible space.

    A. True   B. False

20. The Metro in Washington DC attempted to fight subway crime by adding public restrooms, locker facilities, convenient seating, and fast food restaurants.

    A. True   B. False

FILL IN

1. The view that crime is a function of a decision making process in which the potential offender weighs the potential costs and benefits of an illegal act is called _____ choice.

2. _____ is the view that people's behavior is motivated by the pursuit of pleasure and the avoidance of pain.

3. According to the rational choice approach, the _____ criminal describes when law violating behavior occurs when an offender decides to risk breaking the law after considering both personal factors and situational factors.

4. _____ is the idea that offenders react selectively to the characteristics of particular crimes.

5. _____ is the idea that offenders evaluate their skills, motives, needs, and fears before deciding to commit a crime.

6. _____ is a violation of societal rules of behavior as interpreted and expressed by a criminal legal code created by people holding social and political power.

7. _____ deterrence is a crime control policy that depends on the fear of criminal penalties to deter potential offenders from committing crime.

8. The phenomenon in which a crime prevention effort has an immediate impact which then dissipates as criminals adjust to new conditions is called _____.

9. Crime _____ is an effect of crime prevention efforts in which efforts to control crime in one area shift illegal activities to another area.

10. _____ is an effect which occurs when an effort made to eliminate one type of crime also controls others, because it reduces the value of criminal activity by limiting the access to desirable targets.

11. _____ of benefits refers to an effect that occurs when an effort to control one type of crime has the unexpected benefit of reducing the incidence of another crime.

12. Crime discouragers include _____ who monitor targets.

13. Crime discouragers include _____ who monitor potential offenders.

14. Crime discouragers include _____ who monitor places.

15. _____ is a personality trait of the individual as distinct from a crime which is considered an event.

ESSAY

1. Discuss the basic principles of classical criminology and describe what policies have resulted from this theoretical model.

2. What types of crime are clearly based on rational choice?

3. What is situational crime prevention and how would it be used to prevent crime?

4. What is the difference between general deterrence and specific deterrence?

5. What does research testing the deterrence effects of capital punishment indicate?

CHAPTER FIVE
CHOICE THEORY
ANSWER KEY

MULTIPLE CHOICE ITEMS

1. A	6. B	11. B	16. C	21. C
2. D	7. A	12. D	17. A	22. C
3. C	8. A	13. B	18. A	23. D
4. A	9. A	14. C	19. B	24. A
5. C	10. B	15. B	20. D	25. D

TRUE FALSE ITEMS

1. A	6. B	11. A	16. B
2. B	7. B	12. B	17. A
3. A	8. A	13. B	18. B
4. A	9. B	14. A	19. A
5. A	10. B	15. B	20. B

FILL IN ITEMS

1. rational	6. crime	11. diffusion
2. utilitarianism	7. general	12. guardians
3. reasoning	8. extinction	13. handlers
4. offense specific	9. displacement	14. managers
5. offender specific	10. discouragement	15. criminality

CHAPTER SIX
TRAIT THEORIES

LEARNING OBJECTIVES

1. Recognize the foundations of biological theory.
2. Identify and differentiate between Biosocial and psychological theories of crime.
3. Identify biochemical factors linked to criminality.
4. Identify neurological factors linked to criminality.
5. Identify personality factors linked to criminality.

CHAPTER SUMMARY

The earliest positivist criminologists were biologists. Led by Lombroso, these early researchers believed that people manifested primitive traits that made them born criminals. Today, that research is debunked because of poor methodology, testing, and logic. Biological views fell out of favor in the early 20th century. In the 1970s, spurred by the publication of Wilson's Sociobiology, several criminologists again turned to study of the biological basis of criminality. The effort has focused on the causes of violent crime. Interest has centered on several areas: 1) biochemical factors, such as diet, allergies, hormonal imbalances, and environmental contaminants; 2) neurophysiological factors, such as brain disorders, EEG abnormalities, tumors, and head injuries; and 3) genetic factors, such as the XYY syndrome and inherited traits. There is also an evolutionary branch, which holds that changes in the human condition evolving over time may help explain crime rate differences.

Psychological attempts to explain criminal behavior have their historical roots in the concept that all criminals are insane or mentally damaged. This position is no longer accepted. Today, there are three main psychological perspectives. According to the psycho-dynamic view, originated by Freud, aggressive behavior is linked to personality conflicts developed in childhood. In the view of some psychoanalyst, psychotics are aggressive, unstable people who can easily become involved in crime. According to behavioral and social learning theorists, criminality is a learned behavior; children who are exposed to violence and see it rewarded may become violent as adults. In contrast, cognitive psychologists are concerned with human development and how people perceive the world. They see criminality as a function of improper information processing or moral development.

Psychological traits, such as personality and intelligence, have been linked to criminality. One important subject of study has bene the psychopath, a person who lacks emotion and concern for others. The controversial issue of the relationship of IQ to criminality has been resurrected once again with the publication of studies purporting to show that criminals have lower IQs than noncriminals. Psychologists have developed standardized tests with which to measure personality traits. One avenue of research has been to determine whether criminals and noncriminals manifest any differences in their responses to test items.

CHAPTER OUTLINE

I.   Introduction
      A.   Russell Weston Jr. shooting in Washington DC
            1.   diagnosed as a paranoid schizophrenic
            2.   troubled past beginning in high school
      B.   Media depictions of troubled psychos getting in trouble
            1.   view that criminals are deviant and mentally unstable
            2.   some may develop mental or physical traits from birth or shortly after
            3.   some factors may be associated with low academic achievement
                a.   low academic achievement indirectly linked to crime
II.   Foundations of Trait Theory

A.   Lombroso's born criminal
    1.   used scientific methods to identify physical abnormalities linked to criminals
    2.   Garofalo saw offenders as having a tolerance for pain
        a.   submit to tattooing
    3.   Ferri added the social dimension to the biological perspective
        a.   offenders should not be held personally or morally responsible
    4.   inheritance school examines genetic link of crime
    5.   somatotype school
        a. mesomorphs, ectomorphs, and endomorphs
        b. regarded today as historical curiosity rather than fact

B.   Impact of Sociobiology
    1.   biological school falls out of favor in early 20th century
    2.   impact of biophobia
    3.   reciprocal altruism- people's actions driven by gene survival
    4.   trait theory focuses on genetic influences on human behavior

III.   Modern Trait Theory
    A.   Differences among criminals
        1.   trait theorists not concerned about definitions of crime
        2.   focus more on aggression, violence, and impulsive behavior
        3.   environmental stimuli can suppress or trigger antisocial behavior
        4.   single factor cannot explain all crime
        5.   equipotentiality not the case
    B.   Social interaction
        1.   focus on basic human behavior and drives
        2.   environmental conditions in inner city may influence antisocial behavior
        3.   value in explaining chronic recidivism
    C.   The Nature Assumption
        1.   Harris' book The Nature Assumption
        2.   valued genetics over socialization
        3.   abuse-delinquency link questioned
        4.   home environment not as strong an influence

IV.   Biological Trait Theory
    A.   Biocriminology
        1.   belief that biological, environmental, and social conditions influence behavior
        2.   not all humans have equipotentiality
    B.   Learning potential
        1.   such behavior is learned
        2.   each organism is believed to have a unique potential for learning
        3.   physical and social environment interact to limit or enhance capacity to learn
    C.   Instinct
        1.   some believe that learning is influenced by instinctual drives
        2.   the possess and control instinct

V.   Biochemical Conditions and Crime
    A.   Biochemical and crime
        1.   influence of diet and environment
        2.   White's Twinky defense
    B.   Chemical and mineral influences
        1.   minimal levels of minerals and chemicals needed for normal functioning
        2.   vitamin deficiencies can cause behavioral problems
    C.   Excessive sugar
        1.   glucose processing linked to reasoning power and attention deficit
        2.   violent behavior linked to diet

3.　　　dissenting views fail to establish the causal connection
　　D.　　Hypoglycemia
　　　　1.　　occurs when glucose falls below necessary levels for normal functioning
　　　　2.　　link between hypoglycemia and violent outbursts
　　　　3.　　reactive hypoglycemia found in groups of habitually violent offenders
　　E.　　Hormonal influences
　　　　1.　　Wilson identifies hormones, enzymes, and neurotransmitters as key to behavior
　　　　2.　　evaluating the association between violent behavior and hormonal levels
　　　　3.　　prenatal exposure to testosterone linked to violence and aggression
　　F.　　How hormones can influence behavior
　　　　1.　　hormones cause areas of the brain to become less sensitive to stimuli
　　　　2.　　lowering of seizure thresholds in the limbic system
　　　　3.　　right shift in neocortical functioning
　　G.　　Premenstrual syndrome
　　　　1.　　Dalton research criticized for methodological flaws
　　　　2.　　Fishbein found at least a small number of women prone to PMS hostility
　　H.　　Allergies
　　　　1.　　can cause swelling in the brain and produce sensitivity in the CNS
　　　　2.　　conditions linked to mental, emotional, and behavioral problems
　　I.　　Environmental contaminants
　　　　1.　　copper, mercury, and inorganic gases can influence behavior
　　　　2.　　food dyes and artificial colors linked to antisocial behavior
　　J.　　Lead levels
　　　　1.　　lead levels linked to delinquency, aggression, and lower IQs

VI.　　Neurophysiological Conditions and Crime
　　A.　　Neurological dysfunction
　　　　1.　　first received attention with the case of Charles Whitman
　　　　2.　　had tumor and experienced urges to kill before event
　　　　3.　　studies show link between brain impairment and aggression
　　B.　　Neurological impairments
　　　　1.　　various tests available
　　　　2.　　EEG records electrical brain waves
　　　　3.　　valuable tool for detecting crime-producing physical conditions
　　　　4.　　abnormal patterns linked to aggression
　　C.　　Minimal brain dysfunction
　　　　1.　　examples include dyslexia, visual perception problems, and hyperactivity
　　　　2.　　poor attention span, temper tantrums, and aggression also linked
　　　　3.　　MBD is manifested through episodes of explosive rage
　　　　4.　　seen as a cause of spousal abuse, suicide, aggression, and homicide
　　D.　　ADHD
　　　　1.　　developmentally inappropriate lack of attention, impulsivity, and hyperactivity
　　　　2.　　symptoms of ADHD identified in text
　　　　3.　　treatment can improve life circumstances
　　E.　　Other brain dysfunctions
　　　　1.　　linked to problems in the frontal and temporal regions of the brain
　　F.　　Tumors, injury, and disease
　　　　1.　　linked to personality changes, hallucinations, and psychotic episodes
　　　　2.　　linked to depression, irritability, temper outbursts, and homicidal attacks
　　G.　　Brain chemistry
　　　　1.　　neurotransmitters are chemical compounds which influence brain functions
　　　　2.　　prenatal exposure to androgens and low levels of MOA linked to brain behavior
　　H.　　Arousal theory
　　　　1.　　thrill of getting away with it
　　　　2.　　sensation seekers may seek more stimulation with violence

3. some brains have more nerve cells

VII. Genetics and Crime
    A. Modern resurgence
        1. belief that personality traits are genetically predetermined
        2. Richard Speck and the XYY chromosome controversy
    B. Parental deviance
        1. evidence that children of criminals more likely to become criminal
        2. inter-generational deviance may be learned
    C. Sibling influence
        1. influence of siblings may be genetic or learned
    D. Twin behavior
        1. studies conducted between 1929 and 1961 found pattern
            a. 60% of MZ twins shared patterns
            b. 30% of DZ twins shared patterns
        2. recent findings have supported the pattern
        3. evidence is still not conclusive proof that crime is genetically predetermined
    E. Adoption studies
        1. relationships may exist between biological parents' behavior and children's behavior
        2. criminality of biological father was a strong predictor of child's behavior
    F. Evaluating genetic research
        1. genetic makeup is the key determinant to influence behavior
        2. gene crime relationship is quite controversial

VIII. Evolutionary Views of Crime
    A. Traits have been ingrained
        1. aggressive males have more offspring and pass on genes
        2. characteristics may be responsible for some crime patterns
    B. Evolution of gender and crime
        1. belief that gender roles are genetic for survival
        2. abusive males may fear the potential loss of their younger mates
    C. R/k selection theory
        1. rs reproduce rapidly, ks reproduce slowly
        2. males are more r- orientated
    D. Cheater theory
        1. subpopulation of males use stealth to impregnate females
        2. they mimic more stable males
        3. use criminal methods to acquire resources
            a. seek to impress younger, less intelligent women
    E. Evaluation of the biological branch
        1. perspectives raise questions, especially about rape
        2. perspectives criticized as not explaining certain patterns
            a. regional variations and social influences
        3. lack of adequate empirical testing

IX. Psychological Trait Theories
    A. Goring's English Convict
        1. little physical differences between criminals and non-criminals
        2. crime linked to defective intelligence
    B. Theory of imitation
        1. Tarde was early learning theorist
        2. people learn from each other through a process of imitation
        3. three laws of imitation
        4. psychological experts play active role in development of criminology

X. Psychological Perspective

A.   Freud and psychoanalytic theory
        1.   conscious, precocious, and unconscious minds
        2.   id, ego, and superego
B.   Psychosexual stages of human development
        1.   most basic human drive is eros
        2.   development stages of oral, anal, phallic, latency, and genital
        3.   unsatisfied development can cause fixation
C.   Psychodynamics of abnormal behavior
        1.   neurotics experience feelings of mental anguish
        2.   they are afraid they are losing control of their personalities
        3.   psychotics have lost total control and are dominated by their id
        4.   schizophrenia is the most common form of psychosis
            a.   paranoid schizophrenia
            b.   Adler's inferiority complex
            c.   Erickson's identity crisis
            d.   Aichorn's latent delinquency
D.   Psychodynamics of criminal behavior
        1.   criminals suffer from weak egos and undeveloped superegos
        2.   weak egos can be easily led into crime
        3.   bipolar disorder
        4.   crime is a manifestation of feelings of oppression

XI.   Behavioral Theories
    A.   Social learning theory
        1.   aggressive behavior is learned through life experiences
        2.   Bandura saw rewards for aggressive behavior
        3.   saw violence as being learned through behavior modeling
    B.   Social learning and violence
        1.   three principle sources of learning
            a.   family, environment, and mass media
        2.   physical or verbal assault may trigger violence
        3.   four factors produce violence and aggression

XII.   Cognitive Theory
    A.   Moral and intellectual development theory
        1.   Piaget as founder of approach
        2.   Kohlberg's stages of development
        3.   found that criminals were significantly lower in moral development
        4.   people who obey the law simply to avoid punishment or self interests
            a.   more likely to commit crimes
    B.   Information processing
        1.   make decisions involves sequence of cognitive thought processes
        2.   violence-prone people may use incorrect information in decision making
        3.   has been used to explain date rape
        4.   treatment programs are aimed at problem solving skills
    C.   The Criminological Enterprise: Media and violence
        1.   copycat crimes
        2.   teens watch 23 hours of TV a week
        3.   youths more likely to rent horror films than other groups
        4.   numerous anecdotal cases of violence linked to media
        5.   TV violence seen as a contribution to violence rather than a cause of it
        6.   TV provides aggressive scripts to action
        7.   violence in media copied by viewer
        8.   media violence may increase arousal levels in viewers
        9.   promotes attitude changes

10. helps justify preexisting aggressive attitudes
11. dis-inhibits aggressive behavior
12. research is persuasive but inconclusive
D. Crime and mental illness
1. school shooting case
2. serious violence linked to mental illness
3. 75% of male murderers could be diagnosed as mentally ill
4. mentally ill are arrested in disproportionate numbers
E. Is the link valid?
1. mentally ill more likely to withdraw or harm themselves
2. great majority of known criminals are not mentally ill

XIII. Personality and Crime
A. Definitions and traits
1. personality traits are reasonable stable patterns of behavior
2. can include thoughts and emotions
3. research conducted by the Gluecks
4. Eysenck's personality traits
5. neurotics are anxious, tense, and emotionally unstable
B. Sociopathy
1. traits of hyperactivity, impulsive, conduct disorders, and depression
2. antisocial, sociopathic, or psychopathic personality
C. Research on personality
1. projective techniques and personality inventories
a. Rorschach Inkblot Test and TAT
b. MMPI and CPI
2. Pd scores linked to delinquency
D. Are some people crime prone?
1. use of other measures such as MPQ
2. evidence of criminal personality

XIV. Intelligence and Crime
A. Early thoughts
1. linked a below average IQ to crime
2. testing of prisoners led to nature-nurture controversy
B. Nature Theory
1. argues that intelligence is determined genetically
2. low intelligence linked to criminal behavior
3. additional research associated low intelligence to crime
C. Nurture Theory
1. environmental factors create intelligence
2. evaluation of research discredits intelligence- crime link
3. IQ and crime link downplayed
D. IQ and criminality
1. mainstream criminologists dismiss the link
2. Hirschi and Hindelang revive issue in 1977
3. low IQ increases likelihood of crime through school performance

4. recent research supports their findings
E. Cross national studies
1. link found in several comparative studies
F. IQ and crime reconsidered
1. some research finds the link weak
2. The Bell Curve supports the association

73

XV.   Social Policy Implications
    A.   Impact
        1.   psychological counseling
        2.   diet and mood altering medication

KEY TERMS

anal stage: In Freud's schema, the second and third years of life, when the focus of sexual attention is on the elimination of bodily wastes.

androgens: Male sex hormones.

arousal theory: A view of crime suggesting that people who have a high arousal level seek powerful stimuli in their environment to maintain an optimal level of arousal. These stimuli are often associated with violence and aggression. Sociopaths may need greater than average stimulation to bring them up to comfortable levels of living; this need explains their criminal tendencies.

attention deficit hyperactivity disorder: A psychological disorder in which a child shows developmentally inappropriate impulsivity, hyperactivity, and lack of attention.

behaviorism: The branch of psychology concerned with the study of observable behavior rather than unconscious motives. It focuses on the relationship between particular stimuli and people's responses to them.

biophobia: Sociologists who held the view that no serious consideration should be given to biological factors when attempting to understand human nature.

biosocial theory: An approach to criminology that focuses on the interaction between biological and social factors as they relate to crime.

cerebral allergies: A physical condition that causes brain malfunction due to exposure to some environmental or biochemical irritant.

chemical restraints: Anti-psychotic drugs which help control levels of neurotransmitters, that are used to treat violence prone people; also called chemical straight jackets.

cognitive theory: The study of the perception of reality and of the mental processes required to understand the world we live in.

conduct disorder: A psychological condition marked by repeated and severe episodes of antisocial behavior.

conscience: One of two parts of the superego; it distinguishes between what is right and wrong.

contagion effect: Genetic predispositions and early experiences make some people, including twins, susceptible to deviant behavior, which is transmitted by the presence of antisocial siblings in the household.

defective intelligence: Traits such as feeblemindedness, epilepsy, insanity, and defective social instinct, which Goring believed had a significant relationship to criminal behavior.

disorder: Any type of psychological problem, such as anxiety disorders, mood disorders, and conduct disorders.

ego: The part of the personality, developed in early childhood, that helps control the id and keep people's actions within the boundaries of social convention.

ego ideal: Part of the superego; directs the individual into morally acceptable and responsible behaviors, which may not be pleasurable.

Electra complex: A stage of development when girls begin to have sexual feelings for their fathers.

electroencephalograph: A device that can record the electric impulses given off by the brain, commonly called brain waves.

equipotentiality: View that all individuals are equal at birth and are thereafter influenced by their environment.

eros: The instinct to preserve and create life; eros is expressed sexually.

fixated: An adult that exhibits behavior traits characteristic of those encountered during infantile sexual development.

hypoglycemia: A condition that occurs when glucose in the blood falls below levels necessary for normal and efficient brain functioning.

id: The primitive part of people's makeup, present at birth, that represents unconscious biological drives for food, sex, and other life-sustaining necessities. The id seeks instant gratification without concern for the rights of others

inferiority complex: Peoples who have feelings of inferiority and compensate for them with a drive for superiority.

inheritance school: Advocates of this view trace the activities of several generations of families believed to have an especially large number of criminal members.

latency: A developmental stage that begins at age six. During this period, feelings of sexuality are repressed until the genital stage begins at puberty; this marks the beginning of adult sexuality.

neocortex: A part of the human brain; the left side of the neocortex controls the sympathetic feelings towards others.

neuroallergies: Allergies that affect the nervous system and cause the allergic person to produce enzymes that attack wholesome foods as if they were harmful to the body. They may also cause swelling of the brain and produce sensitivity in the central nervous system, conditions linked to mental, emotional and behavioral problems.

neurophysiology: The study of brain activity.

neurotic: People who fear that their primitive id impulses will dominate their personalities.

Oedipus complex: A stage of development when males begin to have sexual feelings for their mother.

oral stage: In Freud's schema, the first year of life, when a child attains pleasure by sucking and biting.

paranoid schizophrenic: Individuals who suffer complex behavior delusions involving wrongdoing or persecution-they think everyone is out to get them.

phallic stage: In Freud's schema, the third year; when children focus their attention on their genitals.

pleasure principle: According to Freud, a theory in which id dominated people are driven to increase their personal pleasure without regard to consequences.

premenstrual syndrome (PMS): The stereotype that several days prior to and during menstruation females are beset by irritability and poor judgement as a result of hormonal changes.

psychotic: In Freudian theory, people whose id has broken free and now dominate their personality. Psychotics suffer from delusions and experience hallucinations and sudden mood shifts.

reality principle: According to Freud, the ability to learn about the consequences of one's actions through experience.

reciprocal altruism: According to sociobiology, acts that are outwardly designed to help others but that have at their core benefits to the self.

schizophrenia: A type of psychosis often marked by bizarre behavior, hallucinations, loss of thought control, and inappropriate emotional responses.

somatotype: A system developed for categorizing people on the basis of their body build.

superego: Incorporation with the personality of the moral standards and values of parents, community, and significant others.

testosterone: The principal male steroid hormone. Testosterone levels decline during the life cycle and may explain why violence rates decline over time.

trait theory: The view that criminality is a product of abnormal biological and/or psychological traits.

Wernicke- Korsakoff disease: A deadly neurological disorder.

TEST BANK

MULTIPLE CHOICE

1. What led to the re-emergence of biological theories of criminality in the 1970s?
    A. the election of Ronald Reagan
    B. the publication of Sociobiology by Wilson
    C. the publication of Biology and Crime by Smith
    D. the Charles Manson case

2. According to Freud, the primitive part of people's makeup, present at birth, that represents unconscious biological drives for food, sex, and other life-sustaining necessities is called the _____; it seeks instant gratification without concern for the rights of others.
    A. id   C. superego
    B. ego   D. mesomorph

3. Individuals who suffer complex behavior delusions involving wrongdoing or persecution- they think everyone is out to get them are called _____.
    A. neurotics   C. psychotics
    B. paranoid schizophrenics   D. mesomorphs

4. In Freud's schema, the _____ stage occurs during the first year of life, when a child attains pleasure by sucking and biting.
    A. oral   C. genital
    B. anal   D. teething

5. The _____ is a stage of development when males begin to have sexual feelings for their mother.
    A. latency stage   C. Electra complex
    B. genital stage   D. Oedipus complex

6. The _____ is a stage of development when girls begin to have sexual feelings for their fathers.
    A. latency stage   C. Electra complex
    B. genital stage   D. Oedipus complex

7. _____ is a developmental stage that begins at age six. During this period, feelings of sexuality are repressed until puberty.
    A. latency stage   C. Electra complex
    B. genital stage   D. Oedipus complex

8. Which theory stems from Lombroso's work?
    A. rational choice theory   C. biological trait theory
    B. psychodynamic theory   D. labeling theory

9. Which early criminologist believed that criminals' common trait was their ability to withstand pain which he witnessed during their tattoo rituals?
    A. Lombroso   C. Ferri
    B. Garofalo   D. Dugdale

10. In Freud's schema, the _____ occurs during the third year when children focus their attention on their genitals.
    A. latency stage   C. phallic stage
    B. genital stage   D. anal stage

11. In Freud's schema, the _____ occurs during the second and third years of life when the focus of sexual attention is on the elimination of bodily wastes.
    A. latency stage   C. phallic stage
    B. genital stage   D. anal stage

12. Which somatotype was reported to be most likely to become criminal?
    A. mesomorph   C. endomorph
    B. ectomorph   D. mightymorph

13. Which psychological perspective on criminology is best described as focusing on the unconscious conflicts, defenses, tendencies, anger, and sexuality?
    A. psychodynamic   C. cognitive
    B. behavioral   D. parapsychology

14. Which psychological perspective on criminology is best described as focusing on past experiences, stimulus, and rewards and punishment?
    A. psychodynamic   C. cognitive
    B. behavioral   D. parapsychology

15. Which psychological perspective on criminology is best described as focusing on thinking, planning, memory, perspective, and ethical values?
    A. psychodynamic   C. cognitive
    B. behavioral   D. parapsychology

16. Which somatotype was reported to have well developed muscles and an athletic appearance.
    A. mesomorph   C. endomorph
    B. ectomorph   D. mightymorph

17. Which somatotype was reported to have heavy builds and are slow moving; they are associated with lethargic behavior.
    A. mesomorph   C. endomorph
    B. ectomorph   D. mightymorph

18. According to the sociobiologist, what is the true motive of coming to the aid of someone in need?
    A. reciprocal altruism   C. cognitive dissonance
    B. reflective enhancement   D. universal relativism

19. Schoenthaler's research indicates that behavior can be changed by controlling the intake of _____ in the diet of juveniles.
    A. vitamin C   C. sugar
    B. protein   D. alcohol

20. What condition occurs when glucose in the blood stream falls below levels needed for normal and efficient brain functioning?
    A. hypothermia   C. neuroticism
    B. hypomania   D. hypoglycemia

21. Alcoholics often suffer from what deficiency because of their poor diet?
    A. Vitamin E   C. beta carotene
    B. thiamine   D. vitamin C

22. What is the only body organ able to obtain its energy solely from the combustion of carbohydrates?
    A. the liver   C. the heart
    B. the brain   D. the pancreas

23. Harris' book The Nature Assumption caused much controversy because it stated that criminal behavior was more closely related to what?
    A. TV consumption   C. genetics
    B. greed and lust   D. parenting styles

24. Unusual or excessive reactions of the body to foreign substances are known as _____.
    A. contaminants   C. intake disorders
    B. allergies   D. paranoia

25. What contaminant did Denno identify as one of the most significant predictors of delinquency among 900 African American youths in her study?
    A. milk   C. DDT
    B. lead   D. sulphate

TRUE/FALSE

1. According to the author, the work of Lombroso and his contemporaries is regarded today as important scientific fact which is the basis of contemporary justice policy.
    A. True   B. False

2. The publication of Sociobiology by E. O. Wilson led to the re-emergence of biological theories of criminality in the 1970s.
    A. True   B. False

3. Biosocial theorists believe strongly in equipotentiality as a basis for their theories.
    A. True   B. False

4. The author notes that people with vitamin deficiency or dependency do not manifest many physical, mental or behavioral problems; there is also no link to intelligence test scores.
    A. True   B. False

5. The Oedipus complex is a stage of development when males begin to have sexual feelings for their mother.
    A. True   B. False

6. The Electra complex is a stage of development when girls begin to have sexual feelings for their fathers.
    A. True   B. False

7. Individuals who suffer complex behavior delusions involving wrongdoing or persecution- they think everyone is out to get them are called paranoid schizophrenics.
    A. True   B. False

8. In Freud's schema, oral stage occurs during the first year of life, when a child attains pleasure by sucking and biting.
    A. True   B. False

9. Latency is a developmental stage that begins at age six. During this period, feelings of sexuality are repressed until puberty.
    A. True   B. False

10. The author notes that rational choice theory originates with Lombroso's work.
    A. True   B. False

11. Garofalo believed that criminals' common trait was their ability to withstand pain which he witnessed during their tattoo rituals.
      A. True   B. False

12. In Freud's schema, the phallic stage occurs during the first year of life when a child attains pleasure by sucking and biting.
      A. True   B. False

13. In Freud's schema, the oral stage occurs during the second and third years of life when the focus of sexual attention is on the elimination of bodily wastes.
      A. True   B. False

14. In Freud's schema, the anal stage occurs during third year when children focus their attention on their genitals.
      A. True   B. False

15. Behaviorism is the branch of psychology concerned with the study of observable behavior rather than unconscious motives; it focuses on the relationship between particular stimuli and people's responses to them.
      A. True   B. False

16. Cognitive theory is the study of the perception of reality and of the mental processes required to understand the world we live in.
      A. True   B. False

17. The primitive part of people's makeup, present at birth, that represents unconscious biological drives for food, sex, and other life-sustaining necessities is called the id; it seeks instant gratification without concern for the rights of others.
      A. True   B. False

18. According to Freud, the pleasure principle is a theory in which id dominated people are driven to increase their personal pleasure without regard to consequences.
      A. True   B. False

19. The ego is part of the personality developed in early childhood that helps control the id and keep people's actions within the boundaries of social convention.
      A. True   B. False

20. According to Freud, the ability to learn about the consequences of one's actions through experience is called the reality principle.
      A. True   B. False

FILL IN

1. Advocates of the _____ school view trace the activities of several generations of families believed to have an especially large number of criminal members.

2. A system developed for categorizing people on the basis of their body build is called _____.

3. _____ theory is the view that criminality is a product of abnormal biological and/or psychological traits.

4. According to sociobiology, acts that are outwardly designed to help others but that have at their core benefits to the self are known as _____ altruism.

5. _____ refers to sociologists who held the view that no serious consideration should be given to biological factors when attempting to understand human nature.

6. _____ is the view that all individuals are equal at birth and are thereafter influenced by their environment.

7. _____ is a condition that occurs when glucose in the blood falls below levels necessary for normal and efficient brain functioning.

8. _____ allergies are a physical condition that causes brain malfunction due to exposure to some environmental or biochemical irritant.

9. _____ is a part of the human brain; the left side controls the sympathetic feelings towards others.

10. The principal male steroid hormone is _____.

11. Male sex hormones are called _____..

12. The stereotype that several days prior to and during menstruation females are beset by irritability and poor judgement as a result of hormonal changes is called _____.

13. Allergies that affect the nervous system and cause the allergic person to produce enzymes that attack wholesome foods as if they were harmful to the body are called _____.

14. The study of brain activity is called _____.

15. _____ is a device that can record the electric impulses given off by the brain, commonly called brain waves.

ESSAY

1. Identify the focus of the early biological theories of crime. What were identified as the serious flaws of this line of inquiry?

2. Discuss the focus of psychodynamic theory to explain criminality. What is the policy implications of this theory?

3. Explain the relationship between intelligence and crime. Is there an alternative explanation for this association?

4. Define the terms neurotic, psychotic, and paranoid schizophrenic. How do these diagnosis relate to criminality?

5. Discuss the nature - nurture debate. What is the implication for criminology?

CHAPTER SIX
TRAIT THEORIES
ANSWER KEY

MULTIPLE CHOICE ITEMS

1. B	6. C	11. D	16. A	21. B
2. A	7. A	12. A	17. C	22. B
3. B	8. C	13. A	18. A	23. C
4. A	9. B	14. B	19. C	24. B
5. D	10. C	15. C	20. D	25. B

TRUE FALSE ITEMS

1. B	6. A	11. A	16. A
2. A	7. A	12. B	17. A
3. B	8. A	13. B	18. A
4. B	9. A	14. B	19. A
5. A	10. B	15. A	20. A

FILL IN ITEMS

1. inheritance	6. equipotentiality	11. androgens
2. somatotype	7. hypoglycemia	12. premenstrual syndrome
3. trait	8. cerebral	13. neuroallergies
4. reciprocal	9. neocortex	14. neurophysiology
5. biophobia	10. testosterone	15. electroencephalograph

CHAPTER SEVEN
SOCIAL STRUCTURE THEORIES

LEARNING OBJECTIVES

1. Identify and define the three branches of social structure theory.
2. Understand social disorganization theory.
3. Understand anomie theory.
4. Understand general strain theory.
5. Contrast anomie theory and general strain theory.
6. Understand Cohen's theory of delinquent subcultures.

CHAPTER SUMMARY

Sociology has been the main orientation of criminologists because they know that crime rates vary among elements of the social structure, that society goes through changes that affect crime, and that social interaction relates to criminality. Social structure theories suggest that people's places in the socioeconomic structure of society influence their chances of becoming a criminal. Poor people are more likely to commit crimes because they are unable to achieve monetary of social success in any other way. Social structure theory has three schools of thought: social disorganization, strain, and cultural deviance theory.

Social disorganization theory suggests that slum dwellers violate the law because they live in areas in which social control has broken down. The origin of social disorganization theory can be traced to the work of Shaw and McKay. Shaw and McKay concluded that disorganized areas marked by divergent values and transitional populations produce criminality. Modern social ecology theory looks at such neighborhood issues as community fear, unemployment, siege mentality, and deterioration.

Strain theories comprise the second branch of the social structure approach. They view crime as a result of the anger people experience over their inability to achieve legitimate social and economic success. Strain theories hold that most people share common values and beliefs, but the ability to achieve them is differentiated throughout the social structure. The best known strain theory is Merton's theory of anomie, which describes what happens when the means people have at their disposal are not adequate to satisfy their goals. Contemporary researchers have extended this theory by showing that strain has multiple sources.

Cultural deviance theories hold that a unique value system develop in lower class areas. Lower class values approve of such behaviors as being tough, never showing fear, and defying authority. People perceiving strain will bond together in their own groups or subcultures for support and recognition. Cohen links the formation of subcultures to the failure fo lower class citizens to achieve recognition from middle class decision makers such as teachers, employers, and police officers.

CHAPTER OUTLINE

I.   Introduction
      A.   Murder of 13 year old
            1.   assailants believed to be MS 13 gang members
            2.   death stemmed from a gang related party
            3.   confrontations arise over gang recruiting efforts
      B.   Power of social forces on behavior
            1.   sociology primary area of orientation for criminologists
            2.   Chicago School perspective
            3.   significant early research on the influence of social ecology

II.   Socioeconomic Structure and Crime
        A.   Stratified society
                1.   top 20% in US society earn about 50% of the income
                2.   poverty rate dropped to 11.3%
                3.   social ills of poverty
        B.   Child poverty
                1.   25% of children under age 6 live in poverty
                2.   6% of white children described as extremely poor
                3.   50% African American children described as extremely poor
                4.   social and physical ills of child poverty
                5.   poor communities become hollowed out
        C.   The underclass
                1.   Oscar Lewis coins the term culture of poverty
                2.   underclass lack education and skills
                3.   desperate life circumstances interfere with developing skills
                4.   disproportionately impacts minority group members
                5.   William Julius Wilson coins the term the truly disadvantaged
        D.   Bridging the racial divide
                1.   Wilson identifies the truly disadvantaged
                2.   inner city residents who occupy the bottom rung of economic ladder
                3.   live in areas marked by a breakdown of informal social control
                4.   self doubt is neighborhood norm
                5.   most adults in inner city ghetto areas are not working during a typical week
                6.   ghetto residents isolated from mainstream economy
                7.   manufacturing jobs once provided upward mobility for inner city residents
                8.   schools unable to teach basic skills
                9.   few conventional adult role models
                10.   discrimination becoming more subtle and harder to detect
                11.   advocates affirmative opportunities

III.   Social Structure Theories
        A.   Social structure theory
                1.   crime attributed to disadvantaged economic class position
                2.   negative effects of underemployment
                3.   focus on the environmental contribution to crime rates
        B.   Social disorganization theory
                1.   focus on conditions within the urban environment
                2.   breakdown of informal social controls community
        C.   Strain theory
                1.   focuses on the conflict between goals and means
                2.   criminality can result when they choose alternative means to achieve goals
        D.   Cultural deviance theory
                1.   combines strain and social disorganization
                2.   unique lower class culture develops in disorganized areas
                3.   cultural transmission passes values down to next generation

IV.   Social Disorganization Theory
        A.   Theory
                1.   links crime rates to neighborhood ecological characteristics
                2.   areas unable to provide essential services
                3.   residents try to leave area at earliest opportunity
                4.   residents are uninterested in community matters.
        B.   Work of Shaw and McKay
                1.   linked criminality to living in transitional area

84

            2.   influenced by the ecological perspective
            3.   newcomers to Chicago occupied the oldest, most rundown sections

   C.   Transitional neighborhoods
            1.   transitional neighborhoods had high population turnover
            2.   low rents attracted the poor
            3.   residents experienced conflicting norms with old world values
            4.   children left without strong set of values

   D.   Concentric zones
            1.   crime patterns in Chicago followed concentric zone pattern
            2.   stable pattern of crime over decades
            3.   five concentric zones
            4.   high crime rates in zone I and II even as ethnic groups changed

   E.   Legacy of Shaw and McKay
            1.   crime is a function of ecological conditions in cities
            2.   saw crime and delinquency as a normal response to setting
            3.   increase police surveillance in inner city areas

V.   The Social Ecology School
   A.   Social Ecology
            1.   return of the area studies in 1980s

   B.   Community deterioration
            1.   disorder, poverty, and fear linked to crime
            2.   abandoned buildings serve as magnet for crime
            3.   areas with slum lords have high rates of gun crime

   C.   Poverty concentration
            1.   concentration effect with middle class flight
            2.   stable homogenous resident populations trapped in public housing

   D.   Employment opportunities
            1.   relationship between unemployment and crime is unsettled
            2.   long term unemployment rates will produce high levels of antisocial behavior
            3.   reduced employment opportunities destabilize neighborhoods
            4.   old heads replaced by street thugs as socialization force

   E.   Community fear
            1.   areas suffer from social and physical incivilities
             2.   fear of crime becomes contagious
            3.   inevitability of death alters short term behavior
            4.   fear linked to racial and ethnic conflicts
            5.   gang presence takes place in public
            6.   fearful people become suspicious of others
            7.   mistrust of others can lead to a siege mentality

   F.   Community change
            1.   rapid structural changes in areas can produce higher crime rates
            2.   structural changes can be economic or demographic
            3.   as areas decline, those who can leave to more stable areas
            4.   high population turnover has a detrimental impact on community life

   G.   Cycles of community change
            1.   areas undergoing change experience increase in crime rates
            2.   run down areas may lead to gentrification
            3.   never married families and underemployed workers

   H.   Collective efficacy
            1.   common goal among residents
            2.   mutual trust and willingness to intervene in social control
            3.   collective efficacy linked to crime rates, physical and social incivilities
            4.   areas with high collective efficacy have high levels of informal social control
            5.   institutional social control is also effected by collective efficacy

   6. more stable areas are better able to use external agents of social control
   7. social altruism also linked to crime rates
   8. significant negative association between welfare and crime rates
  I. Re-entry blues
   1. imprisonment rates affect neighborhood stability
   2. family and neighborhood lose worker and income
   3. 500,000 prisoners released each year back into communities
   4. only 13% of prisoners with addictions received treatment while incarcerated
   5. after 1 year, 60% of released prisoners are not working

VI. Strain Theories
  A. Definition of anomie
   1. theory traced to Durkheim's work
   2. social rules become ineffective during times of rapid social change
   3. mechanical solidarity characterizes pre-industrial societies
   4. organic solidarity characterizes post industrial societies
   5. anomie threatens social control
  B. Theory of anomie
   1. Merton's emphasis on society's goals and means
   2. means to achieve wealth are stratified by social class
   3. those locked out of accepted means are frustrated
  C. Social adaptions
   1. conformity
   2. innovation
   3. ritualism
   4. retreatism
   5. rebellion
  D. Evaluation of anomie theory
   1. Merton's theory has been influential and enduring
   2. social conditions and not people influence crime rates
   3. some people may have other goals besides wealth
  E. Anomie reconsidered
   1. fell out of favor to social psychology views
  F. Institutional anomie theory
   1. Crime and the American Dream
   2. American dream is process and goal
   3. desire to succeed at any cost drives people apart
  G. Impact of anomie
   1. noneconomic roles have been devalued
   2. in conflict, noneconomic roles subordinate to economic roles
   3. economic terms permeate into noneconomic roles
   4. self interest prevails in times of culture of competition
  H. Supporting research
   1. number of efforts support institutional anomie theory
  I. Relative deprivation
   1. income inequality good predictor of neighborhood crime rates
   2. lower class compare their standing to the more affluent
   3. key point is that deprivation is relative to comparison group
VII. General Strain Theory
  A. GST
   1. helps identify individual sources of strain
   2. criminality is the result of negative affective states
   3. there are multiple sources of strain
  B. Sources of strain
   1. social sources of strain

2.   community sources of strain
3.   works at the individual and community level

C.   Coping with strain
1.   people deal with strain differently
2.   some defenses are cognitive

D.   Strain and criminal careers
1.   some people have traits making them more sensitive to strain
2.   youths may experience more sources of strain
3.   youths may have less skills to deal with strain effectively

E.   Evaluating GST
1.   indicators of strain are linked to criminality
2.   criminality may be a coping strategy to stress

F.   Gender issues
1.   big question of GST
2.   coping strategies may vary by gender

VIII.   Cultural Deviance Theory

A.   Third branch of social structure
1.   lower class subculture stresses different values
2.   its members are unable to meet middle class standards

B.   Conduct norms
1.   criminal law is an expression of the rules of the dominant culture
2.   culture conflict when criminal laws clash with conduct norms

C.   Focal concerns
1.   Miller identifies lower class value system
2.   respect is hard won but easily lost
3.   6 focal concerns identified

IX.   Theory of Delinquent Subcultures

A.   Cohen's work
1.   1955 book Delinquent Boys
2.   lower class youths experience status frustration
3.   act out in non-utilitarian, malicious, and negativistic manner
4.   lower class parents incapable of teaching middle class value system

B.   Middle class measuring rods
1.   lower class youths cannot positively impress middle class authority figures
2.   middle class measuring rods are standards

C.   Formation of deviant subcultures
1.   youth may join available subcultures
2.   corner boy, college boy, and delinquent boy

X.   Theory of Differential Opportunity

A.   Cloward and Ohlin's work
1.   delinquency is a requirement for dominant roles in subculture
2.   differential opportunities key to theory
3.   opportunities for conventional jobs and criminal jobs may be limited
4.   lead to criminal gangs, conflict gangs, and retreatist gangs

XI.   Evaluating Social Structure Theories

A.   Influential
1.   influenced both theoretical development and crime prevention
2.   economic stress and social indicators linked
3.   most members of lower class are not criminal
4.   questions whether lower class value system exists

XII.   Social Structure Theory and Public Policy
         A.   Policies
                 1.   ADC
                 2.   Chicago Area Projects
                 3.   war on poverty programs

KEY TERMS

American Dream: The goal of accumulating material goods and wealth through individual competition; the process of being socialized to pursue material success and to believe it is achievable.

anomie: A condition produced by normlessness. Because of rapidly shifting moral values, the individual has few guides to what is socially acceptable.

at-risk: Children and adults who lack the education and skills needed to be effectively in demand in modern society.

Chicago School: A group of urban sociologists who studied the relationship between environmental conditions and crime.

collective efficacy: Social control exerted by cohesive communities, based on mutual trust, including intervention in the supervision of children and maintenance of public order.

college boy: A disadvantaged youth who embraces the cultural and social values of the middle class and actively strives to be successful by those standards.

concentration effect: As working- and middle-class families flee inner-city poverty areas, the most disadvantaged population is consolidated in urban ghettos.

conduct norms: Behaviors expected of social group members. If group norms conflict with those of the general culture, members of the group may find themselves described as outcasts or criminals.

corner boy: According to Cohen, a role in the lower class culture in which young men remain in their birth neighborhood, acquire families and menial jobs, and adjust to the demands of their environment.

cultural transmission: The concept that conduct norms are passed down from one generation to the next so that they become stable within the boundaries of a culture. Cultural transmission guarantees that group lifestyle and behavior are stable and predictable.

culture conflict: According to Sellin, a condition brought about when the rules and norms of an individuals' sub-cultural affiliation conflict with the role demands of the conventional society.

culture of poverty: The view that people in the lower class of society form a separate culture with its own values and norms that are in conflict with conventional society; the culture is self maintaining and ongoing.

delinquent boy: A youth who adopts a set of norms and principles in direct opposition to middle class values, engaging in short run hedonism, and living for today and letting tomorrow take care of itself.

differential opportunity: The view that lower class youths whose legitimate opportunities are limited join gangs and pursue criminal careers as alternative means to achieve universal goals.

focal concerns: According to Miller, the value orientations of lower class cultures; feature include the needs for excitement, trouble, smartness, fate, and personal autonomy.

general strain theory: The view that multiple sources of strain interact with an individual's emotional traits and responses to produce criminality.

gentrification: A process of reclaiming and reconditioning deteriorated neighborhoods by refurbishing depressed real estate and then renting or selling the properties to upper middle class professionals.

institutional anomie theory: The view that anomie pervades US culture because the drive for material wealth dominates and undermines social and community values.

mechanical solidarity: A characteristic of pre- industrial society which is held together by traditions, shared values, and unquestioned beliefs.

middle class measuring rods: According to Cohen, the standards by which teachers and other representatives of state authority evaluate lower class youths. Because they cannot live up to middle class standards, lower class youths are bound for failure, which gives rise to frustration and anger at conventional society.

negative affective states: According to Agnew, the anger, depression, disappointment, fear, and other adverse emotions that derive from strain.

organic solidarity: Post industrial social systems which are highly developed and dependent on the division of labor; people are connected by their interdependent needs for each other's services and production.

reaction formation: According to Cohen, rejecting goals and standards that seem impossible achieve. Because a boy cannot hope to get into college, he considers higher education a waste of time.

relative deprivation: The condition that exists when people of wealth and poverty live in close proximity to one another.

siege mentality: Residents who become so suspicious of authority that they consider the outside world to be the enemy out to destroy the neighborhood.

social altruism: Voluntary mutual support systems, such as neighborhood associations, that reinforce social and moral obligations.

social disorganization theory: Branch of social structure theory that focuses on the breakdown of institutions such as the family, school, and employment in inner city areas.

social structure theory: The view that disadvantaged economic class position is a primary cause of crime.

status frustration: A form of culture conflict experienced by lower class youths because social conditions prevent them from achieving success as defined by the larger society.

strain theory: Branch of social structure theory that sees crime as a function of the conflict between peoples' goals and the means available to them.

strain: The emotional turmoil and conflict caused when people believe they cannot achieve their desires and goals through legitimate means. Members of the lower class might feel strain because they are denied access to adequate educational opportunities and social support.

stratified society: Grouping according to social strata or levels. American society is considered stratified on the basis of economic class and wealth.

subculture: A group that is loosely part of the dominant culture but maintains a unique set of values, beliefs, and traditions.

transitional neighborhoods: An area undergoing a shift in population and structure, usually from middle class residential to lower class mixed use.

truly disadvantaged: The lowest level of the underclass: urban, inner city, socially isolated people who occupy the bottom rung of the social ladder and are the victims of discrimination.

underclass: The lowest social stratum in any country whose members lack the education and skills needed to successful function in modern society.

TEST BANK

MULTIPLE CHOICE

1. About _____ percent of children in the United States live in poverty.
    A. 7   C. 25
    B. 15   D. 37

2. Who coined the term culture of poverty?
    A. James Q. Wilson   C. James Madison
    B. Oscar Lewis   D. Charles Dickens

3. Which of the following theories focuses on deteriorated neighborhoods, inadequate social controls in communities, law violating gangs and groups, and conflicting social values?
    A. social disorganization   C. cultural deviance
    B. strain   D. rational choice

4. Which of the following theories focuses on unequal distribution of wealth and power, frustration, and alternative methods of achieving cultural goals?
    A. social disorganization   C. cultural deviance
    B. strain   D. rational choice

5. Which of the following theories focuses on the development of subcultures as a result of disorganization and stress and subcultural values in opposition to conventional values?
    A. social disorganization   C. cultural deviance
    B. strain   D. rational choice

6. Members of the lower class are unable to achieve symbols of success through conventional means; consequently, they feel anger, resentment, and frustration which is called _____.
    A. strain   C. relative deprivation
    B. culture conflict   D. hypoglycemia

7. Subcultural values are handed down from one generation to the next generation in a process called _____.
    A. relative deprivation   C. acculturation tendency
    B. cultural transmission   D. trans-generational bonding

8. A group of urban sociologists who studied the relationship between environmental conditions and crime became known as the _____ School.
    A. Chicago   C. New York
    B. Philadelphia   D. Denver

9. According to Cohen, the standards by which teachers and other representatives of state authority evaluate lower class youths are called _____.
    A. school barometers   C. lower class yard sticks
    B. middle class measuring rods D. cultural dipsticks

10. Which mode of adaption occurs when individuals embrace both conventional social goals and they also have the means to achieve the goals at their disposal?
    A. conformity   C. ritualism
    B. innovation   D. retreatism

11. _____ occurs when an individual accepts the goals of society but rejects or is incapable of achieving them through legitimate means.
    A. conformity   C. ritualism
    B. innovation   D. retreatism

12. According to Merton, which mode of adoption gains pleasure from practicing traditional ceremonies regardless of whether they have a real purpose or goal?
    A. conformity   C. ritualism
    B. innovation   D. retreatism

13. According to Merton, _____ reject both the goals of society and the means to achieve them.
    A. conformity   C. ritualism
    B. innovation   D. retreatism

14. According to Merton, _____ involves substituting an alternative set of goals and means for conventional ones.
    A. conformity   C. ritualism
    B. innovation   D. rebellion

15. According to Cohen, the _____ boy is not a chronic delinquent but may be a truant who engages in petty or status offenses; his main loyalty is to his peer group, on which he depends for support, motivation, and interest.
    A. corner   C. delinquent
    B. college   D. retreatist

16. According to Cohen, the _____ boy embraces the cultural and social values of the middle class; he strives to be successful by middle class standards.
    A. corner   C. delinquent
    B. college   D. retreatist

17. According to Cohen, the _____ boy is a youth who adopts a set of norms and principles in direct opposition to middle class values; he engages in short run hedonism, and living for today and letting tomorrow take care of itself.
    A. corner   C. delinquent
    B. college   D. retreatist

18. Which of Cloward and Ohlin's gangs are seen as double failures who are unable to achieve success through legitimate means and are also unable to achieve them through illegal means?
    A. criminal   C. retreatist
    B. conflict   D. souvenir

19. Which of the following social structure theories contends that crime is a product of transitional neighborhoods that manifest social disorganization and value conflict?
    A. concentric zone theory   C. relative deprivation theory
    B. anomie theory   D. cohen's theory of delinquent gangs

20. Which of the following social structure theories contends that crime results when people adopt the goals of society but lack the means to achieve them and then turn to crime as an alternative?
    A. concentric zone theory   C. relative deprivation theory
    B. anomie theory   D. Cohen's theory of delinquent gangs

21. Which of the following social structure theories contends that crime results when the wealthy and the poor live in close proximity to one another?
    A. concentric zone theory   C. relative deprivation theory
    B. anomie theory   D. Cohen's theory of delinquent gangs

22. Which of the following social structure theories contends that crime results when the status frustration of lower class boys, created by their failure to achieve middle class success, causes them to join gangs?
    A. concentric zone theory   C. relative deprivation theory
    B. anomie theory   D. Cohen's theory of delinquent gangs

23. Which of the following social structure theories contends that the conflicts and problems of urban social life and communities, including fear, unemployment, deterioration, and siege mentality, influence crime rates?
      A. social ecology theory   C. institutional anomie theory
      B. general strain theory   D. culture conflict theory

24. Which of the following social structure theories contends that strain has a variety of sources; strain causes crime in the absence of adequate coping mechanisms?
      A. social ecology theory   C. institutional anomie theory
      B. general strain theory   D. culture conflict theory

25. Which of the following social structure theories contends that material goals pervade all aspects of American life?
      A. social ecology theory   C. institutional anomie theory
      B. general strain theory   D. culture conflict theory

TRUE/FALSE

1. About 25 percent of children in the United States live in poverty.
      A. True
      B. False

2. James Q. Wilson coined the term culture of poverty in 1966.
      A. True
      B. False

3. Social disorganization theory focuses on deteriorated neighborhoods, inadequate social controls in communities, law violating gangs and groups, and conflicting social values.
      A. True
      B. False

4. Strain theory focuses on unequal distribution of wealth and power, frustration, and alternative methods of achieving cultural goals.
      A. True
      B. False

5. Cultural deviance theory focuses on the development of subcultures as a result of disorganization and stress and subcultural values in opposition to conventional values.
      A. True
      B. False

6. According to social disorganization theory, residents are uninterested in community matters, try to leave at the earliest possible opportunity, and communities are unable to provide essential services to its residents.
      A. True
      B. False

7. Social ecology theory contends that the conflicts and problems of urban social life and communities, including fear, unemployment, deterioration, and siege mentality, influence crime rates.
      A. True
      B. False

8. General strain theory contends that strain has a variety of sources; strain causes crime in the absence of adequate coping mechanisms.
      A. True
      B. False

9. Institutional anomie theory contends that material goals pervade all aspects of American life.
    A. True
    B. False

10. Cohen's theory of delinquent gangs contends that crime is a product of transitional neighborhoods that manifest social disorganization and value conflict.
    A. True
    B. False

11. Concentric zone theory contends that crime results when people adopt the goals of society but lack the means to achieve them and then turn to crime as an alternative.
    A. True
    B. False

12. Anomie theory contends that crime results when the wealthy and the poor live in close proximity to one another.
    A. True
    B. False

13. Relative deprivation theory contends that crime results when the status frustration of lower class boys, created by their failure to achieve middle class success, causes them to join gangs.
    A. True
    B. False

14. Organic solidarity is a characteristic of pre- industrial society which is held together by traditions, shared values, and unquestioned beliefs.
    A. True
    B. False

15. Mechanical solidarity describes post industrial social systems which are highly developed and dependent on the division of labor; people are connected by their interdependent needs for each other's services and production.
    A. True
    B. False

16. A corner boy is a youth who adopts a set of norms and principles in direct opposition to middle class values, engaging in short run hedonism, and living for today and letting tomorrow take care of itself.
    A. True
    B. False

17. According to Cohen, a corner boy is a role in the lower class culture in which young men remain in their birth neighborhood, acquire families and menial jobs, and adjust to the demands of their environment.
    A. True
    B. False

18. According to Cohen, middle class measuring rods are the standards by which teachers and other representatives of state authority evaluate lower class youths.
    A. True
    B. False

19. A college boy is a disadvantaged youth who embraces the cultural and social values of the middle class and actively strives to be successful by those standards.
    A. True
    B. False

20. A delinquent boy is a youth who adopts a set of norms and principles in direct opposition to middle class values, engaging in short run hedonism, and living for today and letting tomorrow take care of itself.
	A. True
	B. False

FILL IN

1. The view that people in the lower class of society form a separate culture with its own values and norms that are in conflict with conventional society is called the _____.

2. A _____ society refers to the grouping according to social strata or levels.

3. _____ children and adults lack the education and skills needed to be effectively in demand in modern society.

4. The lowest social stratum in any country whose members lack the education and skills needed to successful function in modern society is called the _____.

5. The lowest level of the underclass is called the _____; the members of this group are urban, inner city, socially isolated people who occupy the bottom rung of the social ladder and are the victims of discrimination.

6. A group of urban sociologists who studied the relationship between environmental conditions and crime originated with the _____ School.

7. _____ theory is the view that disadvantaged economic class position is a primary cause of crime.

8. _____ theory is the branch of social structure theory that sees crime as a function of the conflict between peoples' goals and the means available to them.

9. _____ is the emotional turmoil and conflict caused when people believe they cannot achieve their desires and goals through legitimate means.

10. A _____ is a group that is loosely part of the dominant culture but maintains a unique set of values, beliefs, and traditions.

11. _____ theory is a branch of social structure theory that focuses on the breakdown of institutions such as the family, school, and employment in inner city areas.

12. According to Miller, the value orientations of lower class cultures are called _____ concerns; these concerns include the needs for excitement, trouble, smartness, fate, and personal autonomy.

13. _____ transmission is the concept that conduct norms are passed down from one generation to the next so that they become stable within the boundaries of a culture.

14. An area undergoing a shift in population and structure, usually from middle class residential to lower class mixed use is known as a _____ neighborhoods.

15. As working- and middle-class families flee inner-city poverty areas, the most disadvantaged population is consolidated in urban ghettos resulting in a _____ effect of poverty.

ESSAY

1. Discuss social disorganization theory as developed by Shaw and McKay. What are the policy implications of this theory?

2. Discuss anomie theory. What are the policy implications of this theory?

3. Discuss institutional anomie theory. What are the policy implications of this theory?

4. Discuss general strain theory. In what ways is the theory similar and different from Merton's version of anomie theory?

5. Define the concept of relative deprivation. How does it relate to crime rates?

MULTIPLE CHOICE ITEMS

1. C	6. A	11. B	16. B	21. C
2. B	7. B	12. C	17. C	22. D
3. A	8. A	13. D	18. C	23. A
4. B	9. B	14. D	19. A	24. B
5. C	10. A	15. A	20. B	25. C

TRUE FALSE ITEMS

1. A	6. A	11. B	16. B
2. B	7. A	12. B	17. A
3. A	8. A	13. B	18. A
4. A	9. A	14. B	19. A
5. A	10. B	15. B	20. A

MULTIPLE CHOICE ITEMS

1. culture of poverty	6. Chicago	11. social disorganization
2. stratified	7. social structure	12. focal
3. at-risk	8. strain	13. cultural
4. underclass	9. strain	14. transitional
5. truly disadvantaged	10. subculture	15. concentration

CHAPTER EIGHT
SOCIAL PROCESS THEORIES

LEARNING OBJECTIVES

1. Identify and define the three branches of social process theory.
2. Identify and understand the principles of differential association theory.
3. Identify and understand neutralization theory.
4. Identify and understand social bond theory. Identify the four elements of the bond.
5. Differentiate between primary and secondary deviance.
6. Identify and define key terms associated with social reaction theory.

CHAPTER SUMMARY

Social process theories view criminality as a function of people's interaction with various organizations, institutions, and processes in society. People in all walks of life have the potential to become criminals if they maintain destructive social relationships. Social process theory has three main branches: social learning theory stresses that people learn how to commit crimes; control theory analyzes the failure of society to control criminal tendencies; and labeling theory maintains that negative labels produce criminal careers.

The social learning branch suggests that people learn criminal behaviors much as they learn conventional behavior. Control theories maintain that all people have the potential to become criminals but that their bonds to conventional society prevent him from violating the law. Labeling theory holds that criminality is promoted by becoming negatively labeled by significant others. Social process theories have had a great influence on social policy. They have controlled treatment orientations as well as community action policies.

CHAPTER OUTLINE

I. Introduction
A. Non-criminal lower class residents
      1.   calls into question social structure theories
      2.   relatively few go on to become chronic hardcore offenders

II. Socialization and Crime
    A.   Social process theories
        1.   socialization common to all people
        2.   criminality is a function of socialization
        3.   all people have the potential to become criminal
    B.   Family relations
        1.   seen as major determinant to behavior
        2.   family conflict seen as more important that structure of family
        3.   broken home seen as early factor in criminality
        4.   discipline, supervision, attachment and parental deviance critical factors
        5.   35% of children live in married, two parent families
        6.   children living with step-parents exhibits traits as single parent children
    C.   Child abuse and crime
        1.   physical abuse, sexual abuse, and neglect linked to criminality
        2.   corporal punishment linked to antisocial outcomes
        3.   international studies also show support for these links
    D.   Educational experience
        1.   attachment and achievement in school linked to criminality

2. dropping out seen as critical risk factor for criminality
3. school failure and tracking linked to criminality
4. significant amount of crime occurs in schools

   E. Peer relations
1. peer groups have powerful influence on behavior
2. peer conformity concerns are big issue
3. some youths join more than one deviant peer group
4. peer rejection linked to antisocial outcomes
5. deviant friends are sticky- tough to lose

   F. Institutional involvement and belief
1. the influence of religion or high moral values
2. participation in religion inhibits delinquency

   G. Keeping kids in school
1. dropouts earn less money over their lifetime
2. Communities in Schools program to prevent dropping out
3. classroom model and academy model of program
4. positive outcomes associated with the program

   H. Effects of socialization on crime
1. positive self image can inhibit crime
2. branches of social process theory
     a. social learning theory, social control theory, and labeling theory
3. social learning theory assumes people are born good and learn to be bad
4. social process theory assumes people are born bad and learn to be good

III. Social Learning Theory
   A. Basics
1. people learn the norms, values, and behaviors of crime
2. crime is a product of learning
3. three theories of learning crime
     a. differential association
     b. differential reinforcement
     c. neutralization theory

   B. Differential association theory
1. Sutherland's theory
2. refuted social structure theories as cause of crime
3. believed criminality was a function of learning
4. principles of the theory identified
5. become criminal when faced with excess of definitions favorable to violating law
6. learning process is not mere imitation

   C. Testing differential association theory
1. terms and concepts may be seen as vague
2. delinquent friends are powerful force on criminality
3. principles seem relevant to drug use
4. drug users have intimate relationships with other users
5. peer relationships may help explain gender differences

   D. Analysis of differential association theory
1. cultural deviance critique- people improperly socialized into normative society
2. difficulty explaining criminality differences of people from same environment
3. difficulty explaining impulsive violent acts
4. birds of a feather flock together critique

IV. Differential Reinforcement Theory
   A. Proposed by Akers
1. rewards and punishments become key determinants to whether crime continues
2. theory focuses on direct conditioning of the behavior

3.   behavior rationalized as justified is more likely to be continued
4.   normative groups are key- have power to reward or sanction
B.   Testing differential reinforcement
1.   strong association between drug use and social learning variables
2.   rewarded behavior is likely to continue
3.   learning and crime are not static concepts
4.   parental deviance linked to child antisocial behavior
5.   criminal knowledge gained from experience and produces rational choice

V.   Neutralization Theory
A.   Proposed by Sykes and Matza
1.   most delinquents hold conventional values and beliefs
2.   they master techniques to neutralize guilt and shame over violating law
3.   they drift from conventional behavior to criminal behavior
4.   subterranean value system
5.   few people are all good or all bad
6.   criminals sometimes develop a sense of guilt over crime
7.   criminals frequently respect law abiding individuals
8.   sometimes draw a line between acceptable victims and unacceptable victims
9.   criminals are not immune to demands of conformity
B.   Techniques of neutralization
1.   denial of responsibility
2.   denial of injury
3.   denial of victim
4.   condemnation of the condemners
5.   appeal to higher authority
C.   Testing neutralization theory
1.   helps explain aging out of crime- drift back to conventional behavior
2.   criminals excuse behavior more so than general population
3.   if they hold values in opposition to larger society then no need to neutralize them
D.   Are learning theories valid?
1.   fail to account for the origin of criminal definitions
2.   fails to explain spontaneous acts of violence
3.   drug users may not stop to neutralize their feelings of guilt
4.   people may not learn skills of crime before actually committing it

VI.   Social Control Theory
A.   Basics
1.   commitment to conformity or strong moral sense prevents crime
2.   all individuals are potential law violators
3.   weakened bond to society leads to criminality
B.   Self concept and crime
1.   Reckless' containment theory
2.   strong positive self image insulates youth from crime
3.   youths seek out deviant groups if rejected in efforts to develop self esteem
C.   Hirschi's social control theory
1.   developed from Hirschi's Causes of Delinquency
2.   absence of sensitivity to others frees person to commit crime
3.   bond includes attachment, commitment, involvement, and belief
D.   Testing social bond theory
1.   Hirschi first tested theory
2.   youths attached to parents are less delinquent
3.   supported by numerous research efforts
4.   positive attachments help control delinquency
5.   youths who are detached from school are at risk for delinquency

6.   general findings also supported with cross national studies
E.   Opposing views
    1.   more than 70 published studies in support
    2.   delinquents may not be detached losers
    3.   not all the elements of the bond are equal
    4.   attachment to the wrong crowd can be bad
    5.   may be better suited to explaining minor types of deliquency
    6.   bonds change over time
    7.   criminality may weaken bonds to conventional others

VII.   Social Reaction Theory
A.   Labeling theory
    1.   roots in symbolic interaction theory
    2.   people incorporate gestures from others into their self image
    3.   there is no objective reality
    4.   people are given a variety of symbolic labels
    5.   devalued status by authority figure- the label may cause harm
    6.   negative label may strengthen commitment to deviance
    7.   system may help create and maintain deviance with official labels
B.   Crime and labeling theory
    1.   use the interactionist definition of crime
    2.   crime is defined by the reaction to the behavior
    3.   social groups create deviance
    4.   acts are bad because people label them as bad
    5.   moral entrepreneurs create rules
C.   Differential enforcement
    1.   law is applied differently
    2.   minorities and the poor are more likely to be processed by system
    3.   long prison sentences for street crime
    4.   law favors the powerful of society
D.   Becoming labeled
    1.   not concerned with explaining onset of crime
    2.   race, class, and ethnic differences between powerful and powerless groups key
    3.   visibility in the community and tolerance of behavior influences labeling
E.   Consequences of labeling
    1.   creates stigma
    2.   effects of self image
    3.   successful degradation ceremonies
F.   Differential social control
    1.   effects may produce a reevaluation of the self- reflective role taking
    2.   institutions also important
G.   Joining deviant cliques
    1.   labeled youths join other outcasts
    2.   acquire motives to deviate from social norms
H.   Retrospective reading
    1.   label tends to redefine the whole person
I.   Dramatization of evil
    1.   label becomes basis for personal identity
J.   Primary and secondary deviance
    1.   primary deviance has little influence on actor
    2.   secondary deviance when act becomes part of the personality
    3.   secondary deviance involves resocialization into deviant role
K.   Research on social reaction
    1.   poor and powerless are more likely to get labeled
    2.   little evidence exists to clearly demonstrate bias and discrimination in system

<ol start="3">
<li>study documenting contextual discrimination</li>
<li>little evidence showing impact of the label on self image</li>
<li>labeling causes parents to become alienated from their children</li>
<li>labeling plays a significant role in persistent offending</li>
</ol>

L. Is labeling theory valid?
<ol>
<li>ignores the onset of delinquency</li>
<li>some people remain secret deviants</li>
<li>criminality may occur long before deviant label</li>
<li>examines the roles of formal actors in the system</li>
</ol>

VIII. Evaluating Social Process Theories

A. Part of the socialization process
<ol>
<li>social interactions help shape behavior and attitudes</li>
<li>offenders are detached from conventional values</li>
<li>don't consider ecological patterns of crime</li>
</ol>

IX. Social Process Theories and Social Policy

A. Major role since the 1950s
<ol>
<li>more impact on programs for younger offenders</li>
<li>offenders can unlearn criminal habits and traits</li>
<li>diversion programs can avoid official labeling</li>
</ol>

KEY TERMS

commitment to conformity: A strong personal investment in conventional institutions, individuals, and processes that prevents people from engaging in behavior that might jeopardize their reputation and achievements.

containment theory: The idea that a strong self image insulates a youth from the pressures and pulls of criminogenic influences in the environment.

contextual discrimination: A practice in which African Americans receive harsher punishments in some instances (as when they victimize whites) but not in other cases (when they victims other African Americans).

differential association theory: According to Sutherland, the principle that criminal acts are related to a person's exposure to an excess amount of antisocial attitudes and values.

differential social control: A process of labeling that may produce a reevaluation of the self, which reflects actual or perceived appraisals made by others.

direct conditioning: Behavior is reinforced by being either rewarded or punished while interacting with others; it is also called differential reinforcement.

diversion programs: Programs of rehabilitation that remove offenders from the normal channels of the criminal justice process; thus avoiding the stigma of a criminal label.

dramatization of evil: As the negative feedback of law enforcement agencies, parents, friends, teachers, and other figures amplifies the force of the original label, stigmatized offenders may begin to reevaluate their own identities. The person becomes the thing he is described as being.

drift: According to Matza, the view that youths move in and out of delinquency and that their lifestyle can embrace both conventional and deviant values.

moral entrepreneurs: Interest groups that attempt to control social life and the legal order in such a way as to promote their own set of personal moral values. People who use their influence to shape the legal process in ways they see fit.

negative reinforcement: Using either negative stimuli (punishment) or loss of reward to curtail unwanted behaviors.

neutralization theory: The view that holds that offenders hold to conventional values while drifting into periods of illegal behavior. In order to drift, people must first overcome legal and moral values.

normative groups: Groups, such as the high school in-crowd, that conform to the social rules of society.

primary deviance: According to Lemert, deviant acts that do not help to redefine the self- and public image of the offender.

reflective role taking: The phenomenon that occurs when youths who view themselves as delinquents give an inner voice to their perceptions of how significant others feel about them.

retrospective reading: The reassessment of a person's past to fit a current generalized label.

secondary deviance: According to Lemert, accepting deviant labels as a personal identity. Acts become secondary when they form a basis for self concept.

self control: A strong moral sense that renders a person incapable of hurting others or violating social norms.

social bond: Ties a person has to the institutions and processes of society. According to Hirschi, elements of the social bond include attachment, commitment, involvement, and belief.

social control theory: The view that people commit crimes when the forces that bind them to society are weakened or broken.

social learning theory: The view that human behavior is modeled through observation of human social interactions, either directly from observing those who are close and from intimate contact, or indirectly from the media. Interactions that are rewarded are copied, while those that are punished are avoided.

social process theory: The view that criminality is a function of peoples' interactions with various organizations, institutions, and process in society.

social reaction theory: The view that people become criminals when significant members of society label them as such and they accept those labels as a personal identity.

stigma: An enduring label that taints a person's identity and changes him or her in the eye's of others

subterranean values: Morally tinged influences that have become entrenched in the culture but are publically condemned. They exist side by side with conventional values and while condemned in public may be admired or practiced in private.

symbolic interaction theory: The view that people communicate through symbols. People interpret symbolic communication and incorporate it within their personality. A person's view of reality, then, depends on his or her interpretation of symbolic gestures.

MULTIPLE CHOICE

1. What is the name of the program that specifically tries to reduce the number of students who drop out of school?
    A. Up with People   C. Head Start
    B. Communities in Schools   D. Aid to Dependent Students

2. As children go through adolescence, they form _____, small groups of friends who share activities and confidences.
    A. cliques   C. gaggles
    B. crowds   D. groups

3. Recent research shows that _____ is a more significant inhibitor of crime than the mere holding of religious beliefs.
    A. a family history of church attendance
    B. participation in religious activities
    C. rejection of satanic principles
    D. ownership of religious artifacts

4. Which branch of social process theory suggests that people learn techniques and attitudes of crime from close relationships with criminal peers?
    A. social learning theory   C. social control theory
    B. labeling theory   D. rational choice theory

5. Which branch of social process theory suggests that people become criminal when significant members of society label them as criminal and they accept the label as their personal identity?
    A. social learning theory   C. social control theory
    B. labeling theory   D. rational choice theory

6. Which branch of social process theory suggests that when the forces that bind people to society are weak or broken they are then free to commit crimes?
    A. social learning theory   C. social control theory
    B. labeling theory   D. rational choice theory

7. Which of the following theories is not grouped under the social process theory?
    A. social learning theory   C. social control theory
    B. labeling theory   D. rational choice theory

8. What are the three branches of social process theory?
    A. strain, social learning, and labeling
    B. social learning, rational choice, and labeling theory
    C. conflict theory, rational choice, and situational crime prevention
    D. social learning, social control, and labeling theory

9. What is the basic assumption of social learning theories?
    A. people are motivated to crime by internal impulses
    B. people use crime as a way of obtaining blocked goals
    C. people are born good and learn to be bad
    D. people are rational actors who weigh the costs and benefits of their actions

10. Which branch of social process theory contends that people are born bad and must be controlled in order to be good?
    A. social learning theory   C. social reaction theory
    B. social control theory   D. social disorganization theory

11. _____ developed the theory of differential association.
   A. Hirschi   C. Sutherland
   B. Smith   D. Sykes and Matza

12. _____ developed the social bond theory and published the book Causes of Delinquency.
   A. Hirschi   C. Sutherland
   B. Smith   D. Sykes and Matza

13. _____ developed neutralization theory and formulated the techniques of neutralization.
   A. Hirschi   C. Sutherland
   B. Smith   D. Sykes and Matza

14. According to differential association theory, crime is _____.
   A. learned   C. a function of disorganized neighborhoods
   B. genetically determined D. based on rational choice

15. According to differential association, where does the learning of criminal definitions take place?
   A. during interactions with formal institutions
   B. by movies and television
   C. within intimate personal groups
   D. by the actions of the criminal justice system

16. According to differential association, what happens when a person receives an excess of definitions favorable to violating the law over definitions unfavorable to violating the law?
   A. anomie   C. strain
   B. crime   D. cognitive dissonance

17. Ronald Akers developed _____ theory.
   A. social control   C. differential reinforcement
   B. differential association D. rational choice

18. What do delinquents neutralize in order to free themselves to commit crimes?
   A. biochemical bonds   C. conventional social values
   B. neurological connections D. deviant subcultural values

19. What theory maintains that most offenders hold conventional attitudes but adopt techniques which enable them to temporarily ignore these values?
   A. subterranean recruitment theory C. social bond theory
   B. containment theory   D. neutralization theory

20. In neutralization, the process of moving from conventional behaviors and values to criminal values and behaviors is called _____.
   A. swaying   C. anomie
   B. denial   D. drift

21. What technique of neutralization is displayed when offenders claim that unlawful acts were not their fault and resulted from forces beyond their control?
   A. denial of injury   C. denial of victim
   B. denial of responsibility D. condemnation of the condemners

22. What technique of neutralization is displayed when offenders claim that stealing is really like long term borrowing or that no actual damage occurs from fighting?

   A. denial of injury   C. denial of victim
   B. denial of responsibility D. condemnation of the condemners

23. What technique of neutralization claims that the victim had it coming to them?
    A. denial of injury
    B. denial of responsibility
    C. denial of victim
    D. condemnation of the condemners

24. What technique of neutralization claims that it is a dog eat dog world, it is unfair to target youths for delinquency when the cops are corrupt, and there are much more serious offenses committed by the wealth?
    A. denial of injury
    B. denial of responsibility
    C. denial of victim
    D. condemnation of the condemners

25. What technique of neutralization states that everyone has to stick by their friends even if it sometimes means you have to break the law to protect them?
    A. denial of injury
    B. denial of responsibility
    C. denial of victim
    D. appeal to higher authorities

TRUE/FALSE

1. Social process theory is the view that criminality is a function of peoples' interactions with various organizations, institutions, and process in society.
    A. True
    B. False

2. Social control theory is the view that human behavior is modeled through observation of human social interactions, either directly from observing those who are close and from intimate contact, or indirectly from the media.
    A. True
    B. False

3. Social learning theory is the view that people commit crimes when the forces that bind them to society are weakened or broken.
    A. True
    B. False

4. Social reaction theory is the view that people become criminals when significant members of society label them as such and they accept those labels as a personal identity.
    A. True
    B. False

5. According to Sutherland, differential association theory contends that criminal acts are related to a person's exposure to an excess amount of antisocial attitudes and values.
    A. True
    B. False

6. According to Hirschi, elements of the social bond include attachment, commitment, involvement, and belief.
    A. True
    B. False

7. Social reaction theory focuses attention on the initial act, or onset, of delinquency.
    A. True
    B. False

8. In the labeling process, the initial criminal act states that people commit crimes for a number of different reasons.
    A. True
    B. False

9. In the labeling process, the stage of deviance amplification means that people commit crimes for a number of different reasons.
   A. True
   B. False

10. Contextual discrimination is defined as the negative feedback of law enforcement agencies, parents, friends, teachers, and other figures which amplifies the force of the original label, so that stigmatized offenders may begin to reevaluate their own identities.
   A. True
   B. False

11. Primary deviance, according to Lemert, is accepting deviant labels as a personal identity; acts form a basis for self concept.
   A. True
   B. False

12. Secondary deviance, according to Lemert, are deviant acts that do not help to redefine the self- and public image of the offender.
   A. True
   B. False

13. The dramatization of evil is a practice in which African Americans receive harsher punishments in some instances (as when they victimize whites) but not in other cases (when they victims other African Americans).
   A. True
   B. False

14. According to the social bond theory, concern for the opinions of family, friends, and teachers is found in the element of attachment.
   A. True
   B. False

15. According to the US Census Bureau, about 35 percent of children live in families headed by a married couple.
   A. True
   B. False

16. According to the author, children as young as two years old who are the children of drug abusers exhibit personality defects such as excessive anger and negativity.
   A. True
   B. False

17. The author notes that there is no association between crime and negative family issues such as physical abuse, neglect, and sexual abuse.
   A. True
   B. False

18. The labeling perspective identifies and examines the role played by agents of social control in the process of crime causation.
   A. True
   B. False

19. Containment theory contends that society produces pushes and pulls toward delinquency; in some people these forces are counteracted by internal and external containment.
   A. True

B. False

20. Differential association theory contends that people learn to commit crimes from exposure to antisocial definitions.
    A. True
    B. False

FILL IN

1. The view that people commit crimes when the forces that bind them to society are weakened or broken is called _____ theory.

2. According to social learning theory, interactions that are rewarded are copied, while those that are punished are _____.

3. _____ theory is the view that human behavior is modeled through observation of human social interactions, either directly from observing those who are close and from intimate contact, or indirectly from the media.

4. _____ theory is the view that criminality is a function of peoples' interactions with various organizations, institutions, and process in society.

5. _____ theory is the view that people become criminals when significant members of society label them as such and they accept those labels as a personal identity.

6. According to Sutherland, the principle that criminal acts are related to a person's exposure to an excess amount of antisocial attitudes and values is called _____.

7. The connection a person has to the institutions and processes of society is called the _____; according to Hirschi, it includes attachment, commitment, involvement, and belief.

8. Using either negative stimuli (punishment) or loss of reward to curtail unwanted behaviors is called _____ reinforcement.

9. _____ theory is the view that holds that offenders hold to conventional values while drifting into periods of illegal behavior; in order to drift, people must first overcome legal and moral values.

10. Morally tinged influences that have become entrenched in the culture but are publically condemned are called _____ values; they exist side by side with conventional values and while condemned in public may be admired or practiced in private.

11. Behavior is reinforced by being either rewarded or punished while interacting with others; this process is called _____ or differential reinforcement.

12. The connection a person has to the institutions and processes of society is called the social bond. According to _____, elements of the social bond include attachment, commitment, involvement, and belief.

13. _____ theory is the view that people communicate through symbols; people interpret symbolic communication and incorporate it within their personality

14. Moral _____ are interest groups that attempt to control social life and the legal order in such a way as to promote their own set of personal moral values; people who use their influence to shape the legal process in ways they see fit.

15. _____ is an enduring label that taints a person's identity and changes him or her in the eye's of others.

ESSAY

1. Discuss Hirschi's social bond theory. Be sure to describe the four elements of the social bond.

2. Discuss Sykes and Matza's techniques of neutralization. Be sure to describe the five techniques of neutralization.

3. How does stigma influence criminality? Identify a situation in which a person may adopt the role of their label.

4. Explain differential reinforcement theory?

5. Discuss the principles of differential association.

MULTIPLE CHOICE ITEMS

1. B	6. C	11. C	16. B	21. B
2. A	7. D	12. A	17. C	22. A
3. B	8. D	13. D	18. C	23. C
4. A	9. C	14. A	19. D	24. D
5. B	10. B	15. C	20. D	25. D

TRUE FALSE ITEMS

1. A	6. A	11. B	16. A
2. B	7. B	12. B	17. B
3. B	8. A	13. B	18. A
4. A	9. B	14. A	19. A
5. A	10. B	15. A	20. A

MULTIPLE CHOICE ITEMS

1. social control	6. differential association	11. direct conditioning
2. avoided	7. social bond	12. Hirschi
3. social learning	8. negative	13. symbolic interaction
4. social process	9. neutralization	14. entrepreneurs
5. social reaction	10. subterranean	15. stigma

CHAPTER NINE
CONFLICT THEORY

LEARNING OBJECTIVES

1. Identify theoretical elements of social conflict theory.
2. Identify and understand the influence of Marx on conflict theory.
3. Identify the contributions of Bonger, Vold, and Dahrendorf to conflict theory.
4. Identify and understand the principles of power control theory.
5. Identify and understand the principles of peacemaking criminology.

CHAPTER SUMMARY

Social conflict theorists view crime as a function of the conflict that exists in society. Social conflict has its theoretical basis in the works of Marx, as interpreted by Bonger, Dahrendorf, and Vold. Conflict theorists suggest that crime in any society is caused by class conflict. Laws are created by those in power to protect their rights and interests. All criminal acts have political undertones. Quinney has called this concept "the social reality of crime." Unfortunately, research efforts to validate the conflict approach have not produced significant findings. One of conflict theory's most important premises is that the justice system is biased and designed to protect the wealthy. Research has not been unanimous in supporting this point.

Marxist criminology views the competitive nature of the capitalist system as a major cause of crime. The poor commit crimes because of their frustration, anger, and need. The wealthy engage in illegal acts because they are used to competition and because they must do so to keep their positions in society. Marxist scholars have attempted to show that the law is designed to protect the wealthy and powerful and to control the poor, have-not members of society. There are a number of branches of radical theory referred to as instrumental Marxism and structural Marxism

Research on Marxist theory focuses on how the system of justice was designed and how it operates to further class interests. Quite often, this research uses historical analysis to show how the capitalist classes have exerted their control over the police, courts, and correctional agencies. Both Marxist and conflict criminology have been heavily criticized by consensus criminologists, who suggest that Marxists make fundamental errors in their concepts of ownership and class interest.

During the 1990s, new forms of conflict theory emerged. Feminist writers drew attention to the influence of patriarchal society on crime; left realism takes a centrist position on crime by showing its rational and destructive nature; peacemaking criminology brings a call for humanism to criminology; deconstructionism looks at the symbolic meaning of law and culture. Today, the conflict theory approach to crime prevention policy has been translated into the restorative justice movement. Rather than punishing, shaming and excluding those who violate the law, efforts are being made to use humanistic techniques which re-integrate people back into society. Restorative programs rely on victims, relatives, neighbors and community institutions rather than courts and prisons.

CHAPTER OUTLINE

I.   Introduction
        A.   Group of Eight set to meet in Genoa, Italy
                1.   protesters decried international corporations and government control of life
                2.   groups had unique agendas
                3.   demonstrations led to violence and riots
        B.   World is filled with conflict
                1.   conflict is functional when it results in positive social change

2.   view crime as a function of social conflict and economic rivalry

C.   Government role in creating a criminogenic environment
      1.   relationship between personal or group power and shaping of criminal law
      2.   prevalence of bias in justice system operations
      3.   relationship between a capitalist free-enterprise economy and crime rates

D.   View
      1.   conflict theorists view crime as the outcome of class struggle
      2.   conflict theory assumes that intergroup conflict exists in every society causes crime
      3.   Marxist criminology focuses on crime-producing traits of capitalist society

II.   Marxist Thought

A.   Productive forces and productive relations
      1.   Marx lived in an era of unrestrained capitalist expansion
      2.   industrialists could hire workers on their own terms
      3.   conditions in factories were atrocious
      4.   Marx issued his famous communist manifesto in 1848
      5.   contends the character of every civilization is determined by its mode of production

B.   Economic structures
      1.   production has two components: productive forces and productive relations
      2.   class denotes position in relation to others

C.   Surplus value
      1.   capitalists are in constant competition with each other
      2.   goal is to produce goods cheaply
      3.   monopolistic mega-corporations further exploit workers
      4.   capitalist business cycle contained seeds of its own destruction
      5.   Marx used the dialectic method

D.   Marx on crime
      1.   did not write a great deal on the subject of crime
      2.   crime was the product of law enforcement policies
      3.   saw connection between criminality and inequities in capitalist system
      4.   Engels portrayed crime as a function of social demoralization
      5.   collapse of people's humanity reflecting a decline in society

III.   Developing a Conflict Theory of Crime

A.   Contribution of Bonger
      1.   Bonger was born in 1876 in Holland
      2.   crime lies within the boundaries of normal human behavior
      3.   society divided into have and have-nots because of the system of production
      4.   attempts to control law violations through force are a sign of a weak society
      5.   social order is maintained for the capitalists at the expense of the whole
      6.   legal system discriminates against the poor by defending actions of wealthy
      7.   proletariat is deprived of materials monopolized by the bourgeoisie
      8.   distribution of wealth affects crime
      9.   redistribution of property to "each according to his needs" is the demise of crime

B.   Contribution of Dahrendorf
      1.   modern society is organized into imperatively coordinated associations
      2.   society is a plurality of competing interest groups
      3.   workers are divided into the unskilled, semiskilled, and skilled
      4.   the interests of one group may not match the needs of the others
      5.   every society is based on the coercion of some of its members by others

C.   Contribution of Vold
      1.   conflict theory was actually adapted to criminology by George Vold

IV.   Conflict Theory

A.   Developing a conflict criminology

1. came into criminological prominence during the 1960s
2. view that lower class was the subject of discriminatory law enforcement
3. identifying "real" crimes in U.S. society, such as profiteering, sexism, and racism
4. major objective of conflict theory is to show how justice in U.S. society is skewed
B. Power relations
1. crime is defined by those in power
2. unequal distribution of power produces conflict
C. Social reality of crime
1. criminal law represent the interests of those who hold power in society
2. explains harsh punishments for property crime
3. concepts of crime are controlled by the powerful
D. Research on conflict theory
1. compare crime rates of powerless groups with those of elite classes
2. identify laws created with the intent of preserving the power of the elite classes
3. measures of social inequality are highly associated with crime rates
4. as people become economically marginalized they turn to violent crime for survival
5. system is quick to action when victim of crime is wealthy, white, and male
6. unemployed and minorities perceived as "social dynamite"
E. Analysis of conflict theory
1. reject the consensus view of crime
2. some criminologists consider the conflict view naive
3. little evidence that the system is biased

V. Marxist Criminology
A. Overview to Marxist criminology
1. view crime as a function of the capitalist mode of production
2. surplus population provides an excess supply of labor
3. wealthy are immune from prosecution
4. media is owned by the wealthy classes
5. media presents crimes committed by the poor and minorities
B. Development of a Radical Criminology
1. concept of deviance from a labeling perspective
2. U.S. radicals influenced by widespread social ferment during 1960s and 70s
3. many new Marxist criminologists were once positivist criminologists
4. Marxists did not meet with widespread approval at major universities
5. in early 1980s the left realism school was started
6. Sullivan and Tifft created the peacemaking movement
C. Fundamentals of Marxist Criminology
1. Marxist criminologists ignore formal theory construction
2. radicals use the conflict definition of crime
3. criminals are not social misfits but rather a product of society and economic system
D. Economic structure
1. no single view or theory defines Marxist criminology today
2. important aspect of capitalist system is the effect of surplus value
3. economic growth does not have the same benefits for all elements of the population
4. as surplus value increases more people are displaced from productive relationships
5. as the level of surplus value increases so does the level of police expenditures
E. Instrumental Marxism
1. view criminal law and CJS solely as an instrument for controlling the poor
2. poor are driven to crime because a natural frustration exists in a society
3. frustration occurs when affluence is well publicized but unattainable
4. essential to demystify law and justice
5. U.S. society is based on an advanced capitalist economy
F. Integrative-constitutive theory
1. define crime as the application of harm to others

113

2.   two aspects of crime: crimes of reduction and crimes of repression
3.   instrumental Marxism defines state, law, and ruling class as a single entity

G.   Structural Marxism
1.   law is designed to keep the capitalist system operating efficiently
2.   need for legitimacy

H.   Research on Marxist Criminology
1.   real purpose is correctionalism
2.   Marxists investigate both macro-level and micro-level issues
3.   police brutality complaints are highest in minority neighborhoods
4.   capitalism influences the distribution of punishment
5.   corrections' role in suppressing wages and maintaining profits of capitalism
6.   changes in law correspond to the development of a capitalist economy
7.   relationship between convict work and capitalism
8.   police often play an active role in putting down labor disputes

I.   Critique of Marxist Criminology
1.   simple rehash of the old tradition of helping the underdog
2.   most theft is for luxury, not survival
3.   fail to explain why Japan has extremely low crime rates
4.   fail to address problems and conflicts that exist in socialist countries

VI.   Emerging Forms of Conflict Theory

A.   Left Realism
1.   street criminals prey on the poor and disenfranchised
2.   poor are thus making them doubly abused
3.   preemptive deterrence
4.   gang kids may be the ultimate capitalists

B.   Radical Feminist Theory
1.   gender inequality comes from unequal power of men and women in capitalist society
2.   patriarchal system developed and women's work was devalued
3.   dual exploitation of women within the household and in the labor market
4.   double marginality explains female crime rates
5.   powerlessness increases odds women will become the target of violence
6.   struggle to dominate women to prove their manliness is called doing gender
7.   focus on the social forces that shape women's lives and experiences
8.   viewed the great majority of female delinquents as sexually precocious girls
9.   female adolescents have a much narrower range of acceptable behavior

C.   Power-Control Theory
1.   two factors influence crime rates: class position and family functions
2.   parents' work experiences, parenting style, and class position key
3.   egalitarian families and paternalistic families differ in child criminality
4.   girls are controlled more strictly in paternalistic families
5.   daughters of successful and powerful mothers are more at risk for delinquency

D.   Postmodern Theory
1.   critical analysis of communication and language in legal codes
2.   language is value laden

E.   Peacemaking Criminology
1.   main purpose of criminology is to promote a peaceful and just society
2.   mutual aid rather than coercive punishment is the key to a harmonious society

VII.   Social Conflict Theory and Public Policy

A.   Reintegrative shaming
1.   imprisonment rates are not at all related to crime rates
2.   conviction for crimes brings an inordinate amount of shame
3.   shame is a powerful tool of informal social control
4.   most common form of shaming typically involves stigmatization

<ol start="5">
<li>crime control can be better achieved through a policy of reintegrative shaming</li>
</ol>

B. Concept of restoration
1. crime is an offense against human relationships
2. offender has personal responsibility to victims
3. offender has responsibility to the community for crimes committed
4. restoration involves turning the justice system into a healing process

C. Process of restoration
1. most conflicts are better settled in the community than in a court
2. there are many different parties who have a stake in the justice process
3. offender is asked to recognize that they caused injury
4. commitment to both material and symbolic reparation

D. Restoration programs
1. part of the dispute resolution process in European and Asian communities
2. concepts from Native-American and Native-Canadian people
3. schools address problems without resorting to more punitive measures
4. process involves diverting from the formal court process

E. Challenge of restorative justice
1. must be wary of the cultural and social differences
2. differences found throughout our heterogeneous society

KEY TERMS

antithesis: An opposing argument.

capitalist bourgeoisie: The owners of the means of production.

communist manifesto: In this document, Marx focused his attention on the economic conditions perpetuated by the capitalist system. He stated that its development had turned workers into a dehumanized mass who lived an existence that was at the mercy of their capitalist employers.

conflict theory: explain crime within economic and social contexts and to express the connection between the nature of social class, crime, and social control.

correctionalism: Research conducted by mainstream liberal/ positivist criminologists designed to unmask the weak and powerless members of society so they can be better dealt with by the legal system.

deconstructionist analysis: An approach that focuses on the use of language by those in power to define crime based on their own values and biases; also called postmodernist.

dialectic method: For every idea, or thesis, there exists an opposing argument, or antithesis. Since neither position can ever be truly accepted, the result is a merger of the two ideas, a synthesis. Marx adapted this analytic method for his study of class struggle.

doing gender: Men's struggle to dominate women to prove their manliness.

elite deviance: White collar and economic crime.

imperatively coordinated associations: These associations are composed of two groups; those who posses authority and use it for social domination and those who lack authority and are dominated.

instrumentalists: The view that the criminal law and criminal justice system are solely an instrument for controlling the poor, have-not members of society; the state is the tool of the capitalists.

left realism: A branch of conflict theory that holds that crime is a real social problem experienced by the lower classes and that lower class concerns about crime must be addressed by radical scholars.

lumpen proletariat: The fringe members at the bottom of society who produce nothing and live, parasitically, off the work of others.

marginalization: Displacement of workers, pushing them outside economic and social mainstream.

norm resistance: Interactions between authorities and subjects that eventually produces open conflict between the two groups that can take on a number of different forms.

peacemaking movement: A branch of conflict theory that stresses humanism, mediation, and conflict resolution as a means to end crime.

preemptive deterrence: Efforts to prevent crime through community organization and youth involvement.

productive forces: Technology, energy sources, and material resources.

productive relations: The relationships that exist among the people producing goods and services.

proletariat: A term used by Marx to refer to the working class members of society who produced goods and services but who do not own the means of production.

radical theory: The view that crime is a product of the capitalist system.

restorative justice: An approach which relies on nonpunitive strategies for crime prevention and control.

reintegrative shaming: A method of correction that encourages offenders to confront their misdeeds, experience shame because of the harm they caused, and then be reincluded in society.

sentencing circle: People accused of breaking the law will meet with community members, victims if any, to express his or her feelings about the act, the accused can express regret about his or her actions, and people may suggest ways the offender can make things up to the community and those he or she harmed.

semiotics: The use of language elements as signs or symbols beyond their literal meaning.

social reality of crime: The view that the main purpose of criminology is to promote a peaceful, just society.

structural Marxist theory: The view that the law and the justice system are designed to maintain the capitalist system and that members of both the owner and worker classes whose behavior threatens the stability of the system will be sanctioned.

surplus value: The Marxist view that the laboring classes produce wealth that far exceeds their wages and goes to the capitalist class as profit.

synthesis: A merger of two opposing ideas.

TEST BANK

MULTIPLE CHOICE

1. The goal of _____ theorists is to explain crime within economic and social contexts and to express the connection between the nature of social class, crime, and social control.
    A. social disorganization
    C. rational choice
    B. social process
    D. social conflict

2. Conflict theorists view crime as the outcome of _____.
    A. class struggle
    C. disorganized communities
    B. rational choice
    D. disjunction between goals and means

3. According to Marx, production has two components, what are they?
    A. productive forces and productive relations
    B. haves and have-nots
    C. producers and consumers
    D. pushes and pulls

4. According to Marx, what is the most important relationship in industrial culture?
    A. between the buyers and sellers
    B. between the consumers and creditors
    C. between the industrialists and the naturalists
    D. between the bourgeoisie and the proletariat

5. According to Marx, the most important relationship in industrial culture is between the owners of the means of production, the capitalist bourgeoisie, and the people who do the actual labor, the _____.
    A. lumpen rabble
    C. skilled craftsmen
    B. proletariat
    D. inchoate primogeniture

6. According to Marx, the capitalist system will _____ in the end.
    A. destroy itself
    C. lead to plentiful and cheap products
    B. lead to peace and harmony
    D. produce equality

7. Bonger argued that attempts to control law violations through force are a sign of a _____.
    A. strong society
    C. weak society
    B. moral debate
    D. dialectic method

8. According to Bonger, what would lead to the demise of crime?
    A. redistribution of property to "each according to his needs"
    B. maximum unequal stratification of wealth
    C. efficient DNA storage systems
    D. Batman and Spider Man teaming up in real life

9. According to the _____ method, for every idea there exists an opposing argument; since neither position can ever be truly accepted, the result is a merger of the two ideas.
    A. primary
    C. tertiary logic sequence
    B. dialectic
    D. clarity logic indicator

10. According to the author, conflict theory was actually adapted to criminology by _____.
    A. Vold
    C. Quinney
    B. Marx
    D. Sullivan

11. Which of the following terms best identifies when people accused of breaking the law meet with community members and victims to express his or her feelings about the act; the accused can express regret about his or her actions, and people may suggest ways the offender can make things up to the community and those he or she harmed?

    A. sentencing gauntlet   C. sentencing circle
    B. triangle of despair   D. circle of intimidation

12. _____ is a method of correction that encourages offenders to confront their misdeeds, experience shame because of the harm they caused, and then be reincluded in society.

    A. reintegrative shaming   C. stigma
    B. coercive labeling   D. retrograde immersion

13. _____ is an approach which relies on nonpunitive strategies for crime prevention and control.

    A. Marxist theory   C. rational choice
    B. restorative justice   D. social disorganization theory

14. Which of the following is not a type of social conflict theory?

    A. radical feminism   C. left realism
    B. critical theory   D. rational choice

15. What do conflict theorists primarily focus on in their studies of crime?

    A. inherited biological traits   C. government and the wealthy
    B. social strain   D. rational choice

16. Whose writings serve as the basis for conflict theory?

    A. Beccaria   C. Marx
    B. Bentham   D. Shaw and McKay

17. What did Marx call the people who do the actual labor in society?

    A. suckers   C. the chosen few
    B. bourgeoisie   D. proletariat

18. According to Bonger, what is the true purpose of criminal law?

    A. to serve the interests of the dominant class
    B. to create jobs for society
    C. to distract attention from social inequality
    D. to protect the poor from the wealthy

19. According to Bonger, what is the capitalist system held together by?

    A. a very thin thread   C. force
    B. super glue   D. consensus

20. Which of the following would be the best example of restorative justice?

    A. minimum mandatory sentences for drug dealers
    B. capital punishment
    C. graffiti artists apologize to property owners hit by their graffiti
    D. large fines for minor offenses

21. Who is credited with starting the peacemaking perspective?

    A. Sullivan and Tifft   C. Mackey and Courtright
    B. Smith and Jones   D. Siegel and Senna

22. What concept does Messerschmidt identify to explain the lower rates of female criminality?

    A. alienation   C. double marginality
    B. deportation   D. estrogen

23. Men's struggle to dominate women to prove their manliness is called _____.
      A. doing gender   C. gendered crime
      B. anti-chivalry   D. masculinity hypothesis

24. Research conducted by mainstream liberal/ positivist criminologists designed to unmask the weak and powerless members of society so they can be better dealt with by the legal system is called _____.
      A. correctionalism   C. Liberal feminism
      B. structural Marxist theory   D. peacemaking perspective

25. The view that the law and the justice system are designed to maintain the capitalist system and that members of both the owner and worker classes whose behavior threatens the stability of the system will be sanctioned is best associated with _____.
      A. correctionalism   C. Liberal feminism
      B. structural Marxist theory   D. peacemaking perspective

TRUE/FALSE

1. The goal of social disorganization theorists is to explain crime within economic and social contexts and to express the connection between the nature of social class, crime, and social control.
      A. True
      B. False

2. Conflict theorists view crime as the outcome of class struggle.
      A. True
      B. False

3. Conflict theory assumes that intergroup conflict that exists in every society causes crime.
      A. True
      B. False

4. The author notes that Marx's early career as a journalist was interrupted by government suppression of the newspaper where he worked because of the paper's liberal editorial policy.
      A. True
      B. False

5. According to Marx, the most important relationship in industrial culture is between the owners of the means of production, the capitalist bourgeoisie, and the people who do the actual labor, the proletariat.
      A. True
      B. False

6. In his analysis, Marx used the dialectic method, based on the analysis developed by the philosopher Beccaria.
      A. True
      B. False

7. According to the author, Marx did not write a great deal on the subject of crime.
      A. True
      B. False

8. According to Bonger, even though criminal laws may appear to protect members of both classes, hardly any act is punished that does not injure the interests of the dominant ruling class.
      A. True
      B. False

9. Bonger argued that attempts to control law violations through force are a sign of a weak society.
    A. True
    B. False

10. According to the author, conflict theory was actually adapted to criminology by Sullivan.
    A. True
    B. False

11. As a general rule, Marxist criminologists ignore formal theory construction with its heavy emphasis on empirical testing.
    A. True
    B. False

12. The sentencing gauntlet is when people accused of breaking the law meet with community members and victims to express his or her feelings about the act; the accused can express regret about his or her actions, and people may suggest ways the offender can make things up to the community and those he or she harmed.
    A. True
    B. False

13. Reintegrative shaming is a method of correction that encourages offenders to confront their misdeeds, experience shame because of the harm they caused, and then be reincluded in society.
    A. True
    B. False

14. Restorative justice is an approach which relies on nonpunitive strategies for crime prevention and control.
    A. True
    B. False

15. Rational choice theory is the cornerstone of social conflict theory.
    A. True
    B. False

16. Shaw and McKay's writings serve as the basis for conflict theory.
    A. True
    B. False

17. Men's struggle to dominate women to prove their manliness is called doing gender.
    A. True
    B. False

18. The use of language elements as signs or symbols beyond their literal meaning is called semiotics.
    A. True
    B. False

19. Marginalization is the displacement of workers by pushing them outside economic and social mainstream.
    A. True
    B. False

20. According to the instrumentalists, the criminal law and criminal justice system are solely an instrument for controlling the poor, have-not members of society; the state is the tool of the capitalists.
    A. True
    B. False

FILL IN

1. The goal of social _____ theorists is to explain crime within economic and social contexts and to express the connection between the nature of social class, crime, and social control.

2. Conflict theorists view crime as the outcome of _____ struggle.

3. The most important relationship in industrial culture is between the owners of the means of production, the capitalist _____, and the people who do the actual labor, the proletariat.

4. Bonger argued that attempts to control law violations through force are a sign of a _____ society.

5. _____ theory explains crime within the economic and social contexts and expresses the connection between the nature of social class, crime, and social control.

6. _____ is a term used by Marx to refer to the working class members of society who produced goods and services but who do not own the means of production.

7. The capitalist _____ are the owners of the means of production.

8. The relationships that exist among the people producing goods and services are known as productive _____.

9. In the Communist _____, Marx focused his attention on the economic conditions perpetuated by the capitalist system; he stated that its development had turned workers into a dehumanized mass who lived an existence that was at the mercy of their capitalist employers.

10. According to Marxist theory, technology, energy sources, and material resources are known as _____ forces.

11. The fringe members at the bottom of society who produce nothing and live, parasitically, off the work of others are known as the _____.

12. _____ value is the Marxist term which means that the laboring classes produce wealth that far exceeds their wages and goes to the capitalist class as profit.

13. According to the _____ method, for every idea, or thesis, there exists an opposing argument, or antithesis; since neither position can ever be truly accepted, the result is a merger of the two ideas, or a synthesis.

14. _____ is an opposing argument.

15. _____ is a merger of two opposing ideas.

ESSAY

1. What is restorative justice and how does it differ from traditional criminal justice?

2. Discuss the association between patriarchy and capitalism.

3. What are the policy implications of the peacemaking perspective?

4. What are the principles of power control theory?

5. What is the difference between a structural Marxist and an instrumental Marxist?

**CHAPTER NINE
CONFLICT THEORY
ANSWER KEY**

MULTIPLE CHOICE ITEMS

1. D	6. A	11. C	16. C	21. A
2. A	7. C	12. A	17. D	22. C
3. A	8. A	13. B	18. A	23. A
4. D	9. B	14. D	19. C	24. A
5. B	10. A	15. C	20. C	25. B

TRUE FALSE ITEMS

1. B	6. B	11. A	16. B
2. A	7. A	12. B	17. A
3. A	8. A	13. A	18. A
4. A	9. A	14. A	19. A
5. A	10. B	15. B	20. A

FILL IN ITEMS

1. conflict	6. proletariat	11. lumpen proletariat
2. class	7. bourgeoisie	12. surplus
3. bourgeoisie	8. relations	13. dialectic
4. weak	9. Manifesto	14. antithesis
5. conflict	10. productive	15. synthesis

CHAPTER TEN
DEVELOPMENTAL THEORIES: LIFE COURSE AND LATENT TRAIT

LEARNING OBJECTIVES

1. Identify and understand the various developmental theories of criminology.
2. Differentiate between latent trait theories and life course theories.
3. Identify various latent trait factors.
4. Identify and appreciate various factors leading to desistance from crime.

CHAPTER SUMMARY

Latent trait theories hold that some underlying condition present at birth or soon after controls behavior. Suspect traits include low IQ, impulsivity, and personality structure. These underlying traits explain the continuity of offending because, once present, they remain with a person throughout his or her life. The latent trait theories developed by Gottfredson and Hirschi and Wilson and Herrnstein both integrate choice theory concepts: people with latent traits choose crime over noncrime; the opportunity for crime mediates their choice. Mark Colvin and Charles Tittle have developed more recent theories.

Life course theories argue that events that take place over the life course influence criminal choices. The cause of crime constantly changes as people mature. At first, the nuclear family influences behavior; during adolescence, the peer group dominates; in adulthood, marriage and career are critical. There are a variety of pathways to crime: some kids are sneaky, others hostile, and still others defiant. Crime may be part of a variety of social problems, including health, physical, and interpersonal troubles. Life course theories include the social development model, which finds that living in a disorganized area helps weaken social bonds. Important life course theories have been formulated by Terence Thornberry, David Farrington, and John Laub and Robert Sampson

CHAPTER OUTLINE

I.   Introduction
      A.   Gary Sampson
            1.   three murders committed in Massachusetts and New Hampshire
            2.   desperate finale to a troubled life
            3.   once bound, gagged, and beat three elderly women in a candy store
            4.   developed a hair-trigger temper
            5.   Sampson had at least four failed marriages
            6.   took on the identity of Gary Johnson
      B.   Career criminals
            1.   chronic offenders responsible for significant number of all crimes
            2.   career criminals defy the aging-out process
            3.   theories need to explain desistance from crime

II.   The Life Course View
      A.   Developmental theories
            1.   explains the onset and continuation of a criminal career
            2.   provides a more global vision of a criminal career
            3.   addresses the onset, continuation and termination of crime
            4.   two distinct groups: latent trait and life course theories
      B.   Latent trait theories
            1.   hold that human development is controlled by a master trait
            2.   master trait is enduring and stable

C. Life course theory
    1.   views criminality as a dynamic process
    2.   relationships and behaviors will determine their adult life course
    3.   transitions that occur too early or too late are problematic
    4.   disruptions in life's major transitions can be destructive
    5.   rejection of pro-social peers solidifies and escalates his antisocial behavior
    6.   as people mature factors that influence their behavior change
    7.   life course theories are inherently multidimensional
    8.   having criminal relatives is a significant predictor of future crime
    9.   people are influenced by different factors as they mature

III. Glueck Research
  A.   Harvard University in 1930s
    1.   Gluecks popularized research on the life cycle of delinquent careers
    2.   made extensive use of interviews and records in comparisons
    3.   early onset of delinquency as a harbinger of a criminal career
    4.   identified personal and social factors related to persistent offending
    5.   Gluecks measured biological and psychological traits
    6.   Gluecks' research was virtually ignored for nearly 30 years
    7.   methodology and theoretical integration were heavily criticized
  B.   Life course concepts
    1.   Glueck legacy was rediscovered by Sampson and Laub
    2.   evolution of criminal careers is key
  C.   Problem behavior syndrome
    1.   crime results from rather than caused by social problems
    2.   criminality is one of many social problems faced by at-risk youth
    3.   offenders may suffer from one and exhibit symptoms of the rest
    4.   those who suffer PBS are prone to more difficulties
    5.   examples support the existence of PBS
    6.   youths involved in crime have significantly higher mortality rates
  D.   Pathways to crime
    1.   identified three distinct paths to a criminal career
        a.   authority conflict pathway
        b.   covert pathway
        c.   overt pathway
  E.   Age of onset
    1.   early onset strongly predicts later and more serious criminality
    2.   not all persistent offenders begin at an early age
  F.   Oregon Social Learning Center
    1.   poor parental discipline and monitoring was key to onset of crime
    2.   social relations that emerge later in life become key
  G.   Adolescent-limiteds and life course persisters
    1.   adolescent-limited offenders are typical teenagers
    2.   life course persisters to offend well into adulthood
  H.   Supporting research
    1.   research has supported Moffitt's model
    2.   early-onset delinquents also appear to be more violent
    3.   criminal punishment has greater deterrent effect on earlier starters

IV. The Social Development Model
  A.   Overview
    1.   integrate social control, social learning, and structural models
    2.   a child must maintain prosocial bonds
    3.   commitment and attachment to conventional institutions key
    4.   these insulate youths from the crimogenic influences

5.   core assumptions of SDM have been verified empirically

V.   Farrington's theory of delinquent development
     A.   Cambridge Study in Delinquent Development
          1.   followed the offending careers of 411 London boys born in 1953
          2.   participants interviewed eight times over 24 years
          3.   traits present in persistent offenders can be observed as early as age 8
          4.   deviant behavior tends to be versatile
          5.   former delinquent likely to have family problems
     B.   Nonoffenders and desisters
          1.   have backgrounds that put them at risk of becoming offenders
          2.   a relatively good job helped reduce criminal activity
          3.   offenders tend to have large debts and low-paying jobs
          4.   theory is age-graded in nature

VI.   Interactional Theory
     A.   Interactional nature of bonds
          1.   onset of crime traced to a deterioration of the social bond during adolescence
          2.   recognizes the influence of social class and other structural variables
          3.   seriously delinquent youth form belief systems consistent with their deviant lifestyle
          4.   causal influences are bidirectional
     B.   Testing interactional theory
          1.   ample evidence supportive of its core premise
          2.   associating with delinquent peers does increase delinquent involvement
          3.   delinquent behavior further weakens the bonds to family and school
          4.   scoring high on reading and math tests is associated with prosocial behaviors

VII.   Sampson and Laub: Age-Graded Theory
     A.   Turning points
          1.   Sampson and Laub identify the turning points in a criminal career
          2.   formal and informal social controls restrict criminality
          3.   two critical turning points are marriage and career
          4.   attached to a spouse who supports and sustains them
          5.   spending time in marital and family activities reduces exposure to deviant peers
     B.   Social capital
          1.   people build social capital
          2.   it is positive relations with individuals and institutions that are life sustaining
          3.   people can "go straight" if they have positive life experiences
     C.   Marriage factor
          1.   marriage stabilizes people and helps them build social capital
          2.   marriage marks transition from heavy peer involvement to one's spouse
          3.   common-law marriages did not have the same crime-reducing effect
          4.   people who are not married have a lot of free rein to do a lot of what they want
     D.   Future research directions
          1.   connection between military service and desistance
          2.   long-term desistance by interviewing 52 men as they approached age 70
          3.   key for "going straight" is the "knifing off" of individuals
     E.   Early death
          1.   former delinquents desisted from crime
          2.   they also still faced the risk of an early and untimely death
     F.   Policy implications
          1.   early prevention efforts to reduce crime will reduce other antisocial behaviors
          2.   four significant life-changing events:
               a.   marriage
               b.   joining the military

<table>
<tr><td></td><td></td><td>c.</td><td>getting a job</td></tr>
<tr><td></td><td></td><td>d.</td><td>changing one's environment</td></tr>
</table>

VIII. Latent Trait View
- A. Introduction to latent traits
  1. personal attribute controls their inclination to commit crimes
  2. it is established early in life, and it can remain stable over time
  3. positive association between past and future criminality
  4. the opportunity to commit crime fluctuates over time
  5. they lose the strength and vigor to commit crimes
- B. Crime and Human Nature
  1. Wilson and Herrnstein published Crime and Human Nature in 1985
  2. personal traits outweigh social variables as predictors of criminal activity
  3. people weigh the potential gains and losses of each course of action

IX. Latent Trait Theories
- A. General Theory of Crime
  1. book A General Theory of Crime by Gottfredson and Hirschi
  2. consider the criminal offender and the criminal act as separate concepts
  3. crime is rational and predictable
  4. criminal offenders are predisposed to commit crimes
  5. GTC adds a biosocial element to the concept of social control
- B. What makes people crime prone?
  1. a person's level of self-control related to level of criminality
  2. offenders are also more likely to engage in dangerous behaviors
  3. offenders drawn to behavior that provides immediate, short-term gratification
  4. root cause of poor self-control is inadequate child-rearing practices
  5. self-control develops early in life and remains stable
- C. Self-control and crime
  1. all crime stems from a deficiency of self-control
  2. people who lack self-control rarely attain positions to allow white collar crime
- D. Supporting evidence for the GTC
  1. numerous researchers have attempted to test the validity of GTC
  2. low self-control is significantly related to antisocial behavior
  3. association can be seen regardless of culture or national settings
- E. Analyzing the general theory of crime
  1. they integrate the concepts of socialization and criminality
  2. people may forgo criminal careers because there are no criminal opportunities
  3. critics contend the theory is tautological
  4. GTC vision that a single factor causes crime
  5. GTC contends there is a single class of offender
  6. GTC also fails to address individual and ecological patterns
  7. little evidence that males are more impulsive than females
  8. theory ignores the moral concept of right and wrong
  9. kids who lack self-control have trouble maintaining relationships
  10. assumption that criminal propensity does not change
  11. association between variables is at best quite modest
  12. criminals in other countries do not lack self-control
  13. GTC makes flawed assumptions about human character

X. Differential Coercion Theory
- A. Coercion
  1. Colvin's book Crime and Coercion
  2. identifies another master trait called coercion
  3. children experience punitive forms of discipline

126

4.   coercion becomes ingrained and guides reactions to adverse situations

5.   teaches people that they cannot control their lives

    B.   Two sources of coercion

        1.   interpersonal

        2.   impersonal

        3.   experiencing inconsistent or erratic episodes of coercive behavior most damaging

    C.   Coercion and criminal careers

        1.   coercion seems to be intergenerational

        2.   produces a mind-set called coercive ideation

        3.   coercive forces can only be overcome with equal or more coercive responses

    D.   Social support and differential coercion

        1.   social support also comes in two forms

        2.   societies must enhance the legitimate sources of social support

        3.   examples include parent-effectiveness training and paid family leave

XI.   Control Balance Theory

    A.   Tittle's control balance theory

        1.   personal control as a predisposing element for criminality

        2.   concept of control has two distinct elements

        3.   Tittle envisions control as a continuous variable

        4.   three types of behavior to restore balance:

            a.   predation, defiance, or submission

        5.   those who have an excess of control engage in:

            a.   exploitation

            b.   plunder

            c.   decadence

        6.   excessive or deficient control and person will react in an antisocial manner

XII.   Evaluating Developmental Theories

    A.   Theories share some common ground

        1.   evidence supporting both latent trait and life course theories

        2.   maintaining positive social bonds helps reduce criminality

        3.   there are two classes of criminals

KEY TERMS

adolescent-limited offenders: Offenders who follow the most common criminal trajectory, in which antisocial behavior peaks in adolescence and then diminishes.

authority conflict pathway: The path to a criminal career that begins with early stubborn behavior and defiance of parents.

coercive ideation: The world is conceived as full of coercive forces that can only be overcome through the application of equal or even greater coercive responses.

continuity of crime: The view that crime begins early in life and continues throughout the life course. Thus, the best predictor of future criminality is past criminality.

control balance theory: A developmental theory that attributes deviant and criminal behaviors to imbalances between the amount of control that the individual has over others and that others have over him or her.

covert pathway: A path to a criminal career that begins with minor underhanded behavior and progresses to fire starting and theft.

defiance: Challenging control mechanisms but stopping short of physical harm; for example, vandalism, curfew violations, and unconventional sex.

developmental theories: A branch of criminology that examines change in a criminal career over the life course. Developmental factors include biological, social, and psychological change. Among the topics of developmental criminology are desistance, resistance, escalation, and specialization.

general theory of crime (GTC): A developmental theory that modifies social control theory by integrating concepts from biosocial, psychological, routine activities, and rational choice theories.

human nature theory: A belief that personal traits, such as genetic makeup, intelligence, and body build, may outweigh the importance of social variables as predictors of criminal activity.

interactional theory: The idea that interaction with institutions and events during the life course determines criminal behavior patterns; criminogenic influences evolve over time.

interpersonal coercion: The use of force, threat of force, or intimidation by parents, peers, or significant others.

latent trait theory: A stable feature, characteristic, property, or condition, present at birth or soon after, that makes some people crime prone over the life course.

life course persister: One of the small group of offenders whose criminal career continues well into adulthood.

life course theory: The study of changes in criminal offending patterns over a person's entire life. Are there conditions or events that occur later in life that influence the way people, or is behavior predetermined by social or personal conditions at birth.

overt pathway: A pathway to a criminal career that begins with minor aggression, leads to physical fighting, and eventually escalates to violent crime.

predation: direct forms of physical violence, such as robbery, sexual assault, or other forms of physical violence.

problem behavior syndrome (PBS): A cluster of antisocial behavior that may include family dysfunction, substance abuse, smoking, precocious sexuality, and early pregnancy, educational underachievement, suicide attempts, sensation seeking, and unemployment, as well as crime.

prosocial bonds: Socialized attachment to conventional institutions, activities, and beliefs.

self-control theory: According to Gottfredson and Hirschi, the view that the cause of delinquent behavior is an impulsive personality. Kids who are impulsive may find that their bond to society is weak.

social capital: Positive relations with individuals and institutions that are life sustaining.

social development model (SDM): A developmental theory that attributes criminal behavior patterns to childhood socialization and pro- or antisocial attachments over the life course.

turning points: According to Laub and Sampson, the life events that alter the development of a criminal career.

TEST BANK

MULTIPLE CHOICE

1. _____ pathway is the path to a criminal career that begins with early stubborn behavior and defiance of parents.
A. authority conflict   C. overt
B. covert   D. translucent

2. _____ pathway is the path to a criminal career that begins with minor underhanded behavior and progresses to fire starting and theft.
A. authority conflict   C. overt
B. covert   D. translucent

3. _____ pathway is the pathway to a criminal career that begins with minor aggression, leads to physical fighting, and eventually escalates to violent crime.
A. authority conflict   C. overt
B. covert   D. translucent

4. Which one of the following is not one of Loeber's pathways to a criminal career.
A. authority conflict   C. overt
B. covert   D. translucent

5. _____ theory is a branch of criminology that examines change in a criminal career over the life course; it concentrates on the topics of desistance, resistance, escalation, and specialization.
A. developmental   C. interactional
B. latent trait   D. social development model

6. _____theory is a stable feature, characteristic, property, or condition, present at birth or soon after, that makes some people crime prone over the life course.
A. developmental   C. interactional
B. latent trait   D. social development model

7. _____ theory is the idea that interaction with institutions and events during the life course determines criminal behavior patterns; criminogenic influences evolve over time.
A. developmental   C. interactional
B. latent trait   D. social development model

8. _____ attributes criminal behavior patterns to childhood socialization and pro- or antisocial attachments over the life course.
A. developmental   C. interactional
B. latent trait   D. social development model

9. One of the small group of offenders whose criminal career continues well into adulthood is known as _____.
A. life course persister   C. translucent pathways
B. adolescent limited   D. maturation avoiders

10. The author notes that the best predictor of future criminality is _____.
A. high school grades   C. the presence of tattoos
B. EEG readings   D. past criminality

11. The view that crime begins early in life and continues throughout the life course is known as the _____.
A. continuity of crime   C. latent traits
B. spontaneous remission   D. remission tendency

12. Offenders who follow the most common criminal trajectory, in which antisocial behavior peaks in adolescence and then diminishes are known as what?

    A. life course persister
    B. adolescent limited
    C. translucent pathways
    D. maturation avoiders

13. _____ is/are a cluster of antisocial behavior that may include family dysfunction, substance abuse, smoking, precocious sexuality, and early pregnancy, educational underachievement, suicide attempts, sensation seeking, and unemployment, as well as crime.

    A. problem behavior syndrome
    B. latent traits
    C. crime generators
    D. turning points

14. _____ theory is the study of changes in criminal offending patterns over a person's entire life.

    A. life course
    B. latent trait
    C. interactional
    D. social development model

15. How many murders was Gary L. Sampson wanted for when heturned himself in to the Vermont State Police?

    A. three
    B. five
    C. ten
    D. fifteen

16. According to life course theory which of these transitions is expected to take place first?

    A. finishing school
    B. entering the workforce
    C. getting married
    D. having children

17. According to life course theory which of these transitions is expected to take place last?

    A. finishing school
    B. entering the workforce
    C. getting married
    D. having children

18. According to the author, life course theories are inherently what?

    A. multidimensional
    B. unidimensional
    C. convoluted
    D. revolutionary

19. Where did Sheldon and Eleanor Glueck work in the 1930s when they conducted their landmark studies?

    A. Harvard University
    B. University of Massachusetts
    C. UCLA
    D. University of Chicago

20. During the1990s, the Glueck legacy was rediscovered in a series of papers by _____.

    A. criminologists Robert Sampson and John Laub
    B. a man known simply as Charley
    C. Karl and Lenny from the Springfield nuclear plant
    D. Smith and Jones

21. What personal traits are predictors of crime in Wilson and Herrstein's theory of crime?

    A. height, hair, and eye color
    B. intelligence, body build, and genetic make-up
    C. age, ethnicity, and gender
    D. IQ, muscle mass, and EEG readings

22. According to Wilson and Herrstein, what is all human behavior determined by?

    A. perceived rewards and consequences
    B. experiential factors
    C. structural inequalities
    D. unequal distributions of power

23. Hirschi and Gottfredson's General Theory of Crime is a modification of what theory?
      A. social control theory   C. social disorganization theory
      B. strain theory   D. power control theory

24. According to Hirschi and Gottfredson's General Theory of Crime, which of the following is seen as the factor to explain differences in criminality among people?
      A. strain and anomie   C. institutional anomie
      B. relative deprivation   D. levels of self control

25. According to Hirschi and Gottfredson's General Theory of Crime, why do some people with low self control escape leading a life of crime?
      A. high moral upbringing   C. limited opportunities for crime
      B. fear of prison and shame   D. they are too busy drinking and gambling

TRUE/FALSE

1. Adolescent-limited offenders are offenders who follow the most common criminal trajectory, in which antisocial behavior peaks in adolescence and then diminishes.
      A. True   B. False

2. Life course persister are one of the small group of offenders whose criminal career continues well into adulthood.
      A. True   B. False

3. The general theory of crime is a belief that personal traits, such as genetic makeup, intelligence, and body build, may outweigh the importance of social variables as predictors of criminal activity.
      A. True   B. False

4. Human nature theory is a developmental theory that modifies social control theory by integrating concepts from biosocial, psychological, routine activities, and rational choice theories.
      A. True   B. False

5. Gary Sampson turned himself into the Vermont State Police when he was taken into custody.
      A. True   B. False

6. The Gluecks' research was virtually ignored for nearly 30 years as the study of crime and delinquency shifted almost exclusively to social and social-psychological factors.
      A. True   B. False

7. Those who suffer Problem Behavior Syndrome are prone to more difficulties than the general population.
      A. True   B. False

8. According to Wilson and Herrstein's theory of crime, intelligence, body build, and genetic make-up personal traits are predictors of crime.
      A. True   B. False

9. According to Wilson and Herrstein, what is all human behavior determined by perceived rewards and consequences.
      A. True   B. False

10. According to Hirschi and Gottfredson's General Theory of Crime, limited opportunities for crime can explain why some people with low self control escape leading a life of crime.
      A. True   B. False

11. According to the author, research indicates that children who will later become delinquents begin their deviant careers at a very early (preschool) age and that the earlier the onset of criminality the more frequent, varied, and sustained the criminal career.

    A. True   B. False

12. Hirschi and Gottfredson's General Theory of Crime can be used only to explain a small range of criminal behaviors.

    A. True   B. False

13. According to Patterson and findings produced at the Oregon Social Learning Center, poor parental discipline and monitoring was the key to the onset of criminality in early childhood.

    A. True   B. False

14. According to Moffitt, life course persisters combine family dysfunction with severe neurological problems that predispose them to antisocial behavior patterns.

    A. True   B. False

15. According to Moffitt, adolescent limiteds begin offending before age 14, experience (1) poor parenting, which leads them into (2) deviant behaviors and then (3) involvement with delinquent groups.

    A. True   B. False

16. According to Moffitt as they reach their mid-teens, adolescent-limited delinquents begin to mimic the antisocial behavior of more troubled teens, only to reduce the frequency of their offending as they mature to around age 38.

    A. True   B. False

17. Children are socialized and develop bonds to their families through four distinct interactions and processes: Perceived opportunities for involvement in activities and interactions with others, the degree of involvement and interaction with parents, the children's ability to participate in these interactions, and the reinforcement (such as feedback) children perceive for their participation.

    A. True   B. False

18. According to the general theory of crime, adolescents who perceive opportunities and rewards for antisocial behavior will form deep attachments to deviant peers and will become committed to a delinquent way of life.

    A. True   B. False

19. The Cambridge Study in Delinquent Development followed the offending careers of 411 London boys born in 1953; the boys have been interviewed eight times over 24 years, beginning at age 8 and continuing to age 32.

    A. True   B. False

20. The Cambridge Study in Delinquent Development noted that deviant behavior tends to be versatile rather than specialized.

    A. True   B. False

FILL IN

1. _____ theories is a branch of criminology that examines change in a criminal career over the life course; factors include biological, social, and psychological change.

2. _____ is passive obedience to the demands of others, such as submitting to physical or sexual abuse without response.

3. _____ is challenging control mechanisms but stopping short of physical harm; for example, vandalism, curfew violations, and unconventional sex.

4. _____ is direct forms of physical violence, such as robbery, sexual assault, or other forms of physical violence.

5. A developmental theory that attributes deviant and criminal behaviors to imbalances between the amount of control that the individual has over others and that others have over him or her is known as _____ theory.

6. According to the concept _____, the world is conceived as full of coercive forces that can only be overcome through the application of equal or even greater coercive responses.

7. According to Laub and Sampson, _____ are the life events that alter the development of a criminal career.

8. _____ is defined as positive relations with individuals and institutions that are life sustaining.

9. Socialized attachment to conventional institutions, activities, and beliefs is known as _____.

10. _____ coercion is the use of force, threat of force, or intimidation by parents, peers, or significant others.

11. According to Gottfredson and Hirschi, _____ theory is the view that the cause of delinquent behavior is an impulsive personality.

12. A stable feature, characteristic, property, or condition, present at birth or soon after, that makes some people crime prone over the life course is characteristic of the _____ theory.

13. _____ theory is the study of changes in criminal offending patterns over a person's entire life.

14. The _____ of crime is a developmental theory that modifies social control theory by integrating concepts from biosocial, psychological, routine activities, and rational choice theories.

15. _____ is a cluster of antisocial behavior that may include family dysfunction, substance abuse, smoking, precocious sexuality, and early pregnancy, educational underachievement, suicide attempts, sensation seeking, and unemployment, as well as crime.

ESSAY

1. Discuss Gottfredson and Hirschi's general theory of crime?

2. Contrast the latent trait view with that of developmental criminology.

3. What are the major turning points in life and why are they important in criminology?

4. Define problem behavior syndrome. What impact does this concept have in explaining criminality?

5. Identify and define the three pathways to a criminal career identified by Loeber and associates.

CHAPTER TEN
DEVELOPMENTAL THEORIES: LIFE COURSE AND LATENT TRAIT
ANSWER KEY

MULTIPLE CHOICE ITEMS

1. A	6. B	11. A	16. A	21. B
2. B	7. C	12. B	17. D	22. A
3. C	8. D	13. A	18. A	23. A
4. D	9. A	14. A	19. A	24. D
5. A	10. D	15. A	20. A	25. C

TRUE FALSE ITEMS

1. A	6. A	11. A	16. B
2. A	7. A	12. B	17. A
3. B	8. A	13. A	18. B
4. B	9. A	14. A	19. A
5. A	10. A	15. B	20. A

FILL IN ITEMS

1. developmental	6. coercive ideation	11. self-control
2. submission	7. turning points	12. latent trait
3. defiance	8. social capital	13. life course
4. predation	9. prosocial bonds	14. general theory
5. control balance	10. interpersonal	15. problem behavior syndrome

CHAPTER ELEVEN
VIOLENT CRIME: FROM STREET CRIME TO TERRORISM

LEARNING OBJECTIVES

1. Identify and understand the root causes of violence.
2. Differentiate between expressive and instrumental crimes of violence.
3. Identify and understand various forms of terrorism.
4. Identify various types of robbers.
5. Identify and distinguish various levels of homicide.
6. Identify and appreciate the link between gender power relationships, rape, and spousal abuse.

CHAPTER SUMMARY

Violence has become an all too common aspect of modern life. Among the various explanations for violent crimes are the availability of firearms, human traits, a subculture of violence that stresses violent solutions to interpersonal problems, and family conflict.

There are many types of interpersonal violent crime. Rape, the carnal knowledge of a female forcibly and against her will, has been known throughout history, but the view of rape has evolved. At present, close to 100,000 rapes are reported to U.S. police each year; the actual number of rapes is probably much higher. Rape is an extremely difficult charge to prove in court. The victim's lack of consent must be proven; therefore, it almost seems that the victim is on trial. Consequently, changes are being made in rape law and procedure.

Murder is defined as killing a human being with malice aforethought. There are different degrees of murder, and punishments vary accordingly. One important characteristic of murder is that the victim and criminal often know each other. This has led some criminologists to believe that murder is partly victim-precipitated. assault, another serious interpersonal violent crime, often occurs in the home, including child abuse and spouse abuse. There also appears to be a trend toward violence between dating couples. Robbery involves theft by force, usually in a public place. Types of offenders include professional, opportunist, addict, and alcoholic robbers. Robbery is considered a violent crime because it can and often does involve violence.

There are newly emerging forms of violent crime including hate crimes, stalking and work place violence. Terrorism is a significant form of violence. Many terrorist groups exist at both the national and international levels. Hundreds of terrorist acts are reported each year in the United States alone. There are a variety of terrorist goals including political change, nationalism, personal causes, criminality, and environmental protection. Terrorists may be motivated by criminal gain, psychosis, grievance against the state, or ideology. The World Trade Center bombing on September 11, 2001, turned world attention to terrorism. Renewed efforts to combat this threat have included the creation of a cabinet-level Department of Homeland Security.

CHAPTER OUTLINE

I.   Introduction
        A.   Washington, DC area sniper
                1.   six victims were killed with a single shot during a two day period
                2.   sniper reportedly left a tarot death card
                3.   crime scene fingerprint identifies suspect John Lee Malvo
                4.   Muhammad and Malvo taken into custody
                5.   trunk area used as a sniper's perch
        B.   Perception of violence
                1.   UCR tells us that violence rate has been in a recent decline

2.   sniper attacks categorized as expressive violence
3.   instrumental crime is designed to improve the offender's financial or social position

II.   The Roots of Violence
    A.   Personal traits
        1.   Hamilton kills 16 children at a school
        2.   murderous youths suffer signs of major neurological impairment
        3.   death row inmates have history of mental impairment and intellectual dysfunction
    B.   Ineffective families
        1.   variables linked to violent offending include:
            a.   deviant parents
            b.   inconsistent discipline
            c.   lack of supervision
        2.   parents reinforce a child's coercive behavior
        3.   they fail to set adequate limits or to use proper, consistent discipline
        4.   powerful relationship between exposure to physical punishment and later aggression
    C.   Abused children
        1.   children who are abused later engage in delinquent behaviors
        2.   sexual abuse is constant factor in patricide and matricide killings
        3.   greatest effect if abuse is persistent and extends from childhood to adolescence
    D.   The brutalization process
        1.   three groups based on their aggressive tendencies:
            a.   nonviolent
            b.   violent
            c.   incipiently violent
        2.   four distinct types of violent acts:
            a.   physically defensive
            b.   frustrative
            c.   malefic
            d.   frustrative-malefic
        3.   brutalized youth may become belligerent and angry
        4.   violentization process includes belligerence, violent performances, and virulency
    E.   Evolutionary factors/ human instinct
        1.   debate whether violence is inherent in all humans
        2.   violent behavior is committed predominantly by males
        3.   psychologically ingrained need to display virility and toughness
    F.   Exposure to violence
        1.   people exposed to violence may adopt violent methods
        2.   children living in these conditions become crusted over
    G.   Substance abuse
        1.   psychopharmacological relationship
        2.   economic compulsive behavior
        3.   systemic link
    H.   Firearm availability
        1.   two-thirds of all murders involve firearms
        2.   two-fifths of all robberies involve firearms
        3.   firearms in the home increases the risk of suicide among adolescents
    I.   Cultural values
        1.   Wolfgang and Ferracuti subculture of violence concept
        2.   violence has been legitimized by custom and norm
        3.   income inequality and racial disparity may help instill a sense of hopelessness
    J.   Social movements
        1.   membership in radical political and social movements contributes to violence
        2.   local militia groups
    K.   Ganging

        1.   violence rates highest in urban areas where subcultural values support gangs
        2.   gang boys are more likely to own guns and other weapons
        3.   violence is a core value of gang membership
    L   Regional values
        1.   Southern subculture of violence
        2.   regional differences may involve economics
    M.   National values
        1.   national characteristics are predictive of violence

III.   Forcible Rape
    A.   Basics
        1.   forcible carnal knowledge of a female
        2.   other sexual acts or coercion are included in other crime categories
        3.   rape is an act of violence
    B.   History of rape
        1.   rape has been known throughout history
        2.   rape was a common occurrence in early civilization
        3.   practice reflects sexist values and customs
        4.   related to the practice of heiress stealing in the middle ages
    C.   Rape and the military
        1.   rape has been associated with war
        2.   sexual possession of women considered one of the spoils of war
        3.   rape continues to be associated with war
        4.   rape ring at the Aberdeen Proving Grounds in Maryland
        5.   200,000 Korean women into frontline brothels in WWII
        6.   systematic rape of Bosnian and Kosovar women by Serbian army officers
    D.   Incidence of rape
        1.   about 90,000 rapes or attempted rapes were reported to U.S. police in 2001
        2.   rape rate has been in a decade-long decline
        3.   population density influences the rape rate
        4.   racial and age pattern of rape arrests has been fairly consistent for some time
        5.   rape is a warm-weather crime
        6.   rape is frequently underreported
    E.   International sexual violence
        1.   international comparisons vary in the percentage of women who are victimized
        2.   found high rates of reported forced sexual initiation
        3.   sexual violence has significant health consequences
    F.   Types of rape
        1.   Groth's three elements: anger, power, and sadism
        2.   gang versus individual rape
        3.   serial rape
        4.   acquaintance rape: date rape, statutory rape, and marital rape
    G.   Causes of rape
        1.   evolutionary & biological factors
        2.   male socialization
        3.   hypermasculinity
        4.   psychological abnormality
        5.   social learning
        6.   sexual motivation
    H.   Rape and the law
        1.   source of conflict in the criminal justice system
        2.   police and courts are now becoming more sensitive to the plight of rape victims
        3.   proving rape is extremely challenging for prosecutors
        4.   Gary Dotson was convicted of raping a woman in Illinois
        5.   he served more than six years in prison before his alleged victim recanted her story

6.   U.S. sexism causes a cultural suspiciousness of women
7.   prosecutors must establish that the act was forced and violent
8.   no question of voluntary compliance exists
9.   burden of proof is on the victim to show that her character is beyond question
10.   referring to the woman as promiscuous may result in exoneration of the accused
11.   shield laws protect women from being questioned about their sexual history
12.   1991 case, Michigan v. Lucas, Court upheld the validity of shield laws
13.   corroboration is no longer required
14.   Violence Against Women Act passed in 1994
15.   statute allows rape victims to sue in federal court
16.   victim's character was still a critical factor in their decision to file charges

IV.   Murder and Homicide
- A.   Basics
  1.   most serious crime and only one punishable by death
  2.   no statute of limitations on prosecution
  3.   implied or constructive malice
- B.   Degrees of murder
  1.   first degree involves premeditation and deliberation
  2.   second degree has malice but not premeditation and deliberation
  3.   manslaughter is unlawful homicide without malice
  4.   includes non-negligent and negligent
  5.   issue of feticide
  6.   mother whose behavior endangers an unborn child
  7.   successful prosecution for feticide is rare
- C.   Nature and extent of murder
  1.   murder rates peak in early 1990s
  2.   decline of about 33 percent between 1992 and 2001
  3.   about 16,000 citizens were killed in 2001 (excluding the 9-11 casualties)
  4.   murder victims and offenders tend to be males
  5.   the rate per 100,000 peaks in the 18- to 24-year-old age group
  6.   half of all victims are African Americans and the other half white
  7.   murder, like rape, tends to be an intraracial crime
- D.   Murderous relations
  1.   relationship between the murderer and the victim draws attention
  2.   spousal relations
  3.   men kill their spouses or partners because they fear losing control and power
  4.   women who kill out of jealousy aim their aggression at their partners
  5.   men are more likely to kill their mates' suitors
  6.   most murders occur among people who are acquainted.
  7.   many homicides follow a sequential pattern
  8.   violent exchanges and retaliations may be contagious
- E.   Types of murderers
  1.   stranger homicides are most often felony murders
  2.   habitual criminal statutes may be responsible for some increase
  3.   school boards around the nation have adopted similar zero tolerance policies
  4.   though relatively rare events have captured significant media attention
- F.   Serial murder
  1.   Garavito, a 42-year-old drifter, in Colombia
  2.   he killed 140 boys between the ages of 8 and 16 during a five-year killing spree
  3.   there was no one to notice that the children were missing
  4.   Pedro Armando Lopez, known here as the "Monster of the Andes,"
  5.   believed to have killed more than 300 girls and young women
  6.   serial killers distinguished from mass murderers
  7.   research shows that serial killers have long histories of violence

8.   an estimated 10 to 15 percent of serial killers are women
9.   during childhood she suffered from an abusive relationship in a disrupted family
10.   law enforcement officials have been at a loss to control random killers

V.   Assault and Battery
   A.   Basics
      1.   assault and battery are two different offenses
      2.   battery requires offensive touching
      3.   assault requires no touching
   B.   Nature and extent of assault
      1.   pattern of assault is similar to homicide
      2.   road rage on airplanes
      3.   in 2001 the FBI recorded slightly less more than 907,000 assaults
      4.   most common weapons used in assaults are blunt instruments
      5.   victims reported more than 1.2 million aggravated assaults in 2001
      6.   3.6 million simple or weaponless assaults
   C.   Assault in the home
      1.   intra-family violence is an enduring social problem
      2.   70 percent of all female deaths are domestic homicides
      3.   the only way to cleanse the family honor by killing the offending female
      4.   intrafamily violence that has received a great deal of media attention is child abuse
      5.   879,000 children were found to be victims of child maltreatment
   D.   Sexual abuse
      1.   the exploitation of children through rape, incest, and molestation
      2.   most states showed declines of at least 30 percent
      3.   physical and sexual abuse takes a significant toll around the world
   E.   Spousal abuse
      1.   spousal abuse has occurred throughout recorded history
      2.   mid-nineteenth century, severe wife beating fell into disfavor
      3.   between 20 and 40 percent of females experience violence while dating
      4.   batterers tend to fall into one of two categories: Pit Bulls and Cobras

VI.   Robbery
   A.   Basics
      1.   robbery is considered a violent crime because it involves the use of force
      2.   in 2001 the FBI recorded 422,000 robberies
      3.   it is down more than 43 percent since 1992
      4.   ecological pattern for robbery is similar to that of other violent crimes
   B.   Types
      1.   professional robbers have a long-term commitment to crime
      2.   opportunist robbers steal small amounts of money from accessible targets
      3.   addict robbers steal to support their drug habits
      4.   alcoholic robbers steal for reasons related to their excessive consumption of alcohol
      5.   acquaintance robbery focus on people they know
   C.   Rational robbers
      1.   most robbers may be opportunistic rather than professional
      2.   robbers also choose vulnerable victims

VII.   Emerging Forms of Interpersonal Violence
   A.   Hate crimes
      1.   in 1998 Matthew Shepard, a gay college student, was kidnapped and killed
      2.   hate crimes usually involve convenient, vulnerable targets
      3.   Levin identifies three motivations for hate crime
         a.   thrill-seeking hate crimes
         b.   reactive (defensive) hate crimes

                c.   mission hate crimes
        4.   a number of jurisdictions have made a special effort to control hate crimes
B.   Workplace violence
        1.   now considered the third leading cause of occupational injury or death
        2.   number of factors precipitate workplace violence
        3.   unresolved conflict may be compounded by other events causing an eventual eruption
        4.   cost of workplace violence for American businesses runs more than $4 billion
        5.   more than 2 million U.S. residents become victims of violent crime while they work
        6.   advocates the use of mediation to resolve interpersonal disputes
C.   Stalking
        1.   estimated 1.4 one million victims annually
        2.   about 700,000 women are being stalked each year on college campuses alone
        3.   most victims know their stalker
D.   Terrorism
        1.   2 hijacked airliners crashed into the World Trade Center Towers
        2.   terrorism is a political crime
        3.   the intent to disrupt and change the government
E.   Brief history of terrorism
        1.   assassination of Julius Caesar on March 15, 44 b.c., is considered an act of terrorism
        2.   terrorist first became popular during the French Revolution
        3.   Hur Brotherhood in India was made up of religious fanatics
        4.   Internal Macedonian Revolutionary Organization against the Turks
        5.   Irish Republican Army
        6.   resistance to the occupying German troops
F.   Contemporary forms of terrorism
        1.   revolutionary terrorists
        2.   political terrorists
        3.   nationalist terrorism
        4.   cause-based terrorism
        5.   environmental terrorism
        6.   state-sponsored terrorism
        7.   criminal terrorism
G.   Responses to terrorism
        1.   American agents had difficulty in trying to penetrate the al-Qaeda network
        2.   nearly 5,000 trucks entered the United States on the Ambassador Bridge
        3.   creation of the Department of Homeland Security
        4.   1994 Violent Crime Control Act authorized the death penalty for international terrorists
        5.   United States had blocked more than $27 million in assets of the Taliban and al-Qaeda
        6.   USA Patriot Act (USAPA)
        7.   Foreign Intelligence Surveillance Act (FISA)

KEY TERMS

acquaintance rape: Forcible sex in which offender and victim are acquainted with one another.

acquaintance robbery: Robbers who focus their thefts on people they know.

aggravated rape: Rape involving multiple offenders, weapons, and victim injury.

assault: An attack that may not involve physical contact; includes attempted battery or intentionally frightening the victim by word or deed.

battery: A physical attack that includes hitting, punching, slapping, or other offensive touching of the person.

bias crimes: Violent acts directed at a particular person or members of a group merely because the targets share a discernable racial, ethnic, religious or gender characteristic; also called hate crimes.

child abuse: Any physical, sexual, or emotional trauma to a child for which no reasonable explanation, such as an accident, can be found. Child abuse can also be a function of neglecting to give proper care and attention to a young child.

consent: In prosecuting rape cases, it is essential to prove that the attack was forced and that the victim did not give voluntary consent to her attacker. In a sense, the burden of proof is on the victim to show that her character is beyond question. Proving victim dissent is not a requirement in any other violent crime.

convictional criminals: Those who violate the law because they believe their actions will ultimately benefit society.

crusted over: The condition created when children live in situations where they are exposed to violence. They do not let people inside, nor do they express their feelings. They exploit others and in turn are exploited by those older and stronger; as a result, they develop a sense of hopelessness.

date rape: Forcible sex during a courting relationship.

death squads: Government troops used to destroy political opposition parties.

deliberation: Planning a homicide after careful thought, however brief, rather than acting on sudden impulse.

economic compulsive behavior: Drug users resort to violence to support their habit.

eldercide: The murder of a senior citizen.

eros: The instinct to create and preserve life; eros is expressed sexually.

expressive violence: A crime that has no purpose except to accomplish the behavior at hand, such as shooting someone.

felony murder: A homicide in the context of another felony, such as robbery or rape; legally defined as first-degree murder.

feticide: Endangering or killing an unborn fetus.

first-degree murder: The killing of another person after premeditation and deliberation.

gang rape: Forcible sex involving multiple attackers.

guerilla: The term means little war and developed out of the Spanish rebellion against French troops after Napoleon's 1808 invasion of the Iberian Peninsula. Today, the term is used interchangeably with the term terrorist.

hypermasculine: Men who typically have a callous sexual attitude and believe violence is manly. They perceive danger as exciting and are overly sensitive to insult and ridicule. They are also impulsive, more apt to brag about sexual conquests, and more likely to lose control, especially when using alcohol.

infanticide: The murder of a very young child.

instrumental violence: Violence designed to improve the financial or social position of the criminal.

international terrorism: Terrorism involving citizens or the territory of more than one country.

involuntary or negligent manslaughter: A homicide that occurs as a result of acts that are negligent and without regard for the harm they may cause others, such as driving under the influence of alcohol or drugs.

manslaughter: A homicide without malice.

marital exemption: The practice in some states of prohibiting the prosecution of husbands for the rape of their wives.

marital rape: Forcible sex between people who are legally married to each other.

mass murder: The killing of a large number of people in a single incident by an offender who typically does not seek concealment or escape.

mission hate crime: Violent crimes committed by disturbed individuals who see it as their duty to rid the world of evil.

murder: The unlawful killing of a human being with malicious intent.

neglect: Not providing a child with the care and shelter to which he or she is entitled.

premeditation: Consideration of a homicide before it occurs.

psychopharmacological relationship: Violence may be the direct consequence of ingesting mood-altering substances.

rape: The carnal knowledge of a female forcibly and against her will.

reactive hate crime: Perpetrators believe they are taking a defensive stand against outsiders who they believe threaten their community or way of life.

road rage: A term used to describe motorists who assault each other.

robbery: Taking or attempting to take anything of value by force or threat of force and/or putting the victim in fear.

second-degree murder: A homicide with malice but not premeditation or deliberation, as when a desire to inflict serious bodily harm and a wanton disregard for life result in the victim's death.

serial murder: The killing of a large number of people over time by an offender who seeks to avoid detection.

serial rape: Multiple rapes committed by one person over time.

sexual abuse: Exploitation of a child through rape, incest, or molestation by a parent or other adult.

shield laws: Laws designed to protect rape victims by prohibiting the defense attorney from inquiring about their previous sexual relationships.

stalking: A pattern of behavior directed at a specific person that includes repeated physical or visual proximity, unwanted communications, and/or threats sufficient to cause fear in a reasonable person.

statutory rape: Sexual relations between an underage minor female and an adult male; though not coerced, an underage partner is considered incapable of giving informed consent.

subculture of violence: Norms and customs that, in contrast to society's dominant value system, legitimize and expect the use of violence to resolve social conflicts.

sufferance: The aggrieved party nothing to rectify a conflict situation; over time, the unresolved conflict may be compounded by other events that cause an eventual eruption.

systemic link: Violence becomes endemic when drug gangs flex their muscle to dominate territory and drive out rivals.

terrorism: The illegal use of force against innocent people to achieve a political purpose.

terrorist group: Any group practicing, or that has significant subgroups that practice, international terrorism.

thanatos: The death instinct, which produces self-destruction.

thrill-seeking hate crime: Hate mongers who join forces to have fun by bashing minorities or destroying property; inflicting pain on others gives them a sadistic thrill.

virility mystique: The belief that males must separate their sexual feelings from needs for love, respect, and affection.

voluntary or nonnegligent manslaughter: A homicide committed in the heat of passion or during a sudden quarrel; although intent may be present, malice is not.

workplace violence: Irate employees or former employees attack coworkers or sabotage machinery and production lines; now considered the third leading cause of occupational injury or death.

TEST BANK

MULTIPLE CHOICE

1. Which instinctual drive was a life instinct that drove people to self fulfillment and enjoyment?
    A. the thanatos   C. the Xanadu
    B. the eros   D. the superego

2. Which instinctual drive could be used to explain thoughts of suicide?
    A. the thanatos   C. the Xanadu
    B. the eros   D. the superego

3. How did Felton Earls describe the children in his Chicago study that had high levels of exposure to violence?
    A. numb   C. mean-spirited
    B. oblivious   D. crusted over

4. Which region of the United States has been described as having a culture of violence based on the defense of personal honor and ownership of firearms?
    A. south   C. east
    B. north   D. midwest

5. What type of relationship exists when the mood-altering properties of a drug are related to violent acts?
    A. an economic compulsive behavior   C. a structural relationship
    B. a systemic relationship   D. a psychopharmacological relationship

6. What does economic compulsive behavior refer to in regards to substance abuse?
    A. the activities of gangs whose members sell and use drugs
    B. when drug users resort to violence to gain funds to support their habits
    C. drug related deaths caused by drug trafficking conflicts
    D. the direct consequence of ingesting mood altering drugs

7. _____robbers steal to obtain small amounts of money when an accessible target presents itself; they are not committed to robbery but will steal from cab drivers, drunks, the elderly, and other vulnerable persons if they need some extra spending money.
    A. Opportunist   C. Transgendered
    B. Addicted   D. Alcoholic

8. According to Groth, what type of rape involves an attacker who does not want to harm his victim as much as he wants to possess her sexually?
    A. power   C. sadistic
    B. anger   D. dominance

9. What type of men tend to have a callous sexual attitude and believe that violence is manly?
    A. sports-minded   C. hypermasculine
    B. sexually dysfunctional   D. sexually liberated

10. Athens finds that there are four distinct types of violent acts: one of which is called _____, in which the perpetrator sees his violent act as one of self-defense.
A. physically defensive   C. malefic
    B. frustrative   D. frustrative-malefic

11. Athens finds that there are four distinct types of violent acts: one of which is called _____, in which the offender acts out of anger due to frustration when he cannot get his way.
    A. physically defensive   C. malefic
    B. frustrative   D. frustrative-malefic

12. Athens finds that there are four distinct types of violent acts: one of which is called _____, in which the victim is considered to be extremely evil or malicious.

    A. physically defensive   C. malefic

    B. frustrative   D. frustrative-malefic

13. Athens finds that there are four distinct types of violent acts: one of which is called _____, which is a combined type.

    A. physically defensive   C. malefic

    B. frustrative   D. frustrative-malefic

14. _____ is forcible sex in which offender and victim are acquainted with one another.

    A. acquaintance rape   C. rape

    B. serial rape   D. gang rape

15. _____ is multiple rapes committed by one person over time.

    A. acquaintance rape   C. rape

    B. serial rape   D. gang rape

16. _____ is the carnal knowledge of a female forcibly and against her will.

    A. acquaintance rape   C. rape

    B. serial rape   D. gang rape

17. _____ is forcible sex involving multiple attackers.

    A. acquaintance rape   C. rape

    B. serial rape   D. gang rape

18. Forcible sex during a courting relationship is known as _____.

    A. acquaintance rape   C. rape

    B. date rape   D. gang rape

19. Sexual relations between an underage minor female and an adult male; though not coerced, an underage partner is considered incapable of giving informed consent is known as _____.

    A. acquaintance rape   C. statutory rape

    B. serial rape   D. gang rape

20. _____ is forcible sex between people who are legally married to each other.

    A. acquaintance rape   C. marital rape

    B. serial rape   D. gang rape

21. _____ is the practice in some states of prohibiting the prosecution of husbands for the rape of their wives.

    A. marital exemption   C. rape shield law

    B. proximity defense   D. statutory rape

22. _____ violence is designed to improve the financial or social position of the criminal.

    A. instrumental   C. temperamental

    B. expressive   D. transitional

23. _____ violence is a crime that has no purpose except to accomplish the behavior at hand, such as shooting someone.

    A. instrumental   C. temperamental

    B. expressive   D. transitional

24. According to the United Nation's World Health Organization 2002 report, violence kills about people _____ people globally every year.

    A. 350,000   C. 1.6 million

    B. 800,000   D. 10.6 million

25. According to Levin and Fox, it is difficult to estimate the number and extent of serial killings, but a reasoned estimate is that up to 20 serial killers are active in a given year, accounting for up to _____ percent of the total number of homicides.

    A. 240 killings or about 1   C. 1240 killings or about 15

    B. 35 killings or about .10   D. 24 killings or about 5

TRUE/FALSE

1. John Lee Malvo and John Allen Muhammad were taken into custody in connection with the Washington, DC area sniper attacks.

    A. True   B. False

2. Instrumental violence is considered violence designed to improve the financial or social position of the criminal.

    A. True   B. False

3. Expressive violence is a crime that has no purpose except to accomplish the behavior at hand, such as shooting someone.

    A. True   B. False

4. According to the United Nation's World Health Organization 2002 report, violence kills about people 1.6 million people globally every year.

    A. True   B. False

5. According to the United Nation's World Health Organization 2002 report, almost every minute of the day, someone is murdered, an average of 1424 daily murders; adding to this number is an almost equal number of daily suicides.

    A. True   B. False

6. In her 1998 book Guilty by Reason of Insanity, Lewis finds that death row inmates have a history of mental impairment and intellectual dysfunction.

    A. True   B. False

7. A physical attack that includes hitting, punching, slapping, or other offensive touching of the person is called an assault.

    A. True   B. False

8. A battery is an attack that may not involve physical contact; includes attempted battery or intentionally frightening the victim by word or deed.

    A. True   B. False

9. Premeditation is the consideration of a homicide before it occurs.

    A. True   B. False

10. Deliberation is planning a homicide after careful thought, however brief, rather than acting on sudden impulse.

    A. True   B. False

11. Mass murder is the killing of a large number of people over time by an offender who seeks to avoid detection.

    A. True   B. False

12. Serial murder is the killing of a large number of people in a single incident by an offender who typically does not seek concealment or escape.

       A. True   B. False

13. One type of domestic batterer is the cobra, whose emotions are quick to erupt, are driven by deep insecurity and a dependence on the wives and partners they abuse; they tend to become stalkers, unable to let go of relationships once they have ended.

       A. True   B. False

14. One type of batterer is the pit bull, they coolly and methodically inflict pain and humiliation on their spouses; they see violence as an unavoidable part of life

       A. True   B. False

15. The author notes that blended families, such as children who live with a mother's boyfriend, have been linked to abuse.

       A. True   B. False

16. Research by Jones and Finkelhor of the University of New Hampshire's Crimes Against Children Research Center shows that substantiated child sexual-abuse cases in the United States dropped 31 percent between 1992 and 1998.

       A. True   B. False

17. According to the author, in 2001 the FBI recorded 422,000 robberies, a rate of 148 per 100,000 population; robbery is down more than 43 percent since 1992.

       A. True   B. False

18. According to the author, in 2001 the FBI recorded slightly less more than 907,000 assaults, a rate of 318 per 100,000 inhabitants; the number of assaults has been in decline, down 20 percent from 1992.

       A. True   B. False

19. According to Levin and Fox, it is difficult to estimate the number and extent of serial killings, but a reasoned estimate is that up to 20 serial killers are active in a given year, accounting for up to 1240 killings or about 15 percent of the total number of homicides.

       A. True   B. False

20. According to Levin and Fox, expedience killers are out for profit or want to protect themselves from a perceived threat; this is the most common form of serial murderer.

       A. True   B. False

FILL IN

1. A crime that has no purpose except to accomplish the behavior at hand, such as shooting someone is known as _____ violence.

2. _____ is the instinct to create and preserve life; it is expressed sexually.

3. _____ is the death instinct, which produces self-destruction

4. _____ is violence designed to improve the financial or social position of the criminal.

5. The condition created when children live in situations where they are exposed to violence is known as being _____; they do not let people inside, nor do they express their feelings.

6. Violence may be the direct consequence of ingesting mood-altering substances best describes the _____

relationship.

7. Norms and customs that, in contrast to society's dominant value system, legitimize and expect the use of violence to resolve social conflicts is known as the _____ of violence.

8. _____ is the carnal knowledge of a female forcibly and against her will.

9. _____ is forcible sex involving multiple attackers.

10. Violence becomes endemic when drug gangs flex their muscle to dominate territory and drive out rivals best describes the _____ link.

11. _____rape is forcible sex in which offender and victim are acquainted with one another.

12. _____rape is multiple rapes committed by one person over time.

13. _____rape is forcible sex during a courting relationship.

14. _____ rape is sexual relations between an underage minor female and an adult male; though not coerced, an underage partner is considered incapable of giving informed consent.

15. _____ rape is forcible sex between people who are legally married to each other.

ESSAY

1. Identify the potential causes and extent of child abuse.

2. Identify and distinguish various types of terrorism.

3. Discuss the different types of robbers.

4. Identify and define the different types of mass murderers.

5. Discuss the incidence and costs associated with workplace violence.

CHAPTER ELEVEN
VIOLENT CRIME: FROM STREET CRIME TO TERRORISM
ANSWER KEY

MULTIPLE CHOICE ITEMS

1. B	6. B	11. B	16. C	21. A
2. A	7. A	12. C	17. D	22. A
3. D	8. B	13. D	18. B	23. B
4. A	9. C	14. A	19. C	24. C
5. D	10. A	15. B	20. C	25. A

TRUE FALSE ITEMS

1. A	6. A	11. B	16. A
2. A	7. B	12. B	17. A
3. A	8. B	13. B	18. A
4. A	9. A	14. B	19. B
5. A	10. A	15. A	20. B

FILL IN ITEMS

1. expressive	6. psychopharmacological	11. acquaintance
2. eros	7. subculture	12. serial
3. thanatos	8. rape	13. date
4. instrumental	9. gang rape	14. statutory
5. crusted over	10. systemic	15. marital

CHAPTER TWELVE
PROPERTY CRIMES

LEARNING OBJECTIVES

1. Distinguish between the terms fence, street crimes, burglary, occasional criminals and professional criminals.
2. Understand situational inducement and its relationship to the term occasional criminal.
3. Identify the conditions of professional fencing.
4. Describe the different categories of theft.
5. Distinguish between carjacking and auto theft.
6. Define burglary and its various forms.
7. Identify the causes of arson.
8. Understand the relationship between technological developments and changes in criminal behavior.
9. Understand gender differences regarding burglary.

CHAPTER SUMMARY

Economic crimes are designed to bring financial reward to the offender. The majority of economic crimes are committed by opportunistic amateurs. Economic crimes have also attracted professional criminals. A good example of the professional criminal is the fence who buys and sells stolen merchandise. There are also occasional thieves whose skill level and commitment fall below the professional level.

Common theft offenses include larceny, fraud, embezzlement, and burglary. These are common law crimes, created by English judges to meet social needs. Larceny involves taking the legal possessions of another. Petty larceny is theft of amounts typically under $100; grand larceny, of amounts over $100. The crime of false pretenses, or fraud, is similar to larceny because it involves the theft of goods or money, but it differs because the criminal tricks victims into voluntarily giving up their possessions. Burglary, a more serious theft offense, was defined in the common law as the "breaking and entering of a dwelling house of another in the nighttime with the intent to commit a felony within." Most states have modified their definitions of burglary to include theft from any structure at any time of day. Arson is another serious property crime. Although most arsonists are teenage vandals, there are professional arsonists who specialize in burning commercial buildings for profit.

CHAPTER OUTLINE

I.   Introduction
    A.   Basics
        1.   property crime is widespread
        2.   almost thirty million personal and household thefts occur annually
        3.   we can be ambivalent about thieves
        4.   tolerant of property crime because we all do it and it doesn't seriously harm
    B.   A brief history of theft
        1.   surveys indicate that 10-15 percent of US population are victims of theft each year
        2.   theft as a result of the Crusades continues into the Middle Ages
        3.   thieves become more professional with urbanization
        4.   three groups of property criminals by the 18th century
            a.   skilled thieves, pickpockets, forgers, and counterfeiters
            b.   smugglers
            c.   poachers
    C.   Gender, race and culture in criminology
        1.   private police who received rewards for catching thieves
        2.   typically corrupt

3.   Jack Wild was London's most famous thief and thief-taker
4.   Henry Fielding cleaned up the system in 1748

II.   Modern Thieves
    A.   Occasional criminals
        1.   great majority of economic crimes are the work of amateur criminals
        2.   amateur criminals decision to steal is spontaneous
        3.   acts are unskilled, unplanned, and haphazard
        4.   occasional property crime occurs with opportunity or situational inducement
        5.   upper-class have the opportunity for more lucrative business-related crimes
        6.   lower class has opportunity to commit crime and short-run inducements
        7.   occasional criminals will deny any connection to a criminal life-style
        8.   they instead view their transgressions as being out of character
    B.   Professional criminals
        1.   professional criminals make a significant portion of their income from crime
        2.   professional criminals pursue their craft with vigor
        3.   they learn techniques from the older, experienced criminals
        4.   professionals engage in crimes that produce the greater losses to society
        5.   behavior include pocket-picking, burglary, shoplifting, forgery and counterfeiting
        6.   thieves who do not use force and live solely by their wits and skills
        7.   professional criminals as any criminal who:
            a.   identifies with a criminal subculture
            b.   makes the bulk of his or her living from crime
            c.   possesses a degree of skill in his or her chosen trade
    C.   Sutherland's professional criminal
        1.   Sutherland's classic, The Professional Thief
            a.   recording of the life of Chic Conwell
        2.   Conwell and Sutherland's concept has two critical dimensions
        3.   professional thieves engage in limited types of crime
        4.   a requirement to establish professionalism as a thief is the use of wits and skill
        5.   both argue that professional thieves share feelings, sentiments, and behaviors
        6.   professional thief recognized and received as such by other professional thieves
    D.   The criminological enterprise: Transforming theft-train robbers and safe crackers
        1.   professional thieves influenced by technology
        2.   train passengers were easy pickings
        3.   improvements in trains were designed to deter robbers
        4.   untorchable safes led to safe cracking
    E.   Professional criminals: the fence
        1.   Sutherland's view of the professional thief may be outdated
        2.   modern thieves often work alone and are not part of a criminal subculture
        3.   principles still have value in understanding the professional fence
        4.   Carl Klockers study of Vincent Swaggi
        5.   Steffensmeier's Sam Goodman says the fence must meet five conditions:
            a.   up-front cash
            b.   knowledge of dealing
            c.   connections with suppliers of stolen goods
            d.   connections with buyers
            e.   complicity with law enforcers
        6.   fence is much more willing to cooperate with authorities than most other criminals
    F.   The nonprofessional fence
        1.   significant portion of all fencing is performed by "amateur" or occasional criminals
        2.   novice burglars find it difficult to establish relationships with professional fences
        3.   types of occasional criminals include:
            a.   part-timers
            b.   associational fences

neighborhood hustlers
        d.   amateur receivers

III.   Theft Categories
        A.   Larceny/theft
                1.   larceny/theft was one of the earliest common-law crimes
                2.   acts in which one person took for his or her own use the property of another
                3.   goods must have been taken from the physical possession of the rightful owner
                4.   English judges were more concerned with disturbance of the peace
                5.   English judges created the concept of constructive possession
                        a.   persons voluntarily and temporarily gave up custody of their property
                        b.   still believed that the property was legally theirs
        B.   Larceny today
                1.   larceny is usually separated by state statute into petit larceny or grand larceny
                2.   each state sets its own boundary between grand larceny and petit larceny
                3.   larceny/theft is probably the most common criminal offense
        C.   Varieties of larceny
                1.   most small larcenies are not reported and written off
                2.   between 1992 and 1997 thieves stole $20.8 million worth of government equipment
        D.   Shoplifting
                1.   theft involving the taking of goods from retail stores
                2.   shoplifting has increased dramatically in last 20 years
        E.   The shoplifter
                1.   Cameron found that about 10 % of all shoplifters were professional boosters or heels
                2.   majority of shoplifters are amateur snitches
                3.   Cameron and others believe that shoplifters will reform if caught
        F.   Controlling shoplifting
                1.   employees and customers do not see or report shoplifting
                2.   states have passed merchant privilege laws
                3.   laws designed to protect retailers and their employers from litigation
        G.   Prevention strategies
                1.   target removal strategies
                2.   target hardening strategies
                3.   situational measures
        H.   Private justice
                1.   loss prevention units
                2.   state law that allows recovery of civil damages from shoplifters
                3.   target affluent for civil damages and ship poor to the justice system
        I.   Bad checks
                1.   knowingly and intentionally drawn on a nonexistent or under-funded bank account
                2.   majority of check forgers are naive
                3.   few professional or systematic forgers found
        J.   Credit card theft
                1.   amateurs acquire stolen cards through theft or mugging
                2.   use them for two or three days
                3.   Congress passed a law in 1971 limiting a person's liability to $50 per stolen card
                4.   Websites are used to trick people out of their credit card numbers
        K.   Auto theft
                1.   motor vehicle theft is another common larceny offense
                2.   auto thefts data reported
                3.   McCaghy and his associates uncovered five categories of auto theft:
                        a.   joyriding
                        b.   short-term transporation
                        c.   long-term transportation
                        d.   profit

        e.   commission of another crime
        4.   change theft patterns from joyriding to professional thefts

L. Which cars are taken most?
1. luxury cars and utility vehicles
2. Toyota land cruiser
3. cars with few design changes over last few years

M. Carjacking
1. legally is a robbery and accounts for about 2% of auto thefts
2. carjackings involve guns and cause injuries

N. Combating auto theft
1. use of situational crime prevention
2. Lojack system
3. target hardening
4. alarms don't work

O. False pretenses or fraud
1. crime of false pretenses or fraud
        a. involves a wrongdoer's misrepresenting a fact
        b. causes a victim to willingly give his or her property to the wrongdoer
2. false pretenses differs from traditional larceny
        a. victims willingly give their possessions to the offender
        b. crime does not involve a trespass in the taking

P. Confidence games
1. con games and marks
2. most common is the pigeon drop

Q. Modern confidence games
1. telemarketing strategies
2. recent arrest data for fraud

R. Embezzlement
1. occurs when someone who is so trusted with property fraudulently
        a. keeps it for his or her own use or the use of others
2. serious breach of trust before a person can be convicted of embezzlement
3. number of arrests made
4. increases over time

IV. Burglary
A. Basics
1. breaking and entering with intent to commit a felony
2. common law definition has evolved

B. The nature and extent of burglary
1. includes any unlawful entry of a structure to commit theft or felony
2. reported burglary data
3. declines noted
4. NCVS provides description of typical burglarized home

C. Residential burglary
1. craft of burglary learned
2. professionals learn to spot environmental clues

D. Commercial burglary
1. retail stores are a favorite target
2. other locations, like warehouses, require more planning

E. Careers in burglary
1. great variety exists within the ranks of burglars
2. Shover uncovered the existence of the good burglar
3. characteristic of the good burglar include:
        a. technical competence
        b. maintenance of personal integrity

        c.   specialization in burglary

        d.   financial success at crime

        e.   ability to avoid prison sentences

    4.   process of becoming a professional burglar linked to differential association

    5.   learning the techniques of the trade from older, more experienced burglars

F.   The burglary "career ladder"

    1.   burglars go through career stages

        a.   novice stage

        b.   journeyman stage

        c.   professional burglar

    2.   many burglars had serious drug habits

    3.   criminal activity was in part aimed at supporting their substance abuse

G.   Repeat burglary

    1.   some places may be repeatedly burglarized

    2.   some items are indispensable and will be replaced by homeowner

    3.   other factors involve knowledge and familiarity of the home

H.   Gender, race and culture in criminology: the female burglar

    1.   about 9% of arrested burglars are female

    2.   females similar to male burglars but shun auto theft

    3.   females always worked with a partner, started later and committed fewer burglaries

    4.   both genders had drug problems and drank before burglarizing

    5.   females were either accomplices or partners

V.   Arson

A.   Basics

    1.   arson is a young man's crime

    2.   46% of all arrests are for juveniles

B.   The criminological enterprise: What motivates juvenile fire starters

    1.   Wayne Wooden typology

        a.   "playing with matches" firesetter

        b.   "crying for help" firesetter

        c.   "delinquent" firesetter

        d.   "severely disturbed" firesetter

    2.   Garry found firestarting is either accidental, experimentation or intentional

C.   Other forms of arson

    1.   some other reasons for arson include:

        a.   arson for sexual arousal

        b.   arson as an act of revenge

        c.   arson for profit

        d.   arson fraud

KEY TERMS

arson: The intentional or negligent burning of a home, structure or vehicle for criminal purposes such as profit, revenge, fraud, or crime concealment.

arson for profit: People looking to collect insurance money, but who are afraid or unable to set the fire themselves, hire professional arsonists. These professionals have developed the skills to set fires yet make the cause seem accidental.

arson fraud: A business owner burns his or her property, or hires someone to do it, to escape financial problems.

boosters: Professional shoplifter who steals with the intention of reselling stolen merchandise.

burglary: Breaking into and entering a home or structure for the purposes of committing a felony.

carjacking: The theft of a car by force or threat of force.

closure: A term used by Lemert to describe people from a middle class background who have little identification with a criminal subculture but cash bad checks because of financial crisis that demands an immediate resolution.

confidence games: A swindle, usually involving a get-rich scheme, often with illegal overtones, so that the victim will be afraid or embarrassed to call the police.

constructive possession: In the crime of larceny, willingly giving up temporary physical possession of property but retaining legal ownership.

economic crimes: An act in violation of the criminal law that is designed to bring financial gain to the offender.

embezzlement: A type of larceny that involves taking the possessions of another that have been placed in the thief's lawful possession for safekeeping, such as a bank teller misappropriating deposits or a stock broker making off with a customer's account.

false pretenses: Illegally obtaining money, goods or merchandise from another by fraud or misrepresentation.

fence: A buyer and seller of stolen merchandise.

flash houses: Public meeting places in England, often taverns, that served as headquarters for gangs.

flashover: An effect in a fire when heat and gas at the ceiling of a room reach 2,000 degrees and clothes and furniture burst into flame, duplicating the effects of arsonists gasoline or explosives. It is possible that many suspected arson cases are the result of flashover.

fraud: Taking the possessions of another through deception or cheating, such as selling a person a desk that is represented as an antique but is known to be a copy.

good burglar: Professional burglars use this title to characterize colleagues who have distinguished themselves as burglars. Characteristics of a good burglar include: technical competence, maintenance of personal integrity, specialization in burglary, financial success, and the ability to avoid prison sentences.

grand larceny: Theft of money or property of substantial value, punished as a felony.

heels: Professional shoplifter who steals with the intention of reselling stolen merchandise to pawn shops or fences, usually at half of the original price.

larceny: Taking for one's own use the property of another, by means other than force or threats on the victim or forcibly breaking into a person's home or workplace; theft.

mark: The target of a con man.

naive check forgers: Amateurs who cash bad checks because of some financial crisis but have little identification with a criminal subculture.

occasional criminals: Offenders who do not define themselves by a criminal role or view themselves as committed career criminals.

petty larceny: Theft of a small amount of money or property, punishable as a misdemeanor.

pigeon drop: A con game in which a package or wallet containing money is 'found' by a con man or women. A passing victim is stopped and asked for advice about what to do, and soon another 'stranger' who is part of the con approaches and enters the discussion. The three decide to split the money; but first, one of the swindlers goes off to consult a lawyer. The lawyer claims the money can be split up but each party must prove that he or she can reimburse the original owner should one show up. The victim is then asked to give some good faith money for the lawyer to hold. When the victim goes to the lawyer's office to pick up a share of the loot, he or she finds the address is bogus and the money is gone.

poachers: Early English thieves who typically lived in the country and supplemented their diet and income with game that belonged to a landlord.

professional criminals: Offenders who make a significant portion of their income from crime.

professional fence: An individual who earns his or her living solely by buying and reselling stolen merchandise.

shoplifting: The taking of goods from retail stores.

situational inducement: Short term influence on a person's behavior, such as financial problems or peer pressure, that increases risk taking.

skilled thieves: Thieves who typically work in the larger cities, such as London and Paris. This group includes pickpockets, forgers, and counterfeiters, who operate freely.

smugglers: Thieves who move freely in sparsely populated areas and transport goods, such as spirits, gems, gold, and spices, without bothering to pay tax or duty.

snitch: Amateur shoplifter who does not self identify as a thief but who systematically steals merchandise for personal use.

street crimes: Illegal acts designed to prey on the public through theft, damage, and violence.

systematic forgers: Professionals who make a living by cashing bad checks.

target hardening: Making one's home or business crime proof through the use of locks, bars, alarms, and other devices.

target removal: Displaying dummy or disabled goods as a means of preventing shoplifting.

MULTIPLE CHOICE

1. What types of crimes are defined as violations of the criminal law designed to bring financial reward to an offender?
    A. Economic crimes   C. Institutional crimes
    B. Expressive crimes   D. Integrated crimes

2. What is the main reason why the general public feels ambivalent about economic criminals?
    A. Because so many members of society have themselves been involved in economic crimes
    B. Because most victims are insured and do not suffer economic losses
    C. Because the general public admires a clever well planned crime
    D. Because economic criminals are usually poor and need the money from their crimes to survive

3. Approximately what percent of the American public are victims of theft every year?
    A. 0-10%   C. 25-30%
    B. 10-15%   D. 55-60%

4. What were the public meeting places of the 18th century called?
    A. Roadhouses   C. Brothel-houses
    B. Flash houses   D. Stablehouses

5. A thief who lived in the country and supplemented his diet with game that belonged to his landlord was known as what?
    A. Poacher   C. Thief-taker
    B. Smuggler   D. Rustler

6. Which London criminal was also known as the "Thief-taker general of Great Britain and Ireland"?
    A. Vincent Swaggi   C. Edgar Poe
    B. Robert Agnew   D. Jack Wild

7. The private police who caught thieves in eighteenth century England were called what?
    A. Bobbies   C. Bounty hunters
    B. Thief takers   D. Dover boys

8. Who reformed the thief taker system with his "Bow Street Runners"?
    A. Jack Wild   C. Henry Fielding
    B. Tom Jones   D. Jeremy Hillary

9. What is a characteristic of the occasional criminal?
    A. They do not define themselves by a criminal role
    B. They receive informal, peer group support for their crimes
    C. They engage in repetitive convictional rationalization to overcome guilt
    D. They incorporate a secret criminal identity into their daily activities

10. A tax cheat is an example of what type of criminal?
    A. Rebellious   C. Property
    B. Occasional   D. Professional

11. Hepburn would argue that the lower classes are overrepresented in street crime statistics because of what?
    A. Because they are biologically predisposed to commit violent crimes
    B. Because society is structured to insure they are caught at such crimes
    C. Because those types of crimes are the ones they have an opportunity to commit
    D. Because these crimes are suited to the lower-class lifestyle

12. According to Hepburn, lower-class property offenders are motivated to commit crime by available opportunities which he refers to as what?
- A. Unguarded targets
- B. Situational inducements
- C. Routine activities
- D. Suitable targets

13. Which of the following is not a pattern of professional criminals?
- A. Youths are taught by older, experienced criminals
- B. Juvenile gang members don't age out with their peers
- C. Youths learn criminal techniques in prison
- D. Youths engage in crime as a profession until a better opportunity arises

14. What criminologist wrote The Professional Thief?
- A. Travis Hirschi
- B. Edwin Sutherland
- C. John Hepburn
- D. Scott Decker

15. According to Sutherland's concept of professional crime, which of the following could not possibly be included within the ranks of professional criminals?
- A. Safecracker
- B. Sneak thief
- C. Jewel thief
- D. Purse snatcher

16. Of all the behaviors in the professional thief's code of honor, the most important is what?
- A. Never show fear
- B. Never squeal on your partners
- C. Never steal from a fellow criminal
- D. Never use force to steal

17. What type of thief is a penny weighter?
- A. Jewel thief who makes fake gem substitutions for real ones
- B. A shoplifter who leaves his or her own clothes in place of the new ones they wear out of the store
- C. A pickpocket who is only interested in money not jewelry
- D. A social climber who dances with rich older women and removes their necklaces during the dance

18. What was Edwin Sutherland and Chic Conwell's term for a pickpocket?
- A. Pennyweighter
- B. Heel
- C. Cannon
- D. Snitch

19. Why did train robbery flourish in the late nineteenth century?
- A. Trains began carrying large amounts of cash and gold across the country
- B. Law enforcement was not centralized
- C. Train passengers were not allowed to carry weapons
- D. All of the above

20. Why did safe-crackers begin to learn how to crack combinations?
- A. Thieves became more educated
- B. New metals made safes harder to break into
- C. Early locks were based on simple number codes
- D. Using torches was too dangerous and loud

21. What was the alias of the fence that Carl Klockers studied?
- A. Chic Conwell
- B. Al Capone
- C. Jack Wild
- D. Vincent Swaggi

22. What type of crime involves buying and reselling stolen merchandise?
- A. Stooping
- B. Fencing
- C. Boosting
- D. Heeling

23. How did Vincent Swaggi maintain close working relations with influential members of the justice system?
    A. He contributed heavily to their political campaigns
    B. He blackmailed them when their children brought stolen goods into his shop
    C. He helped them purchase items at below-cost bargain prices
    D. He arranged for their residences to be burglarized if they made him mad

24. Klockar's professional fence, Vincent Swaggi, owed part of his success to what factor?
    A. He had a sophisticated knowledge of the law of stolen property
    B. He had a far reaching reputation regarding the number of rivals he had killed
    C. He limited his business dealing to only those he could trust
    D. He fenced only for the police

25. Klockar's work suggests that fences cooperate with law enforcement and also do what?
    A. Act as informers to catch thieves
    B. Cheat their thief-clients on a regular basis
    C. Take jobs as dock workers to scout potential goods
    D. Deal in narcotics but don't use them

TRUE/FALSE

1. The Thomas Crown Affair was first made in 1968 with Steve McQueen in the title role.
    A. True   B. False

2. The crime prevention approach of target removal involves displaying dummy or disabled goods as a means of preventing shoplifting.
    A. True   B. False

3. The crime prevention technique of target hardening involves making one's home or business crime proof through the use of locks, bars, alarms, and other devices.
    A. True   B. False

4. Grand larceny is the theft of a small amount of money or property, punishable as a misdemeanor.
    A. True   B. False

5. Petty larceny is the theft of money or property of substantial value, punished as a felony.
    A. True   B. False

6. Skilled thieves are thieves who typically work in the larger cities, such as London and Paris. This group includes pickpockets, forgers, and counterfeiters, who operate freely.
    A. True   B. False

7. Flash houses were public meeting places in England, often taverns, that served as places where people would buy and sell stolen merchandise.
    A. True   B. False

8. Poachers were thieves who move freely in sparsely populated areas and transport goods, such as spirits, gems, gold, and spices, without bothering to pay tax or duty.
    A. True   B. False

9. Smugglers were early English thieves who typically lived in the country and supplemented their diet and income with game that belonged to a landlord.
    A. True   B. False

10. According to Sutherland's typology of professional thieves, a cannon is a pickpocket.
     A. True   B. False

11. According to Sutherland's typology of professional thieves, a heel is a sneak thief from stores, banks, and offices.
     A. True   B. False

12. According to Sutherland's typology of professional thieves, a penny weighter is a jewel thief who substitutes fake gems for real ones.
     A. True   B. False

13. Sutherland's classic book The Professional Thief is based on the criminal life of Snake Plisken who later was portrayed in the movie Escape From New York.
     A. True   B. False

14. The author notes that the number of train robberies increased steadily from 1900 to 1920.
     A. True   B. False

15. One condition of being a fence is the ability to have upfront cash since all deals are cash.
     A. True   B. False

16. Robbery is breaking into and entering a home or structure for the purposes of committing a felony.
     A. True   B. False

17. According to the author, the Toyota Land Cruiser is 23 times more likely to be stolen than the average vehicle.
     A. True   B. False

18. Carjacking is legally defined as a motor vehicle rather than a robbery since it is a vehicle that is taken.
     A. True   B. False

19. According to the UCR about 2 million burglaries occurred in 2000 while the NCVS reports 3.4 million residential burglaries.
     A. True   B. False

20. According to the author, commercial establishments located within three blocks of heavily traveled thoroughfares have been found to be more vulnerable to burglary than those located farther away.
     A. True   B. False

FILL IN

1. A _____ is a buyer and seller of stolen merchandise.

2. _____ crimes are illegal acts designed to prey on the public through theft, damage, and violence.

3. _____ is breaking into and entering a home or structure for the purposes of committing a felony.

4. The intentional or negligent burning of a home, structure or vehicle for criminal purposes such as profit, revenge, fraud, or crime concealment is called _____.

5. An act in violation of the criminal law that is designed to bring financial gain to the offender are known as _____ crimes.

6. _____ thieves typically work in the larger cities, such as London and Paris; this group includes pickpockets, forgers, and counterfeiters, who operate freely.

7. Public meeting places in England, often taverns, that served as headquarters for gangs are known as _____ houses.

8. Thieves who move freely in sparsely populated areas and transport goods, such as spirits, gems, gold, and spices, without bothering to pay tax or duty are known as _____.

9. _____ were early English thieves who typically lived in the country and supplemented their diet and income with game that belonged to a landlord.

10. Illegally obtaining money, goods or merchandise from another by fraud or misrepresentation is known as _____.

11. A _____ inducement is a short term influence on a person's behavior, such as financial problems or peer pressure, that increases risk taking.

12. _____ is taking the possessions of another through deception or cheating, such as selling a person a desk that is represented as an antique but is known to be a copy.

13. A swindle, usually involving a get-rich scheme, often with illegal overtones, so that the victim will be afraid or embarrassed to call the police is known as a _____ game.

14. The target of a con man is called a _____.

15. Offenders who do not define themselves by a criminal role or view themselves as committed career criminals are known as _____ criminals.

ESSAY

1. Distinguish between the activities of a professional and an occasional criminal.

2. What are the four most common forms of auto theft and discuss the individual characteristics of people who engage in them?

3. Discuss the life-style of the professional fence. In what ways are the fences most like the ideal professional criminal type?

4. What are the major categories of theft?

5. Regarding the history of larceny-theft, how was the concept of constructive possession applied and why?

CHAPTER TWELVE
PROPERTY CRIMES
ANSWER KEY

MULTIPLE CHOICE ITEMS

1. A	6. D	11. C	16. B	21. D
2. A	7. B	12. B	17. A	22. B
3. B	8. C	13. D	18. C	23. C
4. B	9. A	14. B	19. B	24. A
5. A	10. B	15. D	20. B	25. A

TRUE FALSE ITEMS

1. A	6. A	11. A	16. B
2. A	7. B	12. A	17. A
3. A	8. B	13. B	18. B
4. B	9. B	14. B	19. A
5. B	10. A	15. A	20. B

MULTIPLE CHOICE ITEMS

1. fence	6. skilled	11. situational
2. street	7. flash	12. fraud
3. burglary	8. smugglers	13. confidence
4. arson	9. poachers	14. mark
5. economic	10. false pretenses	15. occasional

CHAPTER THIRTEEN
ENTERPRISE CRIME: WHITE-COLLAR CRIME, CYBERCRIME, AND ORGANIZED CRIME

LEARNING OBJECTIVES

1. Identify and define seven categories of white collar crime created by Moore.
2. Appreciate the distinctions between traditional street crime and white collar crime.
3. Identify and appreciate the physical and social costs of white collar crime.
4. Identify various causes and explanations for white collar offending.
5. Identify various ways in which the Internet is used to commit crime.
6. Identify and define various Internet fraud schemes.
7. Understand the role of the RICO statutes for the investigation and prosecution of organized crime.

CHAPTER SUMMARY

Enterprise crimes involve criminal acts which twist the legal rules of commercial enterprise for criminal purposes. They can be divided into three independent yet overlapping categories: white-collar crime, high tech crimes and organized crime. White-collar crime involves illegal activities of people and institutions whose acknowledged purpose is profit through legitimate business transactions. High tech crimes involve people using the instruments of modern technology for criminal purpose. Organized crime involves illegal activities of people and organizations whose acknowledged purpose is profit through illegitimate business enterprise.

There are various types of white-collar crime. Stings and swindles involve the use of deception to bilk people out of their money. Chiseling customers, businesses, or the government regularly is a second common type of white-collar crime. Surprisingly, many professionals engage in chiseling offenses. Other white-collar criminals use their positions in business and the marketplace to commit economic crimes. Their crimes include exploitation of position in a company or the government to secure illegal payments; embezzlement and employee pilferage and fraud; client fraud; and influence peddling and bribery. Further, corporate officers sometimes violate the law to improve the position and profitability of their businesses. Their crimes include price-fixing, false advertising, and environmental offenses.

The demand for illegal goods and services has produced a symbiotic relationship between the public and an organized criminal network. Organized crime supplies alcohol, gambling, drugs, prostitutes, and pornography to the public. It is immune from prosecution because of public apathy and because of its own strong political connections. Organized criminals used to be white ethnics—Jews, Italians, and Irish—but today African Americans, Hispanics, and other groups have become involved in organized crime activities. The old-line "families" are now more likely to use their criminal wealth and power to buy into legitimate businesses.

High tech criminals use emerging forms of technology to commit criminal acts. In some instances, they involve the use of technology to commit common law crimes such as fraud and theft. In other instances, the technology itself is the target, for example, illegal copying and sale of computer software. Law enforcement officials fear that high tech crimes will explode in the future.

CHAPTER OUTLINE

I.   Introduction
        A.   Case of Dr. Samuel Waksal, the founder of ImClone Systems
                1.   pleads guilty to charges of securities fraud, perjury and obstruction of justice
                2.   its application for approval of a cancer drug had been rejected by the FDA
                3.   friends and family sell off company stock prior to public announcement

               4.   enterprise crimes have become more common in a free market economy

B.   High tech crimes
          1.   offenders twist the legal rules of commercial enterprise for criminal purposes
          2.   organizational crimes taint and corrupt the free market system
          3.   more than 200,000 occupational deaths occur each year

II.   White-Collar Crime
    A.   Background
          1.   Sutherland first used the phrase
          2.   conspiracies by members of the wealthy classes
          3.   used their position in commerce for personal gain without regard to the law
    B.   Redefining white-collar crime
          1.   income tax evasion, credit card fraud, and bankruptcy fraud now included
          2.   set up business for the sole purpose of victimizing the general public
          3.   criminal conspiracies designed to improve profitability of corporations
    C.   The white-collar crime problem
          1.   employee theft from businesses alone amounts to $90 billion per year
          2.   destroys confidence and saps the integrity of commercial life

III.   Components of White-Collar Crime
    A.   Stings and swindles
          1.   Gold Club in Atlanta in cahoots with the Gambino organized-crime family
          2.   scheme to overcharge credit cards of unsuspecting customers
          3.   federal government took over the Gold Club
          4.   use their institutional or business position to bilk people out of their money
          5.   BCCI was one of the most notorious swindles in recent history
          6.   religious swindles involving Jonathan Strawder
          7.   fake religious organizations bilk thousands of people out of $100 million per year
    B.   Chiseling
          1.   involves charging for bogus auto repairs or short-weighting
          2.   flow of cash through betting windows to launder money for drug dealers
          3.   pharmacists have been known to alter prescriptions
          4.   chiseling takes place on the commodity and stock markets
          5.   churning, front running, and bucketing
          6.   pressured clients into buying the "house stocks" at artificially inflated prices
          7.   insider trading gives the trader an unfair advantage over the general public
    C.   Individual exploitation of institutional position
          1.   victim has a clear right to expect a service
          2.   offender withholds service unless a bribe is forthcoming
          3.   incident involving former governor of Louisiana, Edwin Edwards
          4.   steering repair work to particular contractors in exchange for kickbacks
          5.   case involving Bayship Management Inc. (BSM)
          6.   in West Germany corporate bribes are actually tax-deductible
    D.   Influence peddling and bribery
          1.   individuals holding positions sell power, influence, and information
          2.   influence peddling is distinguished from exploitation
          3.   officials at HUD defrauded the government of $4 billion to $8 billion
          4.   Robin HUD siphoned off $5 million from the sale of repossessed homes
          5.   Knapp Commission found that police corruption in New York City was pervasive
          6.   Foreign Corrupt Practices Act makes it a criminal offense to bribe foreign officials
    E.   Embezzlement and employee fraud
          1.   individuals use their positions to embezzle company funds for themselves
          2.   systematic theft of company property is called pilferage
          3.   the average restaurant worker now steals $204 in cash or merchandise per year
          4.   converting company assets for personal benefit

5.   fraudulently receiving increases in compensation
6.   fraudulently increasing personal holdings of company stock
7.   retaining one's present position within the company by manipulating accounts
8.   concealing unacceptable performance from stockholders
9.   Enron and Worldcom cases

F.   Client fraud
1.   theft by an economic client from an organization that advances credit to its clients
2.   172 people in New Jersey filed false medical claims totaling more than $5 million
3.   ping-ponging refers patients to other physicians in the same office
4.   bank fraud can encompass such diverse schemes as check kiting
5.   important aspect of client fraud is tax evasion
6.   failure to report income from partnerships could alone be as high as $64 billion per year

G.   Corporate crime
1.   interest in corporate crime first emerged in the early 1900s
2.   perpetrator is a legal fiction—a corporation—and not an individual
3.   illegal restraint of trade and price-fixing
4.   government prosecutes about 100 cases of deceptive pricing in defense work each year
5.   making claims about their products that cannot be justified by actual performance
6.   more than 20 million workers exposed to hazardous materials while on the job
7.   EPA prosecutes significant violations across all major environmental statutes

IV.   Causes of White-Collar Crime
A.   Greedy or needy?
1.   need and greed are motivators
2.   the need to keep or improve their jobs or satisfy their egos
3.   wrong doing is rationalized

B.   Corporate culture theory
1.   some business organizations promote white-collar criminality
2.   Enron scandal as a prime example

C.   Self-control view
1.   white-collar criminals have low self-control

V.   White-Collar Law Enforcement Systems
A.   Basics
1.   detection of white-collar crime is primarily on administrative departments

B.   Controlling white collar crime
1.   white-collar criminals are rarely prosecuted
2.   they receive relatively light sentences
3.   compliance systems seek self-policing among business community
4.   punishment of white-collar crimes should include a retributive component

C.   Is the tide turning?
1.   white-collar crime deterrence strategies have become normative
2.   recent cases created backlash that is resulting in more frequent use of prison sentences
3.   the Sherman Anti-trust act caps fines at $10 million

VI.   High Tech Crime
A.   Internet crimes
1.   Landslide Productions Inc. was a highly profitable Internet-based pornography ring
2.   company made as much as $1.4 million in one month
3.   subscription websites were located in Russia and Indonesia
4.   bogus get-rich-quick schemes, weight-loss scams, and investment swindles
5.   criminals make use of Internet chat rooms in their fraudulent schemes
6.   market manipulation
7.   fraudulent offerings of securities
8.   illegal touting

9. identity theft
B. Computer crimes
1. theft of services
2. use of data in a computer system for personal gain
3. unauthorized use of computers to obtain assets
4. theft of property by computer for personal use or conversion to profit
5. making the computer itself the subject of a crime
6. threat from computer crime is rapidly expanding
C. Controlling high tech crimes
1. Counterfeit Access Device and Computer Fraud and Abuse Law in 1984
2. National Information Infrastructure Protection Act (NIIPA)

VII. Organized Crime
A. Basics
1. great mystique has grown up about organized crime
2. Tony Soprano and his family life has become a national craze
B. Characteristics of organized crime
1. organized crime is a conspiratorial activity
2. organized crime has economic gain as its primary goal
3. organized crime activities are not limited to providing illicit services
4. organized crime employs predatory tactics
5. organized crime is not synonymous with the Mafia
C. Activities of organized crime
1. income are derived from providing illicit materials
2. using force to enter into and maximize profits in legitimate businesses
3. entered the high tech world of internet crime and stock market manipulation
D. The Concept of organized crime
1. alien conspiracy theory concept of organized crime
2. view the alien conspiracy theory as a figment of the media's imagination
3. total membership of about 1,700 made men
4. five families: Gambino, Columbo, Lucchese, Bonnano, and Genovese
5. Eastern European crime groups
6. evades as much as $5 billion a year in state and federal taxes related to gas
7. Chinese criminal gangs dominant in New York City's heroin market
E. Controlling organized crime
1. Racketeer Influenced and Corrupt Organization Act (RICO)
2. RICO is designed to limit patterns of organized criminal activity
3. enterprise theory of investigation (ETI) model as their standard investigative tool
F. The future of organized crime
1. number of the reigning family heads are quite old
2. Mafia has also been hurt by changing values in U.S. society

KEY TERMS

actual authority: The authority a corportation knowingly gives an employee.

alien conspiracy theory: The view that organized crime was imported to the United States by Europeans and that crime cartels have a policy of restricting their membership to people of their own ethnic background.

apparent authority: Authority that a third party, like a customer, reasonable believes that the agent has to perform the act in question.

bucketing: A form of stockbroker chiseling in which brokers skim customer trading profits by falsifying trading information.

churning: A white collar crime in which a stockbroker makes repeated trades to fraudulently increase his or her commissions.

corporate crime: White collar crime involving a legal violation by a corporate entity, such as price fixing, restraint of trade, or hazardous waste dumping.

division of markets: Firms divide a region into territories, and each firm agrees not to compete in the others' territories.

enterprise theory of investigation (ETI): A standard investigation tool of the FBI that focuses on criminal enterprise and investigation attacks on the structure of the criminal enterprise rather than on criminal acts viewed as isolated incidents.

front running: A form of stockbroker chiseling in which brokers place personal orders ahead of a large order from a customer to profit from the market effects of the trade.

group boycott: A company's refusal to do business with retail stores that do not comply with its rules or desires.

influence peddling: Using an institutional position to grant favors and sell information to which their coconspirators are not entitled.

insider trading: Illegal buying of stock in a company based on information provided by someone who has a fiduciary interest in the company. Federal laws and the rules of the Securities and Exchange Commission require that all profits from such trading be returned and provide for both fines and a prison sentence.

La Cosa Nostra: A national syndicate of 25 or so Italian-dominated crime families who control crime in distinct geographic areas.

Mafia: A criminal society that originated in Sicily, Italy, and is believed to control racketeering in the United States.

organizational crime: Crime that involves large corporations and their efforts to control the marketplace and earn huge profits through illegitimate business enterprise.

organized crime: Illegal activities of people and organizations whose acknowledged purpose is profit through illegitimate business enterprise.

pilferage: Theft by employees through stealth or deception.

price-fixing: A conspiracy to set and control the price of a necessary commodity.

Racketeer Influenced and Corrupt Organization Act (RICO): Federal legislation that enables prosecutors to bring additional criminal or civil charges against people whose multiple criminal acts constitute a criminal conspiracy.

Sherman Antitrust Act: Law that subjects to criminal or civil sanctions any person "who shall make any contract or engage in any combination or conspiracy" in restraint of interstate commerce.

tying arrangement: A corporation requires customers of one of its services to use other services it offers.

white-collar crime: Illegal acts that capitalize on a person's status in the market place.

TEST BANK

MULTIPLE CHOICE

1. According to the National Food Service Security Council, the average restaurant worker now steals $_____ in cash or merchandise per year.
    A. 204
    B. 36
    C. 1200
    D. 765

2. There are two principal forms of internet based _____: the pump and dump and the cyber-smear.
    A. stock manipulation
    B. fraudulent offerings of securities
    C. illegal touting
    D. insider trading

3. _____ is a white collar crime in which a stockbroker makes repeated trades to fraudulently increase his or her commissions.
    A. churning
    B. front running
    C. bucketing
    D. illegal touting

4. _____ is a form of stockbroker chiseling in which brokers skim customer trading profits by falsifying trading information.
    A. churning
    B. front running
    C. bucketing
    D. illegal touting

5. _____ is a form of stockbroker chiseling in which brokers place personal orders ahead of a large order from a customer to profit from the market effects of the trade.
    A. churning
    B. front running
    C. bucketing
    D. illegal touting

6. A conspiracy to set and control the price of a necessary commodity is called _____.
    A. churning
    B. front running
    C. bucketing
    D. price-fixing

7. Who defined white-collar crime as "a crime committed by a person of respectability and high social status in the course of his occupation?"
    A. Sutherland
    B. Cressey
    C. Hirschi
    D. Courtright

8. A _____ is a white collar crime in which people use their institutional or business position to bilk people out of their money; offenses in this category range from fraud involving the door-to-door sale of faulty merchandise to passing millions of dollars in counterfeit stock certificates to an established brokerage firm
    A. churning
    B. front running
    C. swindle
    D. illegal touting

9. It is estimated that fake religious organizations bilk thousands of people out of _____ per year.
    A. $100 million
    B. 35,000
    C. 125,000
    D. 950,000

10. Some New York City cab drivers routinely tapped the dashboards of their cabs with pens loaded with powerful magnets to "zap" their meters and jack up the fares; this illustrates _____.
    A. chiseling
    B. swindles
    C. individual exploitation of institutional position
    D. influence peddling

11. A striking example of _____ was when San Francisco 49ers co-owner Eddie DeBartolo Jr. pleaded guilty to concealing an extortion plot by the former governor of Louisiana, Edwin Edwards; according to the authorities, Edwards demanded payments of $400,000 or he would use his influence to prevent DeBartolo from obtaining a license for a riverboat gambling casino.
    A. chiseling   C. individual exploitation of institutional position
    B. swindles   D. influence peddling

12. A number of officials at HUD were later convicted of taking bribes and defrauding the government, including one woman who siphoned off $5 million from the sale of repossessed homes; she was nicknamed _____.
    A. Robin HUD   C. Pete the Plunderer
    B. Slick Willy   D. the Widowmaker

13. Which bank was found to be involved in international loan swindles and laundered money for drug cartels, Saddam Hussein, and Ferdinand Marcos?
    A. Chase Manhattan   C. Citizens Bank
    B. BCCI   D. First Bank of Fargo

14. What does the term ping-ponging refer to?
    A. the practice of referring patients to other physicians in the same office
    B. the practice of using pop up windows to move people to selected websites
    C. the police interrogation practice of switching in fresh interrogators to keep suspects off guard
    D. the practice of long distance carriers to move people to different customer service representatives

15. One type of computer crime is the _____; one computer is used to reprogram another for illicit purposes such as one incident, two high school–age computer users reprogrammed the computer at DePaul University, preventing that institution from using its own processing facilities.
    A. Trojan horse   C. super-zapping
    B. salami slice   D. logic bomb

16. One type of computer crime is the _____; an employee sets up a dummy account in the company's computerized records; a small amount—even a few pennies—is subtracted from customers' accounts and added to the account of the thief.
    A. Trojan horse   C. super-zapping
    B. salami slice   D. logic bomb

17. One type of computer crime is _____; most computer programs used in business have built-in antitheft safeguards, and employees can use a repair or maintenance program to supersede the antitheft program.
    A. Trojan horse   C. super-zapping
    B. salami slice   D. logic bomb

18. One type of computer crime is the _____: A program is secretly attached to the company's computer system; the new program monitors the company's work and waits for a sign of error to appear, causing the program to kick into action and exploit the weakness.
    A. Trojan horse   C. super-zapping
    B. salami slice   D. logic bomb

19. The author notes that before October 30, 1998, when the _____ became law, there was no federal statute that made identity theft a crime.
    A. Identity Theft and Assumption Act of 1998   C. Internet Fraud Avoidance Act
    B. Omnibus Privacy Protection Act   D. Federal Code 224

20. New York City, the most important organized crime area, contains five families: the Gambino, Columbo (formerly Profaci), Lucchese, _____, and Genovese families, named after their founding "godfathers".
    A. Smith   C. Bonnano
    B. Siegel   D. Capone

21. Some white-collar criminals become involved in criminal conspiracies designed to improve the market share or profitability of their corporations; this type of white-collar crime, which includes antitrust violations, price-fixing, and false advertising, is known as _____.
- A. corporate crime
- B. organized crime
- C. the Mafia
- D. occupational crime

22. The author notes that the loss due to employee theft from businesses alone amounts to _____ per year.
- A. 1.2 million
- B. 90 billion
- C. 1.2 billion
- D. 600 trillion

23. The _____ manager, Steven Kaplan, was in cahoots with the Gambino organized-crime family of New York in a scheme to overcharge and/or double-billed credit cards of unsuspecting customers; Kaplan plead guilty and received a three- to five-year prison sentence, a $5 million fine and the federal government took over the club.
- A. Gold Club
- B. Golden Banana
- C. Slippery Naval
- D. Lust Haven

24. According to the typology created by Moore, which category of white collar crime involves stealing through deception by individuals who have no continuing institutional or business position and whose entire purpose is to obtain money illegally?
- A. swindle
- B. chiseling
- C. exploitation
- D. bribery

25. A recent survey by the Computer Security Institute found that _____ percent of the employers they contacted had detected employee abuse of Internet access privileges.
- A. 12
- B. 24
- C. 78
- D. 94

TRUE/FALSE

1. One type of computer crime is the Trojan horse; One computer is used to reprogram another for illicit purposes such as one incident, two high school–age computer users reprogrammed the computer at DePaul University, preventing that institution from using its own processing facilities.
- A. True
- B. False

2. One type of computer crime is the salami slice: An employee sets up a dummy account in the company's computerized records; a small amount—even a few pennies—is subtracted from customers' accounts and added to the account of the thief.
- A. True
- B. False

3. One type of computer crime is super-zapping: Most computer programs used in business have built-in antitheft safeguards; employees can use a repair or maintenance program to supersede the antitheft program.
- A. True
- B. False

4. One type of computer crime is the logic bomb: A program is secretly attached to the company's computer system; the new program monitors the company's work and waits for a sign of error to appear, causing the program to kick into action and exploit the weakness.
- A. True
- B. False

5. One type of computer crime is data leakage: A person illegally obtains data from a computer system by leaking it out in small amounts.
- A. True
- B. False

6. One type of computer crime is impersonation: An unauthorized person uses the identity of an authorized computer user to access the computer system.

    A. True   B. False

7. Dr. Samuel Waksal's, who was the founder of ImClone Systems, brother Harlan, sold $50 million worth of shares of the company stock prior to the public announcement that the company application for FDA approval for a drug was denied.

    A. True   B. False

8. F. Hoffmann-La Roche, the vitamin cartel, paid $500 million in 1999 for violations of the Sherman Antitrust Act.

    A. True   B. False

9. A recent survey by the Computer Security Institute found that seventy-eight percent of the employers they contacted had detected employee abuse of Internet access privileges.

    A. True   B. False

10. A January 2001 study by Meridien Research reports that payment-card fraud on the Internet will decrease worldwide from $16 billion in 2000 to $1.5 billion by 2005.

    A. True   B. False

11. Stock market manipulation occurs when an individual tries to control the price of stock by interfering with the natural forces of supply and demand.

    A. True   B. False

12. The Business Software Alliance (BSA) a professional watchdog group estimated 11 billion or more dollars is lost each year to the unauthorized use of software.

    A. True   B. False

13. Sutherland defined white-collar crime as "a crime committed by a person of respectability and high social status in the course of his occupation."

    A. True   B. False

14. A swindle is a white collar crime in which people use their institutional or business position to bilk people out of their money; offenses in this category range from fraud involving the door-to-door sale of faulty merchandise to passing millions of dollars in counterfeit stock certificates to an established brokerage firm

    A. True   B. False

15. A striking example of chiseling was when San Francisco 49ers co-owner Eddie DeBartolo Jr. pleaded guilty to concealing an extortion plot by the former governor of Louisiana, Edwin Edwards; according to the authorities, Edwards demanded payments of $400,000 or he would use his influence to prevent DeBartolo from obtaining a license for a riverboat gambling casino.

    A. True   B. False

16. Churning is the illegal buying of stock in a company based on information provided by someone who has a fiduciary interest in the company.

    A. True   B. False

17. Ponzi/Pyramid Schemes are investment schemes in which investors are promised abnormally high profits on their investments; early investors are paid returns with the investment money received from the later investors, eventually the system collapses.

    A. True   B. False

18. According to a survey by the Computer Security Institute CSI with the participation of the Federal Bureau of Investigation's Computer Intrusion Squad, 90 percent of respondents (primarily large corporations and government agencies) detected computer security breaches within the last twelve months.
    A. True   B. False

19. The Business Software Alliance (BSA) a professional watchdog group estimated 11 billion or more dollars is lost each year to the unauthorized use of software; software piracy was highest in Asia ($4.7 billion) and amounted to about $2 billion in North America.

    A. True   B. False

20. The author notes that before October 30, 1998, when the Identity Theft and Assumption Act of 1998 became law, there was no federal statute that made identity theft a crime.
    A. True   B. False

FILL IN

1. _____ crime is defined as illegal acts that capitalize on a person's status in the market place.

2. _____ crime refers to illegal activities of people and organizations whose acknowledged purpose is profit through illegitimate business enterprise.

3. _____ is defined as a white collar crime in which a stockbroker makes repeated trades to fraudulently increase his or her commissions.

4. _____ crime is defined as white collar crime involving a legal violation by a corporate entity, such as price fixing, restraint of trade, or hazardous waste dumping.

5. _____ is a form of stockbroker chiseling in which brokers place personal orders ahead of a large order from a customer to profit from the market effects of the trade.

6. _____ is a form of stockbroker chiseling in which brokers skim customer trading profits by falsifying trading information.

7. A _____ occurs when a corporation requires customers of one of its services to use other services it offers.

8. When firms divide a region into territories, and each firm agrees not to compete in the others' territories, it is called _____.

9. The _____ Act is a law that subjects to criminal or civil sanctions any person "who shall make any contract or engage in any combination or conspiracy" in restraint of interstate commerce.

10. _____ authority is authority that a third party, like a customer, reasonable believes that the agent has to perform the act in question.

11. _____ authority is the authority a corporation knowingly gives an employee.

12. _____ crime is defined as crime that involves large corporations and their efforts to control the marketplace and earn huge profits through illegitimate business enterprise.

13. Using an institutional position to grant favors and sell information to which their coconspirators are not entitled is known as _____.

14. _____ is theft by employees through stealth or deception.

173

15. _____ is the illegal buying of stock in a company based on information provided by someone who has a fiduciary interest in the company.

ESSAY

1. Identify and define the seven typologies of white collar crime.

2. Differentiate corporate crime from the concept of white collar crime.

3. Differentiate between individual exploitation of institutional position and influence peddling. Provide examples of each.

4. Identify and discuss the social and economic costs of white collar crime for society.

5. Identify and discuss recent trends influencing organized crime.

CHAPTER THIRTEEN
ENTERPRISE CRIME: WHITE-COLLAR CRIME, CYBERCRIME, AND ORGANIZED CRIME
ANSWER KEY

MULTIPLE CHOICE ITEMS

1. A	6. D	11. C	16. B	21. A
2. A	7. A	12. A	17. C	22. B
3. A	8. C	13. A	18. D	23. A
4. C	9. A	14. A	19. A	24. A
5. B	10. A	15. A	20. C	25. C

TRUE FALSE ITEMS

1. A	6. A	11. A	16. B
2. A	7. A	12. A	17. A
3. A	8. A	13. A	18. A
4. A	9. A	14. A	19. A
5. A	10. B	15. B	20. A

FILL IN ITEMS

1. white-collar	6. bucketing	11. actual
2. organized	7. tying arrangement	12. organizational
3. churning	8. division of markets	13. influence peddling
4. corporate	9. Sherman Antitrust	14. pilferage
5. front running	10. apparent	15. insider trading

CHAPTER FOURTEEN
PUBLIC ORDER CRIMES

LEARNING OBJECTIVES

1. Identify and discuss the controversy surrounding the criminalization of moral offenses.
2. Understand the various perspectives of legalization and criminalization of prostitution, pornography and substance abuse
3. Identify some issues regarding the enforcement of illegal sexual behavior, particularly in regard to some negative attitudes toward homosexuality.
4. Understand efforts to control the drug problem, and the difficulties involved in doing so.
5. Define paraphilia and identify the major types.
6. Describe the process of becoming a prostitute.
7. Discuss the problems of controlling pornography.
8. Describe the cycle of addiction and provide a typology of drug addicts.
9. Define and give examples of public order crimes and discuss some of the complexities inherent in legislating morality.
10. Understand the case for drug legalization.

CHAPTER SUMMARY

Public order crimes are acts considered illegal because they conflict with social policy, accepted moral rules, and public opinion. There is usually great debate over public order crimes. Some charge that they are not really crimes at all and that it is foolish to legislate morality. Others view such morally tinged acts as prostitution, gambling, and drug abuse as harmful and therefore subject to public control. Many public order crimes are sex-related. Although homosexuality is not a crime per se, homosexual acts are subject to legal control. Some states still follow the archaic custom of legislating long prison terms for consensual homosexual sex.

Prostitution is another sex-related public order crime. Studies indicate that most prostitutes come from poor, troubled families and have abusive parents. There is little evidence that prostitutes are emotionally disturbed, addicted to drugs, or sexually abnormal. Although prostitution is illegal, some cities have set up adult entertainment areas where commercial sex is tolerated by law enforcement agents. Pornography involves the sale of sexually explicit material intended to sexually excite paying customers. The depiction of sex and nudity is not illegal, but it does violate the law when it is judged obscene. Obscenity is a legal term that tody is defined as material offensive to community standards. There is no conclusive evidence that pornography is related to crime or aggression, but data suggest that sexual violence by those who view it.

Substance abuse is another type of public order crime. Debate continues over the legalization of drugs, usually centering on such nonaddicting drugs as marijuana. Numerous studies have found that drug addicts commit enormous amounts of property crime. Alcohol is another commonly abused substance. Although it is legal to possess, it has been linked to crime.

CHAPTER OUTLINE

I.   Introduction
        A.   Public order crimes or victimless crimes
                1.   mala prohibition crimes
                2.   prohibit the manufacture and distribution of morally quesstionable goods and services
                3.   outlaw sin and vice
        B.   Law and morality
                1.   the question of willing victims

2. society as a victim
C. Debating morality
1. criminal definitions based on morality--but whose morality?
2. culture conflict
3. the legislation of morality motivated by power
D. Criminal or immoral?
1. violations of conventional morality may serve a useful function
2. good motives do not make a criminal act noncriminal
E. Social harm
1. immoral acts can be distinguished from crimes
2. criteria is the social harm they cause
3. harmful acts may be difficult to enforce
F. Moral crusaders
1. vigilance committees attempted to keep the immoral out of San Francisco
2. vigilante goes on moral crusades without legal authorization
3. moral entrepreneurs become rule creators
4. define deviant as "evil"

II. Homosexuality
A. Murder of Matthew Shepard
B. Homosexuality-the basics
1. erotic interest in members of one's one sex
2. homosexuality is more than having sex with same-sex partners
3. exists in most societies, 3-16% of males and 2-6% of females
C. Attitudes toward homosexuality
1. term sodomy comes from ancient city of Sodom
2. Bible forbids homosexuality
3. Hitler killed nearly a half million homosexuals
4. homophobia is a negative overreaction to homosexuals
5. usually based on religious beliefs, ignorance, insecurity or fear of disease
6. constant reminders of anti-gay sentiments
D. Homosexuality and the law
1. Robinson v. California prohibits criminalization of status
2. same-sex marriages are forbidden and sodomy laws exist in half the states
3. Bowers v. Hardwick upheld Georgia law forbidding consensual sodomy
4. gay rights ordinances aare extremely varied and controversial
5. don't ask, don't tell military policy
E. Is the tide turning?
1. survey shows that a majority of Americans support equal rights for homosexuals
2. anti-discrimination laws and Georgia's sodomy law was struck down in 1998

III. Paraphilias
A. Background
1. The case of Marc Dutoix
B. Paraphilia
1. abnormal sexual practices focused on nonhuman objects, humiliation
2. includes giving or receiving of pain, or non-consensual
3. specific types are:
a. autoerotic asphyxia
b. frotteurism
c. voyeurism
d. exhibitionism
e. sadomasochism
f. pedophilia
4. most states ban indecent exposure or voyeurism

IV.   Prostitution
    A.   Background
          1.   derived from the Latin term prostutuere
          2.   historical background in Greece
          3.   reformation ended the religious tolerance
          4.   includes elements of sexual significance for the customer
          5.   an economic transaction and emotional indifference
    B.   Incidence of prostitution
          1.   difficult to estimate the actual number of prostitutes on the street today
          2.   number of male customers has declined
          3.   sexual options, disease might explain decline
          4.   UCR indicates about 100,000 arrests for prostitution occur each year
    C.   Types of prostitution
          1.   streetwalkers
          2.   bar girls
          3.   brothel prostitutes
          4.   call girls
          5.   escort services/call houses
          6.   circuit travelers
          7.   rap booth prostitutes
          8.   skeezers; bartering sex for drugs
          9.   other varieties include massage parlors, photo studios, hotel prostitutes
    D.   Becoming a prostitute
          1.   Contributing factors include:
               a.   growing up in a slum neighborhood
               b.   broken homes
               c.   sex abuse
               d.   drugs
               e.   money
               f.   survival
          2.   little evidence that prostitution results from psychological problems
    E.   Legalize prostitution?
          1.   prostitution is illegal in all states except Nevada
          2.   misdemeanor offense
          3.   Mann Act prohibits transporting women across state lines for prostitution
          4.   sexually equality view
          5.   free choice view

V.   Pornography
    A.   Background
          1.   derived from the Greek
          2.   15% of all video rentals
          3.   First Amendment concerns and the definition of obscenity
          4.   Justice Potter Stewart "I know it when I see it"
    B.   Dangers of pornography
          1.   degradation of men, women, and children
          2.   exploitation may include underage children
    C.   Child pornography rings
          1.   adults who use position of trust to recruit and exploit children
          2.   contains between three and eleven predominantly male children
          3.   solo, transition, and syndicated rings
    D.   Does pornography cause violence?
          1.   Attorney General's Commission on Pornography
          2.   erotic material may act as a safety valve
    E.   Violent pornography, violent crime

            1.   little correlation between porno and violent crime
            2.   stronger evidence exist linking the viewing of violent erotic material
            3.   seen to cause more aggressive attitudes toward females

F.   Pornography and the law
            1.   all states and the federal government prohibit sale and production
            2.   child pornography is a separate category

G.   Punishing obscenity
            1.   Mapplethorpe and the 2 Live Crew examples of obscenity
            2.   Roth v. U.S. and Alberts v. California cases
            3.   Miller doctrine refers to state or local definitions of obscenity
            4.   community standards doctrine was modified with the reasonableness doctrine

H.   Controlling sex for profit
            1. $10 billion a year industry
            2.   get tough approaches may make sex-related goods and services more desirable
            3.   alternate approach is to control pornography by zoning
            4.   threat of governmental regulation may convince the industry to police itself

I.   Technological change
            1.   influence of videotapes, CD-ROMs, cable and the internet
            2.   Communications Decency Act ruled as unconstitutional

VI.   Substance Abuse

A.   Modern emphasis
            1.   arrests and incarceration rates are increasing
            2.   some still view drug use as a victimless public order offense

B.   When did drug use begin?
            1.   traced as far back as Mesopotamian writings
            2.   cocaine and opium widely used at the turn of the century
            3.   drug prohibition in the United States is a history of moral crusades

C.   Alcohol and is prohibition
            1.   temperance movement
            2.   belief that the purity of U.S. culture was being destroyed by city growth
            3.   drinking considered to be a cause of immigrant, degenerate life styles

D.   Commonly abused drugs
            1.   anesthetics are used as nervous system depressants
            2.   volatile liquids
            3.   barbiturates depress central nervous system and produce a sleep-like condition
            4.   tranquilizers reduce levels of anxiety
            5.   amphetamines are synthetic drugs that stimulate action in the CNS
            6.   cannabis (marijuana and hashish)
            7.   hallucinogens are natural or synthetic drugs which produce vivid distortions
            8.   cocaine is an alkaloid derivative of the coca leaf
            9.   derivatives of cocaine include freebase and crack
            10.   narcotics produce a tolerance to pain and free the mind of emotion or anxiety
            11.   steroids are used to gain muscle strength for body building
            12.   designer drugs are chemical substances
            13.   alcohol abuse is a major substance abuse problem

E.   The criminological enterprise: Careers in crack
            1.   federally funded project to systematically analyze crack use
            2.   substance abusers but abuse crack at elevated daily consumption rates
            3.   crack was not associated with non-drug crimes
            4.   crack epidemic went through distinct phases

F.   The extent of substance abuse
            1.   national surveys show drug use has declined in recent years
            2.   National Drug Control Policy
                    a.   crack use is declining because it is a burnout drug

b.   heroin use increasing
3.   ISR survey results
     a.   decline from high points in 1970's and early 80's
     b.   increased reports among younger children
4.   household survey
     a.   general population drug use is increasing
     b.   marijuana use is up and cocaine use is down
G.   How can the trends in drug use be explained?
1.   changing perceptions about the harmfulness of drugs
2.   peer disapproval is down and it is easier to obtain drugs now
3.   easier to obtain drugs
H.   Are the surveys accurate?
1.   self-report problem areas noted
2.   specific subpopulations are not sampled
3.   use of statistical-estimating methods are problematic
I.   AIDS and drug use
1.   AIDS-drug use relationship is due to sharing of needles and multiple sex partners
2.   estimated that one-third of IV drug users are AIDS carriers
3.   fear of contracting AIDS may be a factor in the decline of drug using population

VII.   The Cause of Substance Abuse
A.   Subcultural view
1.   environmental basis
2.   peer pressure and lower socioeconomic status
B.   Psychodynamic view
1.   middle-class substance abuse
2.   personality and emotional problems
3.   addiction-prone personality
C.   Genetic factors
1.   biological predisposition towards addiction
2.   children of addicts likely to have substance abuse problems
D.   Social learning
1.   observation of parental drug use
2.   children learn drugs provide pleasurable sensations
E.   Drug gateways
1.   progression of drug involvement
2.   path begins with early experimentation
F.   Problem behavior syndrome
1.   substance abuse is one of many problems
2.   deviant life-styles
G.   Rational choice
1.   use drugs because they feel good
2.   may be seen
H.   Is there a single cause of drug abuse?
1.   drug users suffer from a variety of family and socialization difficulties
2.   no single path or cause
I.   Types of drug users
1.   adolescents who distribute small amounts of drugs
2.   adolescents who frequently sell drugs
3.   teenage drug dealers who commit other delinquent acts
4.   adolescents who cycle in and out of the justice system
5.   drug-involved youth who continue to commit crimes as adults
6.   outwardly respectable adults who are top-level dealers
7.   smugglers
8.   adult predatory drug users who are frequently arrested

9.   adult predatory drug users who are rarely arrested
10.   less predatory drug-involved adult offenders
11.   women who are drug-involved offenders
- J.   Drugs and crime
  1.   drug users do commit an enormous amount of crime
  2.   4 in 10 violent crimes involve alcohol
  3.   abusers have criminal histories before onset of drug abuse
- K.   User surveys
  1.   drug users report extensive involvement in crime
  2.   property crimes linked to heroin addiction
- L.   Surveys of known criminals
  1.   inmates report regular use of drugs
  2.   ADAM program
- M.   The drug-crime connection
  1.   intoxicated subjects may be easier to arrest
  2.   drug abusers may have weak social bonds
  3.   some may commit crimes to support drug habits
- N.   Close up: How substance abuse provokes violence
  1.   Fagan's multi-stage research
  2.   alcohol can shape dynamics, decisions and strategies
  3.   effects of drugs less clear
- O.   Drugs and the law
  1.   drug laws in America begins with the 1906 Pure Food and Drug Act
  2.   culminates in the 1988 Anti-Drug Abuse Act
- P.   Controlling alcohol
  1.   highway fatalities and drunk driving
  2.   get tough laws reduce traffic fatalities but overcrowd courts and jails
  3.   harsh punishments have little effect on alcoholics

VIII.   Drug Control Strategies
- A.   Source control
  1.   deter sale and importation
  2.   target overseas sources
  3.   massive amounts of drugs produced
  4.   drug trade important source of foreign revenue
  5.   eradication may encourage crop develoment
- B.   Interdiction strategies
  1.   direct efforts at large-scale drug rings
  2.   nontraditional groups replace traditional organized crime families
- C.   Punishment strategies
  1.   crack crackdown
  2.   result in court backlogs
- D.   Community strategies
  1.   drug prevention awareness programs
  2.   four categories include
     a.   law-enforcement type efforts
     b.   civil justice system harassment
     c.   community-based treatment efforts
     d.   community efforts to enhance the quality of life
- E.   Policy and practices in criminology: Drug Abuse Resistance Education (DARE)
  1.   Aimed at convincing youth not to get involved with drugs
  2.   DARE programs
     a.   providing accurate info on substance abuse
     b.   teaching peer pressure resistance
     c.   teaching respect for law

d.providing alternatives to drug use
e.building self esteem
F.Drug testing programs
1.drug-testing programs in private industry and public employment are common
2.defendants are tested at all stages in the criminal justice process
3.little evidence to support the effectiveness of treatment programs
G.Treatment strategies
1.focus on building self-esteem
2.residential programs
3.long term effects of treatment still uncertain
H.Employment programs
1.employment correlated with decreased drug use
2.vocational rehabilitation programs listed
I.Legalization
1.control strategies have not worked because the drug trade is very profitable
2.proponents argue that drug use should be legalized or decriminalized
3.Naddelman and reasons to legalize
4.legalization would destroy black markets
J.Consequences of legalization
1.possible increased consumption of drugs
2.adolescent drug use increases because of forbidden fruit phenomenon

KEY TERMS

brothels: A house of prostitution, usually run by a madam who sets prices and handles business arrangements.

call girls: Prostitutes who make dates via the phone and then service customers in hotel rooms or apartments.

gateway model: A explanation of drug abuse that posits that users begin with a more benign drug and progress to ever more potent drugs.

gay bashing: Violent hate crimes directed towards people because of their sexual orientation.

homophobia: Extreme negative overreaction to homosexuals.

homosexuality: Erotic interests in members of one's own sex.

madam: A women who employs prostitutes, supervises their behavior, and receives a fee for her behavior.

moral crusaders: Efforts by interest group members to stamp out they find objectionable.

moral entrepreneurs: Interest groups that attempt to control social life and the legal order in such a way as to promote their own set of moral values.

obscenity: According to current legal theory, sexual explicit material that lacks a serious purpose and appeals solely to the prurient interests of the viewer.

paraphilias: Bizarre or abnormal sexual practices that involve recurrent sexual urges focused on objects, humiliation, or children.

pornography: Sexual explicit books, magazines, films, or tapes intended to provide sexual titillation and excitement for paying customers.

prostitution: The granting of nonmarital sexual access for renumeration.

182

public order crimes: Acts that are considered illegal because they threaten the general well-being of society and challenge its accepted moral principles.

skeezers: Prostitutes who trade sex for drugs.

social harm: A view that behaviors harmful to other people and society in general must be controlled.

sodomy: Illegal sexual intercourse.

temperance movement: An effort to prohibit the sale of liquor in the United States that resulted in the passage of the Eighteenth Amendment to the US Constitution in 1919.

victimless crimes: Crimes that violate the moral order but in which there is no actual victim or target.

vigilantes: Individuals who go on moral crusades without any authorization from legal authorities.

TEST BANK

MULTIPLE CHOICE

1. What is true of a public order crime?
    A. They are only violations or crimes at the local level of government
    B. It is an act that will be considered a crime in all fifty states
    C. They are crimes which have no victims but often are sexual in nature
    D. They are considered to be mala prohibitum crimes

2. Which wealthy young Californian was charged with running the most exclusive call girl ring in Hollywood?
    A. Heidi Fleiss   C. Heda Nesbaum
    B. Sandra O'Connor   D. Charlie Sheen

3. Who said "What may be trash to me may be prized by others"?
    A. Sir Patrick Devlin   C. Alice Walker
    B. Justice William O. Douglas   D. Bill Clinton

4. What is Howard Becker's label for people who go on moral crusades in order to control the definition of morality?
    A. Vigilantes   C. Moral entrepreneurs
    B. Morality engineers   D. Debauchees

5. It is estimated that between 3% and 16% of the male American population is what?
    A. Homosexual   C. Frequent abusers of violent pornography
    B. Homophobic   D. Problem gamblers

6. An extremely negative overreaction to homosexuals is referred to as what?
    A. Identity insecurity   C. Homophobia
    B. Asphyxiophilia   D. Frotteurism

7. Which Supreme Court decision upheld a Georgia statute making it a crime to engage in consensual sodomy?
    A. Illinois v. Gates   C. Robinson v. California
    B. Bowers v. Hardwick   D. Miranda v. Arizona

8. Is it a crime to be a homosexual?
    A. It depends on the state jurisdiction
    B. No, although homosexual acts are illegal in most states
    C. No, a person may legally be a homosexual and practice homosexual acts
    D. Yes, according to the Supreme Court decision Robinson v. California

9. About how many states have decriminalized private, consensual sodomy between adult homosexuals?
    A. 25   C. 39
    B. 35   D. 50

10. As of 1998, how many states have passed anti-discrimination laws protecting gays?
    A. 5   C. 27
    B. 11   D. 42

11. Bizarre or abnormal sexual practices involving recurrent sexual urges focused on nonhuman objects, humiliation, or children is known as what?
    A. Pedophilia   C. Voyeurism
    B. Frotteurism   D. Paraphilia

184

12. Examples of paraphilia would include what?
    A. Homosexuality and deep interest in pornography
    B. Rape and incest
    C. Dyspareunia and sex aversion disorder
    D. Pedophilia and exhibitionism

13. What are you engaging in if you rub against or touch men in crowded elevators?
    A. Pedophilia   C. Frotteurism
    B. Voyeurism   D. Exhibitionism

14. Attaining sexual pleasure through sexual activity with prepubescent children is known as what?
    A Pedophilia   C. Frotteurism
    B Voyeurism   D. Exhibitionism

15. What is a subset of masochistic behavior called where a noose, plastic bag or mask is used to attempt partial oxygen deprivation to the brain for the purpose of enhancing sexual gratification?
    A. Asphyxiophilia   C. Paraphilias
    B. Sadomasochism   D. Simulated strangulation

16. The earliest records of prostitution appear in the writings of what ancient country?
    A. Greece   C. Egypt
    B. Rome   D. Mesopotamia

17. Modern commercial sex appears to have its roots in what ancient country?
    A. Greece   C. Egypt
    B. Rome   D. Mesopotamia

18. In the early 19th century England, prostitution was linked to what?
    A. The rise of English brewery companies
    B. The male-dominated society
    C. The backlash to religious reformation
    D. The availability of drugs such as heroin and opium solutions

19. Which of the following is not an element in the amplified definition for prostitution in the text?
    A. An activity that has sexual significance for the customer
    B. A behavior that has been criminalized in the jurisdiction where it occurs
    C. An economic transaction
    D. A state of emotional indifference exists between the parties

20. Who initiated twenty percent of college-educated men into sex fifty years ago?
    A. Girlfriends   C. Teachers
    B. Relatives   D. Prostitutes

21. Approximately how many females arrested for prostitution tested positively for drug abuse?
    A. 15%   C. 65%
    B. 35%   D. 85%

22. What type of prostitute barters sex for drugs?
    A. Streetwalker   C. Skeezer
    B. Madam   D. Call girl

23. Which type of prostitute has the highest rate of drug abuse and larceny arrests?
    A. Bar girls   C. Brothel prostitutes
    B. Streetwalkers   D. Escorts

24. The high paid "aristocrats" of prostitution are known as what?
    A. Call girls   C. Streetwalkers
    B. Brothel prostitutes   D. Bar girls

25. What state has legalized prostitution?
    A. New York   C. Nevada
    B. Utah   D. Arkansas

TRUE/FALSE

1. The United Nations estimates that 130 million African women have undergone genital mutilation; the procedure is done to ensure virginity, remove sexual sensation, and render the women suitable for marriage.
    A. True   B. False

2. The author notes that there is no law against lust, gluttony, avarice, sloth, envy, pride, or anger, even though they are considered the seven deadly sins.
    A. True   B. False

3. In our society, the author notes that immoral acts can be distinguished from criminal acts on the basis of the social harm they cause.
    A. True   B. False

4. In 1993, Baylor University regents voted against allowing nude modeling in art classes after school officials were swamped with phone calls objecting to nudity in the classroom.
    A. True   B. False

5. Howard Becker is credited with coining the term moral entrepreneurs.
    A. True   B. False

6. The author notes that, according to the US Census Bureau 2000 data, there were 2.4 million gay partnerships in the United States.
    A. True   B. False

7. According to the author, the Bible expressly forbids homosexuality.
    A. True   B. False

8. In 1986, the United States Supreme Court, in Bowers v. Hardwick, upheld a Georgia statute making it a crime to engage in consensual sodomy, even within one's own home.
    A. True   B. False

9. In 1998, the Georgia Supreme Court reaffirmed the state's 182 year old sodomy law that was the basis for the Bowers v. Hardwick case.
    A. True   B. False

10. The author notes that autoerotic asphyxia is defined as sexual gratification by means of a noose, plastic bag, mask, or similar item.
    A. True   B. False

11. About 60 percent of all cases of autoerotic asphyxia involve males.
    A. True   B. False

12. Frotteurism is rubbing against or touching a non-consenting person in a crowd, elevator, or other public area.
    A. True   B. False

13. Voyeurism is obtaining sexual pleasure from spying on a stranger while he or she disrobes or engages in sexual behavior with another.
     A. True   B. False

14. Exhibitionism is obtaining sexual pleasure from exposing the genitals to surprise or shock a stranger.
     A. True   B. False

15. According to the author, modern commercial sex appears to have its roots in modern France during World War I.
     A. True   B. False

16. According to the UCR data, there are about 90,000 prostitution arrests made annually.
     A. True   B. False

17. The author notes that it is likely that the amount of men who hire prostitutes has increased slowly over the last 30 years.
     A. True   B. False

18. The author notes that most streetwalkers are similar to the character played by Julia Roberts in Pretty Woman.
     A. True   B. False

19. The Mustang Ranch has an official website that sells souvenirs.
     A. True   B. False

20. A madam is a womAn who employs prostitutes, supervises their behavior, and receives a fee for her behavior; her cut is usually 40 to 60 percent of the prostitute's earnings.
     A. True   B. False

FILL IN

1. Acts that are considered illegal because they threaten the general well-being of society and challenge its accepted moral principles are called _____ crimes.

2. _____ is a view that behaviors harmful to other people and society in general must be controlled.

3. _____ are individuals who go on moral crusades without any authorization from legal authorities.

4. Violent hate crimes directed towards people because of their sexual orientation is known as _____.

5. Moral _____ are interest groups that attempt to control social life and the legal order in such a way as to promote their own set of moral values.

6. Efforts by interest group members to stamp out they find objectionable are known as _____.

7. _____ is erotic interests in members of one's own sex.

8. _____ is defined as illegal sexual intercourse.

9. _____ is defined as the granting of nonmarital sexual access for renumeration.

10. A house of prostitution, usually run by a madam who sets prices and handles business arrangements is known as a _____.

11. Bizarre or abnormal sexual practices that involve recurrent sexual urges focused on objects, humiliation, or

children is defined as _____.

12. _____ is defined as an extreme negative overreaction to homosexuals.

13. A _____ is a woman who employs prostitutes, supervises their behavior, and receives a fee for her behavior.

14. Prostitutes who make dates via the phone and then service customers in hotel rooms or apartments are known as _____.

15. _____ are prostitutes who trade sex for drugs.

ESSAY

1. What are victimless crimes? Are these crimes really victimless, why or why not?

2. Take the role of a Supreme Court justice and describe how you would have decided the Bowers v. Hardwick case.

3. What are morally-tinged statutes and why are they a problem for law enforcement agencies?

4. According to the text, where do negative attitudes toward homosexuality come from?

5. What are paraphilias? What is one deadly form of paraphilia? Can it be treated?

MULTIPLE CHOICE ITEMS

1. D	6. C	11. D	16. D	21. D
2. A	7. B	12. D	17. A	22. C
3. B	8. B	13. C	18. A	23. B
4. C	9. A	14. A	19. B	24. A
5. A	10. B	15. A	20. D	25. C

TRUE FALSE ITEMS

1. A	6. B	11. B	16. A
2. A	7. A	12. A	17. B
3. A	8. A	13. A	18. B
4. A	9. B	14. A	19. A
5. A	10. A	15. B	20. A

FILL IN ITEMS

1. public order	6. moral crusaders	11. paraphilias
2. social harm	7. homosexuality	12. homophobia
3. vigilantes	8. sodomy	13. madam
4. gay bashing	9. prostitution	14. call girls
5. entrepreneurs	10. brothels	15. skeezers